COUNSELLING
SKILLS

Sara Miller McCune founded SAGE Publishing in 1965 to support the dissemination of usable knowledge and educate a global community. SAGE publishes more than 1000 journals and over 800 new books each year, spanning a wide range of subject areas. Our growing selection of library products includes archives, data, case studies and video. SAGE remains majority owned by our founder and after her lifetime will become owned by a charitable trust that secures the company's continued independence.

Los Angeles | London | New Delhi | Singapore | Washington DC | Melbourne

COUNSELLING
SKILLS

TRACI POSTINGS

bacp | counselling changes lives

$\circledS$ SAGE

Los Angeles | London | New Delhi
Singapore | Washington DC | Melbourne

SAGE

Los Angeles | London | New Delhi
Singapore | Washington DC | Melbourne

SAGE Publications Ltd
1 Oliver's Yard
55 City Road
London EC1Y 1SP

SAGE Publications Inc.
2455 Teller Road
Thousand Oaks, California 91320

SAGE Publications India Pvt Ltd
B 1/I 1 Mohan Cooperative Industrial Area
Mathura Road
New Delhi 110 044

SAGE Publications Asia-Pacific Pte Ltd
3 Church Street
#10-04 Samsung Hub
Singapore 049483

Editor: Susannah Trefgarne
Assistant editor: Ruth Lilly
Production editor: Rachel Burrows
Copyeditor: Sarah Bury
Proofreader: Lynda Watson
Indexer: Silvia Benvenuto
Cover design: Naomi Robinson
Typeset by: KnowledgeWorks Global Ltd.

Library of Congress Control Number: 2021939783

British Library Cataloguing in Publication data

A catalogue record for this book is available from the
British Library

ISBN 978-1-5297-3378-5
ISBN 978-1-5297-3377-8 (pbk)

Contents

About the Author

Traci is an experienced Counsellor, supervisor and tutor who has also worked extensively in homelessness and addiction settings. Over the years she has taught counselling at all levels and worked at CPCAB for over ten years to promote high standards in counselling training and qualification development. Traci currently works at BACP (British Association for Counselling and Psychotherapy) as a strategic project manager within the professional standards team.

Foreword

Most people who are hurting or struggling emotionally or psychologically will never have the opportunity to see a professional counsellor even though acceptance of counselling as a way of supporting individuals at different points in their life is growing. The British Association for Counselling and Psychotherapy (BACP) Public Perceptions Survey 2019 found that 88% of people would seek counselling for a problem before it gets out of hand and nine out of ten people believe that counselling should be readily available to everyone who needs it (BACP Public Perception Survey 2019, www.bacp.co.uk/about-us/about-bacp/public-perception-survey-2019, accessed 7 January 2021). However, the reality is that counselling services are limited and often not free at the point of delivery, which makes services out of reach for many people. Moreover, not everybody who is experiencing difficulties needs or wants to see a professional counsellor but may benefit from skilled help and support, which can come from many sources.

We know that many people suffering with mental health difficulties come into contact with a wide range of professionals and individuals in other roles whose ability to recognise and respond to them in helpful ways can be life-changing. That moment of being seen, heard and responded to as a human being in pain remains deep in the memory and can in itself be healing and restorative. A friend of mine with a troubled history of addiction and multiple experiences of professionals in addiction services remembered the kindness and the compassion of the cleaner in her hostel as the person who made the biggest difference to her recovery. These moments and these opportunities happen all the time. Offering compassion and care, even in the most difficult circumstances, is a way of respecting that person's life experience and common humanity.

Carl Rogers, the founder of client-centred counselling, understood the power of the relationship in enabling the best possible conditions for human flourishing. He was suspicious and disillusioned with psychological professionals and the medicalisation of human distress, and created a quiet revolution by suggesting that the quality of the relationship offers a way of bringing therapeutic help to those in psychological and emotional pain. His focus on compassion, humanity and the power of the person-to-person encounter as being the engine of healing underpins not only the person-centred approach to counselling, but also the many less formal interactions between those in pain and those seeking to help.

> It is that the individual has within himself or herself vast resources for self-understanding, for altering his or her self-concept, attitudes and self-directed behavior – and that these resources can be tapped if only a definable climate of facilitative psychological attitudes can be provided. (Rogers, 1980, p. 115)

People who are able to use counselling skills safely and effectively as part of another role – whether it be cleaner, nurse, teacher, key worker, care worker or probation officer – are part of the host of people who touch and impact on the lives of many. They are not professional therapists in terms of their core role or identity, but their ability to listen and respond to psychological distress is no less important because of the potential for their response to have a profound impact on others.

Recognising the signs of mental and emotional distress is the first step, but it is equally important to be able to respond appropriately and effectively as well as knowing when it is appropriate to refer an individual to other sources of help if this is required. This is what the BACP counselling skills framework is all about.

Policy makers may have recognised the importance of mental health but in practice there has not been the commitment to provide the necessary resources to ensure parity of esteem between physical and mental health. The response to the obvious and growing need for more mental health support is often to look at upskilling people in existing roles by giving them basic knowledge and information about mental health. What is significant about the counselling skills framework is that the focus is not just on psychological awareness or 'knowing about' mental health, but also about how to 'be' with another human being in psychological distress in ways which are helpful and healing. This is not only about academic learning or 'doing' something to/for another person; it is about being able to draw close to an individual in emotional distress and offering support without being overwhelmed, taking on too much or burning out – within the role contact you have with that individual. It's about 'seeing' the person, not just the problem, and bringing an emotional focus, understanding and skills to support that interaction.

Counselling skills training is very demanding because it calls upon people to draw upon their own inner resources and to examine and challenge their own attitudes. It demands that we recognise and seek to understand the whole range and diversity of people whatever their age, gender, sex, sexual orientation, race, colour, religion, culture or specific individual needs. This is not easy and is a continuing and constant endeavour, rather than a task to be achieved. This book sets out all the different elements of counselling skills training and offers scenarios where these skills can make a difference within the parameters of many different roles in a range of different contexts.

The book will also offer a solid introduction to the core relational skills that counsellors and psychotherapists learn as part of their training as professional therapists. These skills form part of a wider professional training of theory, skills and practice aimed at bringing about therapeutic change within a formal counselling relationship.

The BACP became involved in the development of the counselling skills framework which this book supports because of our belief that counselling skills are critically important. In the past, the BACP had a separate Code of Ethics for those who use counselling skills, in recognition of the importance of this work alongside, but separate from, the work of counsellors and psychotherapists. One important change was when the different BACP Codes of Ethics were brought together into a single document in the 2001 major revision, resulting in the consolidated *BACP Ethical Framework for the Counselling Professions* (BACP, 2018). It incorporates all those who use counselling skills in recognition that the same values and ethics underpin counselling interactions in other professional roles.

The BACP decision to put resources into developing a counselling skills competence framework in 2019 was in response to the expansion of roles – both new and existing roles – where people are expected to have these skills with minimal training and support, or any real recognition of the demands on the individual of working with people who are vulnerable and in distress. This is why the competence framework includes the need for self-care, the need for consultative support, the importance of recognising the limits of one's own ability and knowing how and when to refer to other sources of support or professional help. The framework captures the standards expected of people using counselling skills so that they can use them safely and effectively. This is important both for the safety of the public and the safety of the person using counselling skills as part of another role. The framework itself was developed with the help and support of an Expert Reference Group from a wide range of backgrounds and settings. BACP resources include the Counselling Skills Framework itself, an associated guide for users, trainers and employers, and a background document on the methodology of the project (www.bacp.co.uk/events-and-resources/ethics-and-standards/competences-and-curricula/counselling-skills).

On a broader note, the BACP sees the widening acceptance and adoption of standards for those using counselling skills as a way of increasing the understanding and importance of emotional and psychological awareness and relational skills in every day interactions. This in turn drives and increases the understanding of the value of therapeutic support and has the potential to increase referral routes and opportunities for counsellors and psychotherapists.

This book brings to life the BACP counselling skills competence framework for both audiences – those using counselling skills as part of another professional role and for trainee therapists starting their counselling journey.

Fiona Ballantine Dykes
BACP Chief Professional Standards Officer

ONE

What are counselling skills?

The British Association for Counselling and Psychotherapy (BACP) defines counselling skills as

> Counselling skills are a combination of values, ethics, knowledge and communication skills that are used to support another person's emotional health and wellbeing. They are not exclusive to counsellors since a wide range of people use them, often to enhance a primary role. Their use is therefore dependent on who is using them and the setting in which they're used. (BACP, 2000, p. 7)

This definition suggests that counselling skills are far more than just communication skills, and that is true. Using counselling skills is a way of being, a way of using knowledge, skills, experience and values to understand someone and offer support and care that is in the other person's best interest. Counselling skills equip someone to be able to support someone safely and ethically in order to:

- Recognise when someone needs to talk
- Respond using appropriate skills to facilitate a safe listening space
- Refer by sensitively signposting or referring when someone needs further help or assistance.

Counselling skills training

Counselling skills training is the first step to becoming a professional counsellor and forms the foundations on which therapeutic counselling training can take place. Counselling skills training also equips people with the necessary knowledge, skills, attitudes and qualities to work with people in a range of different roles and settings. In this instance, the skills are used to enhance someone's primary professional role. It is important to acknowledge that counselling skills enhance but do not change the primary role, e.g. nurse, teacher, support worker, social worker, etc. Another reason some people undertake counselling skills training is for personal development and/or to enhance and improve their personal and collegiate relationships with family, friends and colleagues. A foundation of counselling skills is therefore appropriate for many professional roles, e.g. social worker, doctor, police officer or healthcare professional.

As an analogy: most houses have foundations, but they are generally hidden from view. The house itself is what is noticed and there are many different types of house. If counselling skills are the foundations, and all the different houses are the professional roles that can be safely built on them, solid foundations form the basis for safe and reliable houses and professionals! A wide range of roles that offer support, care and assistance can be built on a foundation of counselling skills. Understanding the relationship between the primary professional role and the counselling skills ensures that the support and care offered will have an additional layer of quality, skill and safe, ethical understanding. Most professionals will already have the skills, knowledge and abilities related to their primary role; counselling skills and values enhance the relational aspects. For example, a doctor will have medical knowledge and counselling skills will support effective and empathic communication with patients.

Activity – Why do I want to learn about counselling skills?

Reflect on the questions in the table below and fill in your answers.

Why am I interested in counselling skills?
What is it about counselling skills that interests me?
What is my long-term goal?
How do I plan to meet that goal?
What qualities do I already have that are supportive to others?
What qualities do I feel I need to cultivate in myself?
What are my fears and doubts about learning and using counselling skills?
What do I need while I am learning?
What can I tell myself if I struggle or feel defeated?
What gives me joy when I forget how to be joyful?

A rose by any other name

Counselling skills are also referred to as helping skills, active listening skills, support skills, skilful communication skills, etc. The professions that benefit from counselling skills are diverse and numerous. Although the philosophy underpinning counselling skills remains the same, the application and purpose vary from role to role. A police officer would use counselling skills differently from a nurse, but the spirit of care and empowerment would remain the same. To return to the previous analogy about the house, where counselling skills are like the foundations, without solid foundations a house is open to the vagaries of the elements and is at risk of falling down. There are many different houses and buildings (professions) that can be built ethically and safely on these strong foundations. The houses can be modest or colourfully flamboyant, single storey or skyscrapers. Counselling skills enhance them all and of course are the foundations for the beautiful mansion we know as counselling and psychotherapy.

The BACP has developed a competence framework for counselling skills (see Appendix 1). This framework identifies five different areas that contribute to the competent use of counselling skills. These areas are like the ingredients of a cake; they are all required to produce a tasty and well-risen bake.

These ingredients are:

- Listening and responding skills
- Empathy
- Working alliance
- Professional issues
- Personal qualities

This book will take a journey through counselling skills training and the five ingredients identified above. Most counselling skills training programmes require students to keep a learning journal, which is an account of thoughts, feelings and opinions in relation to the learning experience. A learning journal is an opportunity for a student and tutor to build a relationship away from the main learning group. This book will also focus on a student's learning journal and the dialogue between student and tutor in relation to the topics and skills work covered.

Learning Journal

The first session of the counselling skills course was a real eye opener for me. We began the session by getting into pairs and introducing ourselves to each other. We then had to introduce our partner to the group. It was harder than I expected and I tried not to forget anything.

I thought that we would all be on the course for the same reason, to train to become a counsellor, but a lot of the students were on the course to help them in their current job. A couple were carers, someone worked with people with drug problems, some people worked in schools and others came from a church background. A real mix of people.

We agreed the ground rules for the group and someone offered to write them up and send us all a copy. The first task we were set was to come up with a definition for counselling and a definition for counselling skills and what the difference was. I think counsellors are more qualified than people just using counselling skills, they have done more training. Some people thought counsellors give advice but others thought that counsellors never gave advice. Some thought that counsellors speak very rarely and use mainly nods and body language. Some thought counsellors were there to solve problems and set goals and others thought counsellors listened and didn't try to sort things out. The whole group agreed that counsellors are there to help people and that the help can take different forms but must always be in the best interests of the client.

When we tried to define counselling skills, we got in a muddle. Counselling skills are skills that counsellors use but they are also skills that can be used by lots of other people. They are definitely specific listening and responding skills that are designed to support someone. We thought that counselling skills are also about understanding and respect and acceptance, but we also agreed that counselling is also about these things too. The tutor asked if counselling skills can stand alone and some of us thought they could, but actually, counselling skills must live inside another role. I hope to go on to train as a counsellor or psychotherapist and of course counselling skills will live inside that role.

On this course we will practise counselling skills with each other and will be known as a helper and a helpee to identify the person using counselling skills and the person being helped. That made sense to me. At the end of the session we had to have a closing circle, which meant going around the group and each of us had to say how we were feeling and what we would take away from the session.

Tutor feedback

Welcome to the course and to a new journey of learning and discovery. You have written a very good factual account of the first session. However, in your learning journal, I don't want to read very much about facts. I want to read about you; your thoughts, feelings and opinions about what happens in the sessions and how you think and feel about the topics we cover and how what we discuss impacts on you, your life and your situation.

From what you have written in your journal, I would like you to reflect on:

- *How it felt to be part of the group and in a new situation? For example, how did you feel about starting the course? How did you feel on the way to the first session and when you met your peers for the first time?*
- *I'd be interested to hear what you thought about the ground rules. I noticed you were very quiet during their negotiation and wondered why that was.*
- *You wrote that the introductions were harder than you expected and you didn't want to forget anything. How were you feeling in that exercise? How would you have felt if you had forgotten something?*

When writing about the definitions, you write about the group rather than yourself. I want to read about you in your journal.

In the closing circle you said you felt fine and would take away wisdom. I would be very interested in reading more about that and what wisdom you took away with you.

In your learning journal: YOUR thoughts, YOUR feelings, YOUR opinions are very important... the good, the bad and the ugly. In a nutshell, I would like to get to know you better.

You have taken the first step on your journey to become a counsellor... I wish you well.

A journey of a thousand miles begins with a single step. Tzu Lao

The three Rs

The three Rs are:

- Recognise when someone needs to talk
- Respond using appropriate skills to facilitate a safe listening space
- Refer by sensitively signposting or referring when someone needs further help or assistance.

Recognise when someone needs to talk

Someone might use body language or non-verbal cues to signal a need to talk or they might verbally express what they are experiencing or what is happening. It can be hard to spot difficulties and recognise an opportunity for discussion, so vigilance and careful attention are important. Branch and Malik (1993) described the ways in which skilled doctors are able to make use of windows of opportunity within ongoing clinical consultations to enable patients to express and work through emotional issues. These windows of opportunity offer professionals a chance to use counselling skills to provide a safe and understanding listening space, where someone can talk through their feelings and difficulties. These windows of opportunity can also be seen as empathic openings. The big challenge for professionals using counselling skills is to know how to recognise that someone wants to talk and to be able to respond in an appropriate way, while remaining in their primary professional role.

A study by Jansen et al. (2010) found that when a nurse acknowledged the emotional expression of the patient, it was more likely that the patient would later recall the content of their discussion. However, when the nurse distanced himself or herself from the patient's emotion, by not acknowledging it, the patient was less likely to recall what happened in the consultation. This highlights the need for attention and focus to recognise when someone needs emotional support.

There are certain signs that can indicate when someone needs support. The signs include:

> **Changes in physical appearance**: Less care is taken with dress and personal hygiene; evidence of weight loss or gain; fidgety, jumpy or restless behaviour.
> **Physical health**: Sleep problems, headaches, aches and pains for no physical reason, palpitations, panic attacks.
> **Emotions**: Anxiety and worry, stress, tiredness, irritability and anger, feeling overwhelmed by things that are usually manageable, being tearful.
> **Thoughts**: Negative and pessimistic, a lack of hope and gratitude, taking things personally, being irrational and reactive.
> **Behaviour**: Alcohol or drug use; isolation and withdrawal; finding it hard to focus and concentrate; a lack of motivation; avoiding friends, family and social situations.

Some or all of the above could indicate that someone needs support, but they could also be indicative of a range of other things. It is important not to make assumptions and to make gentle and tentative enquiry about whether or not someone would like to talk and receive emotional support. If there is already a relationship in place, it could be easier to identify when someone needs additional help.

Respond using appropriate skills to facilitate a safe listening space

Once someone indicates that they need some emotional support, it is important to respond in a timely and sensitive manner, by offering a private, safe and boundaried space for them to talk. The rest of this book focuses on listening and responding skills, the working alliance, facilitating a helping session, offering empathic understanding and adopting those qualities and attitudes in line with the values of counselling skills.

Refer by sensitively signposting or referring when someone needs further help or assistance

Oftentimes professionals will notice when someone needs further support that they are not qualified or equipped to provide. In these cases, a sensitive referral or signposting needs to take place.

Signposting is offering someone information about where they can go or who they can contact for additional advice, guidance or support. Examples could include:

- A housing officer could give information about the Citizen's Advice Bureau (CAB) for assistance with debt
- A police officer could give information to someone about domestic violence services in the area
- A doctor could signpost someone struggling with their sexuality to relevant organisations
- A play worker at a mother and baby group could offer a leaflet on immigration issues
- A youth worker could give a young person information on local colleges.

A referral is when the professional takes responsibility for contacting other professionals, agencies or organisations. A referral takes place when someone needs further help, assistance or guidance that is beyond the original professional's levels of competence, knowledge and experience. Other reasons for a referral could include a conflict of interest or a dual role. Examples of referral include:

- A GP referring a woman who has found a lump in her breast to a consultant at a local hospital
- A child psychologist making a referral to a paediatric consultant for an autism assessment
- A schoolteacher making a referral to a community mental health team when a student's mental health declines
- A support worker in an alcohol recovery drop-in refers someone who has disclosed childhood sexual abuse to a counsellor for long-term therapeutic work.

It is important that referrals take place smoothly, within a circle of confidentiality and with respect for the person's autonomy and privacy. The person should be supported throughout the referral process and not be left without any support while between professionals or organisations. For example, a GP referring someone to a hospital could have telephone contact with the patient until they receive a firm appointment with someone at the hospital. A home carer supporting someone who was waiting for a bed in a care home could still visit regularly while the referral went through. The person should not be left without support during the referral process.

To summarise, referrals should be appropriate and made in the person's best interest. Wherever possible, they should be with their consent and agreement. The person should have clear and detailed information about the referral process, understanding what to expect and to whom they are being referred. It can be helpful to talk through the referral to give someone the opportunity to say how they feel about it. It might be important to clarify that the referral is not a rejection.

A brief history of counselling skills

The power of listening, caring and understanding is as old as time. From as far back as can be remembered, solace has been found in being listened to with understanding and acceptance, and in being able to speak honestly and candidly with someone who will hear us without judgement and without their own thoughts and feelings getting in the way of the listening space. It is homage perhaps to the old saying, 'a problem shared is a problem halved'.

There is a modern-day focus on counselling and counselling skills which came into play in the 19th and 20th centuries, but the principles

Table 1.2 Timeline

Date	Events
Ancient times	The ancient Greeks challenged the idea that mental illness was caused by the gods. They recognised the healing value of encouraging and consoling words. They saw one person helping another as a virtue. Some of their ideas were a little odd. For example, they thought only women suffered from hysteria because it was caused by having a wandering uterus and magic was seen as complimentary to medicine.
	c. 400 BCE – Hippocrates (Kos, Greece) believed that it was black bile that caused depression and melancholia!
	c. 500 BCE – Siddhartha Gautama (Lumbini, Nepal) founded the psychotherapeutic practices of Buddhism, believing that the origin of mental suffering is ignorance, which causes attachment and craving.
	c. 300 BCE – In China the relationship between organs and emotions was identified. The theory of a life force (Qi) was born, alongside the need to balance the primal forces of Yin and Yang.
Middle Ages	Returned to the belief that the supernatural caused mental illness and used torture to get confessions of demonic possession.
	c. 900 – Ahmed ibn Sahl al-Balkhi (Balkh, Afghanistan) introduces the term 'mental hygiene'. He observed that illness could have both physiological and psychological causes. A concept similar to psychotherapy was called 'al-ilai al-nafs'. Nafs means self or psyche.
	1386 – The word 'counselling' found its way into Geoffrey Chaucer's *The Wife of Bath's Tale* in 1386.
	1403 – The first mentally ill patients were admitted to a hospital called The Bethlem Royal in London. Commonly known as Bedlam, the treatment offered was mainly forced restraint. The public were allowed to pay a fee to enter the hospital and stare at the insane.
	1567 – Philippus Aureolus Theophrastus Bombastus von Hohenheim, aka 'Paracelsus' (Einsiedeln, Switzerland) wanted more humane treatment for the mentally ill. He saw them as people struggling with something that could be treated with care and understanding rather than being possessed by evil spirits.
18th century	1770 – An interesting treatment approach was posited by Johann Joseph Gassner, whose practice included a mix of hypnotherapy and exorcism.
	1793 – The Bicetre Hospital in France led the way in humane treatment for the mentally ill. Patients were freed from shackles and chains. This work was pioneered by Jean-Baptiste Pussin, working with Philippe Pinel, and known as 'The Moral Treatment', which considered emotions and social interactions.
	In the late 1800s the term 'psychotherapy' was formalised. The Mayo Clinic in America stated that it was a 'general term for treating mental health problems by talking with a psychiatrist, psychologist or other mental health provider' (www.Mayo.com).

Table 1.2 (Continued)

Date	Events
19th century	1826 – Justinus Kerner appeared to continue the work of Johann Joseph Gassner, whose practice included a mix of hypnotherapy and exorcism, by treating patients with a combination of 'animal magnetism' (hypnotherapy) and exorcism. 1853 – The English psychiatrist Walter Cooper Dendy introduced the term 'psycho-therapeia', meaning 'the helpful influence of a healer's mind upon that of a sufferer' (Jackson, 1999, p. 9). 1879 – The Lancet, an international medical journey, published an article suggesting that supportive telephone calls could reduce unnecessary doctor visits. 1886 – Sigmund Freud, who became known as the grandfather of therapy, began therapeutic practice and research in Vienna. Treatment was primarily listening to the patient and providing interpretations.
20th century	Talking and listening as a kind of treatment was identified as a way of alleviating emotional problems and distress; the people who offered this treatment generally worked as educators, social advocates, employment guides and in other professional roles. This could be seen as the birth of counselling skills being embedded within other professional roles. In the very early 20th century, Clifford Whittingham Beers (1876–1943) founded the mental hygiene movement in America. He had been a patient in the mental health system and vowed to change the appalling conditions of mental institutions. 1908 – In America, Frank Parsons founded Boston's vocational bureau, which highlighted the importance of support and guidance. He believed that the more people knew themselves, the better able they became to make choices that healed rather than harmed. It is important to note that guidance in this instance does not mean telling someone what to do; it means using skills and knowledge that acts as a guide or guiding light that helps someone find their own way. The person using counselling skills shines a light on the path so that someone can work out which way to go. 1940s and 1950s – The interpersonal therapy developed by Carl Rogers focused on the communication of warmth, genuineness and acceptance from the therapist to the individual (Rogers, 1957). It is known today as person-centred counselling and has a major influence in teaching, therapy, helping and counselling skills and a wide range of other professions.

Date	Events
	1943 – The famous hierarchy of need was developed by Abraham Maslow, the founder of Humanistic psychology (Maslow, 1943).
	1945 – Virginia Axline and Carl Rogers published an account of the role undertaken by a teacher, over a period of several months, in response to the emotional and social needs of a disabled six-year-old boy (Axline & Rogers, 1945). It illustrated how the teacher was able to make use of counselling skills to play a key role in the recovery of a seriously troubled young person, mainly through a series of brief, 15-minute listening conversations.
	1960 – Thomas Szasz initiated the anti-psychiatry movement and R. D. Laing published *The Divided Self* (Laing, 1960), which saw mental illness as valid communications of lived experiences rather than symptoms of a mental illness.
	1967 – Aaron Beck developed a psychological model of depression. Doctors, midwives and other health professionals still use the Beck Inventory today to identify and respond to symptoms of depression (Beck, 1967).
	1977 – The birth of the British Association for Counselling (BACP). A professional body for the counselling professions, including those who use counselling skills. In 2019, BACP developed a competence framework for counselling skills.
	1993 – Branch and Malik explored how skilled physicians use skills to make use of windows of opportunity within consultations, to help patients with emotional issues (Branch & Malik, 1993).
	1998 – Egan's Skilled Helper Model, which is a three-stage model using counselling skills in a wide range of roles and settings (Egan, 1998). In line with other models, its aim is to empower people to manage life more effectively and to make lasting changes to engage with opportunities to meet their full potential.
21st century	2008 – Høigaard and Mathisen developed a model for counselling skills that are used by a range of professionals other than counsellors (Høigaard & Mathisen, 2008). A model of informed, situated counselling.
	2011 – McLeod and McLeod proposed a framework for training and research in embedded counselling using counselling skills (McLeod & McLeod, 2011).
	Today counselling and counselling skills are offered in almost every corner of the world. Counselling skills are used in relief work in most countries and add value and effectiveness to professional roles in all areas of health, social care and helping.

and values of counselling and counselling skills started centuries before. Around the time of Jesus Christ, there was a Roman philosopher called Seneca who spoke of the beauty of being understood and understanding others. Perhaps this acknowledges the meaning and value of what we understand today as empathy.

Over centuries, women sat in circles telling stories and weeping for each other's pain and sorrows. A talking stick would be held by the person talking and all others in the circle would be silent and listen. When the person had finished talking and felt rested within the group, the listening stick would be passed onto the next person who needed to talk and be heard. The church has long offered a listening ear in the confessional box, where someone could talk through their wrongdoings and leave the burden of guilt and shame behind.

Historically, care for the mentally ill and emotionally wounded was harsh and often barbaric. People suffering in this way were often seen as bad or, in some cases, possessed by evil spirits. Table 1.2 shows a timeline of how helping others by listening, caring and understanding has evolved to become the counselling skills and counselling profession we know today.

Learning Journal

I've sat for ages trying to write this journal and am finding it really hard to get started. I'm not sure how to write about my feelings and how much to write about myself. I thought a lot about the feedback I got for my first journal entry and realised that I didn't want to write about my feelings and thoughts in case they were wrong. What if I'm not meant to think and feel the way I do? What if I'm not the right sort of person? What if I'm not strong enough and well-rounded enough? I do want to carry on and learn how to be a counsellor but if I'm this scared on a counselling skills course, maybe I'm just not up to it.

The truth is I was very scared before the session, during the session and even after the session. There are professional, academic people in the group and I feel very inadequate and stupid. I haven't worked for many years and when I did work, I worked in shops or as a cleaner. I feel ashamed and not good enough in the group. One woman is a social worker, I am just not in that league.

I stopped work to raise my children and somewhere in those years, my marriage ended and I ended up seeing a counsellor because I just couldn't cope. That was a few years ago, but it was such a help to me at that time that I hoped that one day I could give back what I had been given. It has been such a long time since I'd done anything – anything for myself that is – that I think I forgot how to be. So I just tried to blend in with the others and hope I wouldn't make a fool of myself. I must have been really tense because my neck and shoulders hurt for days after. I feel very silly after writing this journal. I noticed a poster on the wall that said, 'The truth will set you free'. Well, what I've written is the truth. I just wish it were a bit better.

Tutor feedback

Thank you for your honesty and genuineness. It sounds as if you sat with a lot of very difficult and challenging feelings... and you still came back. That tells me about your courage and determination. I don't want to rescue you and offer platitudes, but I do want to tell you that the helping and counselling professions aren't built on intellect and mental ability. These things can be important, but more important are the other things we bring to the work. You already bring honesty, vulnerability and a belief in the therapeutic process.

Your own hard-won experience is as important as reading academic tomes. Your understanding and willingness are just as important as an impressive title. I can hear your fear and trepidation and can tell you that even those things are incredibly valuable.

> Anyone who is going to see a patient tomorrow should, at some point, experience fear. In every consulting room there ought to be two rather frightened people; the patient and the psychoanalyst. If there are not, one wonders why they are bothering to find out what everyone knows. (Bion, 1990, p. 5)

So, you are frightened ... Guess what? Me too.

It becomes clear that counselling skills can enhance most health and social care roles as well as being the bedrock upon which the counselling and psychotherapy professions are built.

The remaining chapters in this book explore and discuss the different elements to counselling skills. Example case studies, exercises and activities to help build competence and confidence accompany each chapter.

TWO

Listening

Listening is often assumed to be an easy thing to do but this is far from true. Listening is, however, arguably the most important of the counselling skills. It is about giving attention, and when using counselling skills, it is about giving undivided attention – to be open to hearing someone else's story, experience and feelings. It is an invitation into the private, sensitive life of someone else and, as such, it needs to done with great care and respect.

According to *Oxford Living Dictionaries*, to listen is:

> To give attention to sound or action. When listening, one is hearing what others are saying, and trying to understand what it means. The act of listening involves complex affective, cognitive, and behavioural processes.

When using counselling skills, of course we listen to the words, but we also listen to what is not said; we listen to feelings and facial expressions. We also need to listen to ourselves, in order to be able to put that to one side and give someone our full attention so that we listen carefully to their unfolding story. It can be difficult to listen carefully. Often our own thoughts and feelings get in the way and we can find ourselves going off on a tangent in our heads. Someone might mention something we disagree with, which stirs up feelings, perhaps of irritation, fear or identification. We can get caught up in these things and stop listening to what someone has to say. Someone might be distressed and cry as they tell us about painful things that have happened to them. We can easily stop listening as we think frantically about how we can make them feel better, offer a pearl of advice or solve their problems and challenges. However, counselling skills are not about solving problems, giving advice or finding solutions. They are about listening and understanding.

If we are really honest with ourselves, we know we cannot change or 'fix' other people; that transition must come from them. We actually patronise other people if we think we can solve their problems better than they can. We can listen carefully and we can work hard to understand how that person feels. That can feel as if it is not enough, and we can wonder how just listening and understanding can help someone. In truth, just listening and being with someone is a lot harder to do than giving advice, making suggestions and offering platitudes.

Activity – How well do you listen?

Listen to 20 minutes of a television programme or radio programme you do not usually watch or listen to.

As you listen, be mindful of when your mind wanders. Where did your thoughts go? What caused the distraction?

Notice your opinions and judgements. What effect do they have on your ability to listen?

Did how you feel about the different characters (like or dislike) impact on how well you were able to listen? Explain in what way.

At the end of 20 minutes, recall what you can remember of the content.

What have you learnt about listening? Was it easier or harder than you expected?

Many things can get in the way of listening attentively and these things can be grouped into two main categories:

* Things inside us
* Things outside us.

Interestingly, blocks to listening can relate and link to each other. A good example of this is when someone's appearance or presentation (external) triggers the listener's prejudice, which in turn causes the listener to make a judgement, which blocks listening and understanding.

It can be quite funny to think of things like wanting a pee and having tight shoes on as blocks to listening, but physical discomfort is very capable of dragging our attention away from everything except our own

Table 2.1   Barriers to listening

Internal barriers to listening	External barriers to listening
Personal feelings, e.g.	Distractions, e.g.
• Resentments and hurts can capture our thoughts, excluding anything else	• Lack of privacy
• Fears, perhaps of not being good enough or of doing things wrong	• Computer screens
	• Mobile phones
• Fears of not being liked or being judged	• Other people's conversations
• Feeling frightened of who we are listening to	• Noise outside the room; perhaps building work or cleaning
• Fears that our own life events cause our hearts to be heavy and closed	• Cars, lorries outside
	• Television
• Anger at a perceived injustice	• Telephone ringing
Personal thoughts, e.g.	
• Getting caught up in what to reply rather than just listening	An unsafe space, e.g.
	• Hearing loud, aggressive-sounding conversations just outside the room
• Trying to think of something clever or helpful to say instead of listening	• Thinking someone will interrupt
• Being preoccupied with people, places or things in our life	• Hearing loud noises of any kind
	• There is nowhere to sit or the seating is inappropriate
• Being reminded of something in our own experience and thinking about that instead of listening to what the person is saying	• Being unable to lock door
	• Being too close or too far away from who you are listening to
	• A messy or chaotic environment
Prejudice and stereotyping, e.g.	The person we are listening to, e.g.
• Making judgements and/or assumptions about someone's	• Someone wearing unusual or 'outlandish' clothes
- Culture	• Someone wearing very revealing clothes
- Race	
- Sexuality	• Someone we find visually attractive or repulsive
- Disability	
- Age, size, gender, etc.	• An unpleasant body odour
• Assuming we know what someone is about to say before they say it	• Strong perfume or cologne
Physical discomfort, e.g.	The actual words or sound, e.g.
• Being too hot or too cold	• Whispering
• Uncomfortable clothing – maybe too tight or itchy	• Shouting
	• Covering mouth and muffling the sound
• Being hungry or thirsty	
• Needing to go to the toilet	• Speaking quickly
• Feeling ill	• Strong accent
• Feeling tired	

physical needs. Checking these physical needs goes a long way in freeing us up to be present and open to what someone else is thinking and feeling. It is not always deep emotional issues that are the problem; something as simple as itchy clothes can make it impossible to listen to anything but the itch. It can often be the case the little things can cause the biggest blocks. It isn't necessarily the hard, emotional and dramatic things that cause blocks; rather, seemingly trivial things do that too and it can be all too easy to dismiss or overlook these.

Personal thoughts and feelings

The most challenging barriers to listening can be our own thoughts and feelings, of which we are often unaware. Table 2.2 outlines some other possible blocks to listening and how we can understand them. Identify your main blocks and reflect on what causes the blocks and what you can do to overcome them.

Table 2.2 Personal blocks to listening

Block to listening	Why
Day dreaming	Something has triggered chains of thought and you zone out for a few seconds or even minutes. When you come back to the present, you have no idea what the person has said.
Judging	You don't like something someone has said or disagree with their behaviour, values and beliefs.
Rehearsing	You are too busy thinking about what you are going to say to really listen to what the other person is saying.
Identification	Someone shares a similar experience to your own and you think you know the way out of their predicament.
Triggered	Someone talks about an experience or situation that reminds you of a painful and unhealed aspect of yourself.
Comparing	You are trying to work out whether the other person is cleverer, better looking, nicer and more together than you are.
Dislike	You simply don't like the person you are listening to.
Personal situation	You are in pain, perhaps a bereavement or an ending or a painful relationship that consumes your thoughts.
Feeling bored	Perhaps at the end of a long day, after supporting and listening to others over a long period of time, it is too hard to care anymore.

(Continued)

Table 2.2   (Continued)

Block to listening	Why
Derailing	You might change the subject or talk about something randomly to avoid the subject the person is talking about.
Mind reading	You think you know about the person before they know themselves.
Rescuing	You feel sorry for someone and offer platitudes to stop them feeling the way they do and try to force them to stop being in pain by telling them things you can't possibly know, e.g. to stop feeling scared, because there's nothing to be scared of.
Placating	You might fear conflict and have a strong need to be liked and admired which makes you agree with everything just to appear nice and caring.
Being right	You are intent on getting your point across and feel certain you know what is right for someone.
Inadequacy	Your mind is flooded with thoughts of how rubbish you are and how you are doing everything all wrong and making a fool of yourself.
Asking questions	You ask question after question either out of personal nosiness or because you can't think of anything else to do.
Advising	You directly tell someone what to do.
Self-disclosure	You talk at length about your own experiences and what helped or worked for you.
Interrupting	You think you have such important things to say, you are too impatient to let the person finish. It could be because you are nervous and your thoughts are going so quickly that they fly out of your mouth without you being able to stop them.
Promising	You want to help so much that you start making promises that you might not be able to keep and overstepping your role and responsibilities, giving false hope.
Minimising	You play down the person's difficulties, e.g. It's not that bad.

It is easy to misinterpret the *meaning* of a message if you are defensive, judgmental, bored, or emotionally upset. (S. K. Ferrett, 2008, p. 157)

Listening really is the crown of counselling skills and to be an attentive listener takes commitment and hard work. The following activity highlights the challenges and difficulties of simply listening.

Activity – Listening skills

In a pair, listen to your partner for five minutes only. During this time, you can say everything you want to EXCEPT you cannot:

- Ask questions
- Offer advice
- Make suggestions
- Talk about yourself
- Try to make the other person feel better, e.g. tell them they will be OK
- Dismiss how the person is feeling, e.g. don't be scared, there's nothing to be scared of.

How did that activity feel?

Were you able to listen and respond for five minutes without resorting to using any of the bullet points?

Which of the bullet points were you tempted to use or did you use?

* * *

The bullet points above are all things we can do to avoid really listening to what someone is saying and feeling. Often, they are the responses we offer when we don't know what else to do. They are often things we do to make ourselves feel better. Simply listening can be painful and anxiety-provoking. Just being quiet and not filling every space with words can be incredibly healing.

Can you remember a time in your life when someone just listened without trying to get you to do, feel or think a certain way? What was that experience like?

Most of us will be able to recall times when, in the middle of a conversation, we become aware of the other person staring expectantly at us, waiting for a response, and we realise that we have absolutely no idea what they have been talking about. Somehow our mind has wandered and we are in the awful position of not knowing whether to agree, disagree or just smile hopefully to try and avoid admitting we weren't listening and risk hurting the other person's feelings. By building awareness of blocks to listening and causes of distraction, we can hopefully rule out or at least minimise these mind-wandering times.

Learning Journal

Listening

I have generally thought of myself as being a good listener, which is part of the reason for me being on the course in the first place. I am beginning to realise that when I think I am listening to someone else, I am often listening to myself and my own thoughts and opinions. When someone is talking, my head is busy thinking what to say next, what the solution could be, what the person needed to do, was I talking rubbish, etc. My head can be so full of my own thoughts that there isn't any room for anyone else. If someone talks about something I've experienced, my thoughts seem to go in a million different directions. I know my experience is not necessarily the same as someone else's and I do try to challenge myself when I identify and make assumptions, but that just makes my head busier. Then I have to contend with the thoughts that tell me I'm doing everything wrong, that I'm talking rubbish and sitting nodding my head frantically, like one of those little dogs sitting in car windows.

No matter how hard I try, my mind wanders. In a skills practice session, I even found myself thinking about what to cook for tea and if I would have time to get to the shops before they closed. I felt disrespectful and ashamed of myself, but I couldn't help it. I try to really concentrate but that seems to make things worse – the words just dance in my head. I also find myself checking that I'm sitting right, checking that I have good posture and haven't crossed my arms or legs. I find eye contact really hard to get right... either there's no eye contact or I find myself staring into the eyes of the other person, which freaks us both out. My body feels really awkward in the chair and I feel self-obsessed and uncomfortable. This in itself is a barrier to listening and supporting someone. It all becomes about me and how I am thinking and feeling – the complete opposite to how it should be.

I try to practise 'watching and waiting' and just providing a safe space for someone to talk at their pace, but I find this almost impossible. I think my anxiety makes me speed up and rush, and I find myself jumping in with questions or comments rather than leaving a little silence for someone to think. I think my internal pace is too quick due to nerves and that just spills out of me.

This might sound a bit silly but I've been thinking of how I can listen better; how I can get out of my own way. I've come up with a little ritual and so far it seems to be helpful. I imagine I have three babies all clamouring for attention. The babies' names are fear, shame and judgement. I take a few minutes to imagine feeding and changing the babies and then wrapping them in the softest of blankets and laying them down to sleep with a gentle lullaby playing in the background and a night-light for comfort. I have gone through this little ritual before the last couple of skills practice sessions and I have definitely felt calmer and also more confident. I feel a bit silly now I've written that.

Up until now, I just assumed that we listen with our ears, but actually I think we listen with other senses too. Body language and non-verbal communication is seen, not heard. Empathy can be felt as well as heard. Even touch can communicate a lot in certain circumstances.

Wow, I never knew listening was such hard work.

Tutor feedback

Thank you for a very self-aware and honest journal. I especially like your analogy about the three babies that you feed and comfort before taking on a listening role. How would you feel about sharing that with the group?

Listening is not easy, especially active listening – listening with the heart as well as the mind. You are learning a whole new way to listen and, like a lot of new things, it feels difficult and uncomfortable. When intrusive thoughts and opinions get in the way of listening, they remind me of mosquitos, distracting and annoying. I spray symbolic mosquito repellent to keep them at bay. The ways we find to help ourselves be better listeners can be innovative and amusing.

It sounds as if you are just beginning to notice how critical you are towards yourself, hopefully you will be able to begin to quieten that harsh voice as the course unfolds.

The environment and listening

A safe and private setting or room is essential for effective listening. It is important that a space is found that will not be interrupted by others. Mobile phones need to be turned off or be on silent, and computer screens should also be turned off. Use comfortable seating, ideally of similar height. If one seat is higher than another, it can suggest a power imbalance, which is not helpful. The space between the seats needs to be close enough to hear each other but not uncomfortably close, which can feel frightening and overwhelming. It can be helpful to place chairs at a slight angle rather than side by side or opposite each other. If the chairs directly face each other, it can feel confrontational and intrusive, whereas placing them side by side impedes communication. But placing chairs at an angle can aid and enhance communication. Of course, sometimes a listening opportunity can happen ad hoc and without the availability of seats or a private room. However, for most listening and helping activities, a safe space and appropriate seating enhances the experience.

The space between you and the person you are listening to is related to both ethical and personal boundaries. Experiment with what feels comfortable for you and others by practising with friends and family, identifying what feels comfortable and uncomfortable and arriving at a happy medium. The space between the two chairs needs to allow both people to be comfortable in a social sense. We like our personal space and need a distance that feels natural. The space between the seats is important and the space in which you meet with someone is also important. We can use the room and the logistics of it to begin to offer someone a listening space where they will feel safe and comfortable enough to talk about the hurts in their heart. Some people like to have a table between the two chairs, while many believe that this creates a barrier. What do you think?

An untidy or cluttered room can be a distraction for both people, and for some people, a sterile, bare room can feel intimidating and cold. It is important that the room is airy and well ventilated to reduce the risk of feeling claustrophobic and becoming overheated. What's next door? The noises from adjoining rooms can be very distracting.

Activity – A listening space

Design an ideal listening space. Reflect on what blocks to listening can be addressed via the environment.

What sort of room would you feel comfortable in and able to talk?

THREE

Responding skills

Circular breathing is a technique used by players of some wind instruments to produce a continuous tone without interruption. It is accomplished by breathing in through the nose while pushing air out through the mouth using air stored in the cheeks. When using counselling skills, we can practise a similar technique. Listening allows us to take in what someone is saying and hold on to what we are hearing; responding skills allow us to reply using the information and feelings we are holding on to. We can then let someone know that we have heard and understood and would like to hear and understand more. There is a rhythm to the art of careful listening and responding that sets the pace and tone for offering a safe and supportive space for someone to open up and share their thoughts, feelings and problems.

This chapter will concentrate on a range of responding and communication skills. The following chapters will focus on how and when to use them. Appropriate use of counselling skills allows us to respond to someone's situation accurately and sensitively in order to meet them, where they are, in any given moment. We will explore and understand the 'Ws' of how to use counselling skills.

When offering counselling skills in a helping role, there are seven simple questions we can ask ourselves to ensure we are working as safely and effectively as possible. The '7 Ws' invite us to reflect on: the setting we are working in, the person we are working with, the purpose or goal of the work, the skills we can use to facilitate this interaction, how and when we use the skills to best support the person, the reasons we do what we do, and how effective and helpful our support is. These questions will help us to use our skills to the best of our ability and also to support us to reflect on how effective they were, in order to inform and improve future helping work.

> ### The 'Ws' of counselling skills
>
> ## Questions to consider
>
> Where are we?
>
> Who are we with?
>
> What are we doing?
>
> Which skills are we using?
>
> When are we using them?
>
> Why are we doing what we are doing?
>
> Will what we are doing help?

Paraphrasing

Paraphrasing is a very important counselling skill, with several uses. It involves listening to what someone has said and then repeating that back to them using different words but without changing the meaning. A paraphrase is often a shorter, more condensed version of what the helpee said. It is important that pertinent details are not omitted, but sometimes the meaning of what someone is saying can get lost in the detail. A paraphrase identifies the heart of the content and does not need to clutter the conversation with minutiae and chatter.

> **Helpee**: I was awake for such a long time, I tried everything, counting sheep, essential oils to help me relax, a hot bath and a warm milky drink, fresh sheets, everything I could think of, but none did any good.

> **Helper**: You tried many different things but were still unable to sleep.

This is quite a simplistic example but it illustrates that paraphrasing shows the person what they have said in clear and concise terms, simply feeding back the essence of what has been said.

Paraphrasing has several benefits.

- It lets someone know they have been listened to carefully
- It communicates attention and understanding

- It helps someone to hear what they have said
- It helps someone to see the heart of things without being distracted by details and stories that can sometimes hide the real problem
- It clarifies confusing content
- It highlights the important issues
- It checks that what you have heard is accurate.

When paraphrasing, it is very important not to change the actual meaning of what the person is saying, by adding your opinion or personal thoughts and feelings on the issue. It is equally important not to ignore any important elements. The following examples show that although a seemingly simple skill, it can be very easy to get things wrong, either by adding to it or taking something away.

> **Helpee**: I am tired of being so busy, my son needs me to drop his packed lunch off, I have to pick up my mother's dry cleaning, I have several reports to write for work and somewhere in all that I have to clean the house and prepare for my daughter's birthday party. I haven't even mentioned that my mother expects me to arrange transport for my sister's children to visit. I also have to buy a new outfit and get my hair done for a friend's wedding next week.

Responses:

> **You are feeling angry with all the burdens being put on you**... This may be true but we don't know that yet. The person has not said they are angry and this response is therefore an assumption. In counselling skills, this could be seen as a premature response, and one that could potentially put words in the helpee's mouth.

> **It sounds as if you want to look your best for your friend's wedding**... Again, this could be true but the person hasn't told us that and the wedding is only a small part of what the person was speaking about.

> **People are taking advantage of you and I think it would help you to tell them you aren't a doormat**... Giving advice is not helpful. It suggests that the person is incapable of deciding what they need to do, which is simply untrue. Giving advice also suggests that we know better than the other person does, which is again simply untrue in most situations. Often, we give advice when it is us who do not know what to do or say.

Could you just sort out what your daughter needs and leave the rest for another time… Part of the work with someone might involve prioritising and thinking about manageable tasks, but it is not your role to do that for the person. This response suggests that you know what the most important thing is for the person and what is best for them. Suggestions can also be a way of feeling important and powerful in the interaction, but it is not helpful to the helpee.

I need you to choose two things only to concentrate on… This puts pressure on the person to do what you want them to do, rather than what they want to do. It may be that it would be helpful to agree a focus on what's important, but that is for the person to decide, not for you. The big risk of telling someone what to do is that they might not want to do it or feel able to do it, and this could cause them to avoid you (and the help they might need), or to lie to avoid feeling guilty or bad.

There are so many demands on your time, the busyness is exhausting… Although not perfect, this is an adequate paraphrase, capturing the heart of what has been said.

Another very important function of paraphrasing is to facilitate a smooth conversation that allows the person to continue speaking without interruption. Using paraphrasing when there is a pause lets the person know they have been heard and understood, and also encourages them to continue speaking and say more about what is troubling them. The length of a paraphrase is important. If the paraphrase is too long, the person may lose focus and even interest while they wait for you to finish talking. If the paraphrase is too short, it may not communicate enough of what was said to show understanding. If the paraphrase is inaccurate, it can put someone in the uncomfortable position of either having to disagree with you or agreeing with you because they feel unable to challenge what you have said. They may also start to feel it's not worth speaking because they aren't being understood. It is important to practise paraphrasing as much as possible. Paraphrasing can be practised in all conversations with others, not just in conversations with those you are helping or supporting. When talking to friends and family, hold back your own personal thoughts, feelings and opinions and simply paraphrase back to them what you have heard them say. You might be surprised at the outcomes.

In the table below, offer a paraphrase in response to each statement. The first couple are done for you.

Statement	Paraphrase
I don't understand him. One minute he's really friendly, and the next time I see him he just ignores me.	He doesn't seem very consistent.
I love going on cruise holidays, there's never a dull moment, always stuff going on, fitness classes, talks, dancing, films, crafts, massage, games, quizzes.	It sounds like there's lots of activities for you to choose from.
I don't think I will ever pass my driving test. I've had so many lessons and I still make loads of mistakes and get the controls mixed up.	
My partner wants a baby and I don't know if I do. I like the idea of us making that commitment together but what if we break up. I don't want to be a single parent.	
I have decided to leave my wife. I haven't loved her for many years but have stayed out of a sense of responsibility, but time is ticking by and I can't stand the thought of being trapped like this for the rest of my life.	
I need to go to the doctor. I keep having pains in my chest but the thought of having to have tests and being poked and prodded puts me off and I just think that I'll leave it alone and see if things sort themselves out on their own.	
Both my son and my daughter are using drugs and are in a pretty bad state. I just don't know what to do and how I can help them. It must be my fault. What sort of mother ends up with both her children on drugs? People must think I'm an awful person.	
I'm gay, I've known for a long long time but I have never told a living soul. My family are very old-fashioned and I don't think they would accept this. I don't know what to do. I am sick and tired of feeling like I'm living a lie.	

Although paraphrasing is a very important skill, it is one skill among many. Paraphrasing focuses on the content and meaning of what someone is saying and if there is an over-reliance on paraphrasing to the exclusion of other skills, it can keep the conversation on a surface level, avoiding hearing and responding to someone's feelings and emotions. This has the potential to discourage someone from being emotionally expressive.

Reflecting

The person's story is important but we also need to hear and be able to explore and understand someone's feelings. It is easier to listen to a story than to hear someone's distress, pain and sadness. The skill of 'reflecting' is similar to paraphrasing, but whereas paraphrasing focuses on content, reflection focuses on emotion and lets the person know that you understand how they are feeling. When working with feelings, our blocks to listening and other unhelpful responses can come to the fore as we try to move from painful feelings by advising, avoiding, suggesting, advising, rescuing, criticising, placating and patronising – to name just a few! Using reflecting as a skill helps us to stay with someone's feelings without our own responses and feelings getting in the way.

> **Helpee**: I can't do this, I really can't, how could he do this to me, my heart is breaking.

> **Helper**: This is so incredibly painful.

Reflecting acknowledges, respects and honours the feelings, full stop. Unlike paraphrasing, reflection picks up on non-verbal as well as verbal cues. Body language and non-verbal communication often say more than words can, but it is all too easy to interpret non-verbal cues incorrectly, make assumptions and make wild guesses. It seems prudent to spend some time looking at non-verbal communication before moving onto the skill of reflection.

When you notice someone's body language or non-verbal communication, it is important to simply offer an observation of what you see, rather than a concrete statement of what you think it means. For example, it is better to say 'You put your head in your hands when you spoke of your mum', rather than 'You put your head in your hands when you spoke of your mum as if you were angry'. The person may be angry, or they may not be, but we don't know that. What we do know is that they put their head in their hands. It is better to offer the observation and either to ask the person how they are feeling or to gently enquire about their body language. For example, 'You put your head in your hands when you spoke of your mum and it looked as if you were feeling some difficult emotions'. This gives the person the opportunity to explain further. Less is more when using counselling skills, but it can often feel insufficient or inadequate in the face of someone's distress. Part of counselling skills training is to learn to trust the process, the skills and also to trust yourself and the person you are working with. It is sometimes a hard ask.

As already stated, reflection focuses on and listens to feelings, not just to the content. It requires listening to emotions such as anger, disappointment, discouragement, guilt, shame, fear, joy, elation, disgust, etc. When using counselling skills, it is often the feelings that need to be explored, understood and accepted in order to help someone manage them. It is vital to be accepting of all emotion – the good, the bad and the ugly. If you find some feelings unacceptable or 'bad', the person you are supporting may feel unable to talk about how they really are, as they may feel bad for having certain thoughts and/or feelings.

The good, the bad and the ugly – all feelings acceptable here!

If you are uncomfortable with certain feelings, the reason and the response lie inside you and are nothing to do with the person you are supporting. When using the skill of reflection, you become like a mirror in front of someone, simply showing them the emotions they are feeling. If they are feeling sad and tearful, holding up a jolly mirror will not be helpful and could well make the person feel even worse.

Benefits of reflection

Reflection is helpful for several reasons:

- It lets someone know their feelings have been heard and understood
- It is non-judgemental and therefore offers empathy and acceptance
- It can help someone make sense of their situation and feelings
- It can reassure and normalise what someone is feeling and that they aren't weird or strange or horrible.

As a race, we humans can tend to think there is something wrong with who we are and how we feel. Reflection can help this by simply accepting and acknowledging how someone is feeling. It is important not to run screaming from the room if someone shares their feelings... unless they are a cannibal and they express a desire to eat you! Then it might be appropriate to run screaming from the room, but this would be the only exception ☺.

Carl Rogers notes:

> When the other person is hurting, confused, troubled, anxious, alienated, terrified; or when he or she is doubtful of self-worth, uncertain as to identity – then understanding is called for. The gentle and sensitive companionship offered by an empathic person ... provides illumination and healing. In such situations deep understanding is, I believe, the most precious gift one can give to another. (Rogers, 1980, pp. 160–1).

He went on to say that a person who receives a response at the emotional level has

> the satisfaction of being deeply understood and can go on to express more feelings, eventually getting 'directly to the emotional roots' of their problem. (ibid.)

Tips for reflecting

- Be natural – there is no need to be an expert
- Listen for the basic message – consider the feeling and meaning expressed by the person you are helping
- Use simple terms and language when reflecting back
- Look for non-verbal as well as verbal cues that confirm or deny the accuracy of your paraphrasing
- Check that what you have reflected is accurate and be aware that some people will agree with you because it is too difficult to be assertive and say you were wrong
- Facilitate a safe and calm space that invites honesty and openness and where you are able to cope with being wrong
- Do not question unnecessarily

- Do not add or subtract from the speaker's meaning; just stay with what the person is feeling
- Do not change the subject or take a diversion to avoid uncomfortable feelings
- Do not take the speaker's topic in a new direction
- Be 'a-non', i.e. be non-directive and non-judgemental.

Non-verbal communication

There are many different types of non-verbal communication or body language. Body language and non-verbal communication actually account for the majority of how we communicate. There are some almost universal cues which include smiling, nodding, waving, etc. We can sometimes pick up on someone's mood simply by looking at their non-verbal cues and body language. Have you ever walked into a room and picked up on the mood without anyone saying a word? No non-verbal cue is completely universal. We are a diverse population: culture, gender, age, sexuality, and race are just some of the things that can influence how we communicate, both with and without words. Let's consider some areas of non-verbal communication.

Facial expressions

The human is able to convey countless emotions without saying a word. And unlike some forms of non-verbal communication, facial expressions tend to be similar for all people. Darwin (1872) suggested that some facial expressions are universal. In the 1960s, Tomkins (1962, 1963) conducted studies demonstrating that some facial expressions are indeed universal, and this has been backed up by many more research studies. This was refuted by Ekman, Friesen, and Ellsworth (1972), who believed that each culture had its own set of meanings for facial expressions.

Overall, the outcome is that there is strong evidence for universal facial expressions for seven emotions – anger, contempt, disgust, fear, joy, sadness, and surprise. What is your opinion on this? Do you agree or disagree?

Body movement and posture

This covers many things: how we sit, walk, stand and move. This type of non-verbal communication includes posture, bearing, stance and the more subtle movements we make. It can be easy to misinterpret body language. Someone moving fast with a heavy footfall and strong, deliberate movements could indicate anger or aggression, but equally someone who is very confident but who is also fearful, anxious or stressed.

Gestures

We wave, point, beckon or use our hands when arguing or speaking animatedly. Some people are very expressive with their hands when speaking, while others keep their hands completely still. Often gestures are unconscious and sit outside awareness, and can vary widely across cultures. Remember that what is a compliment in one culture can be an insult in another.

Eye contact

This is another element that differs wildly across cultures. Sometimes direct eye contact can mean respect and sometimes it can be viewed as disrespectful. Maintaining eye contact can be very uncomfortable for some people, regardless of culture, and it is not helpful to try to make eye contact with someone who clearly doesn't want to. Interestingly, the eyes can communicate many things, including interest, affection, hostility, or attraction. In appropriate circumstances, eye contact is helpful in allowing us to acknowledge what someone has said and the feelings expressed in what they have said, and to maintain the flow of conversation and to check for engagement and ease.

Touch

We communicate a great deal through touch. Think about the very different messages given by a weak handshake, a hug, a pat on the head, or being grabbed by the arm. Touch is a very sensitive issue when it is used in counselling skills and should be used extremely sparingly, if at all. Touch can be a comfort, but it can also be frightening and even threatening, and it can be misinterpreted too.

Space

This is another important issue that was mentioned in Chapter 2 on listening. Have you ever felt uncomfortable during a conversation because someone was standing too close to you? We all have a need for physical space, although that need differs depending on the individual, the situation, and the closeness of the relationship. You can use physical space to communicate many different non-verbal messages, including closeness, hostility, affection, aggression or to engage with issues of power and control.

Voice

It's not just what you say, it's *how* you say it. Tone is very important. Tone is listened to as much as the actual words used and a harsh tone could close someone down and make them withdraw. A warm tone can enable someone to relax and feel safe. Things to be mindful of are timing and pace, how loud or how quietly you speak, your tone and inflection.

It is fair to say that we rely on a variety of information, including tone of voice (Paulmann & Uskul, 2014), body language (Aviezer et al., 2012), and contextual cues (Aguert et al., 2013), to try to make sense of what someone is saying and what they are thinking and feeling. There are no hard-and-fast rules to understanding the majority of non-verbal communications and it is all too easy to make assumptions based on our own current and past experiences. It can be helpful to pay attention to inconsistencies. Is the person saying one thing, while their body language is conveying something else? For example, are they telling you 'yes' while shaking their head 'no'? It can be helpful simply to notice this: 'It's interesting your words are saying one thing but your body language seems to be saying the opposite'.

There is an old television game show called *Catchphrase*. The game show host would invite the contestants to: 'Say what you see'. This is very apt and fitting when using counselling skills:

Say what you see, not what you think you see.

Activity – I have lost my voice

This is a fun activity and shows that a lot of communication takes place without words.

> For a whole day, pretend you have lost your voice completely. All interactions and conversations must take place without you using your voice. You are not allowed to cheat and write anything down either! At the end of the day, reflect on the following:
>
> How did you find communicating without words?
>
> Were you able to make yourself understood?
>
> Were you able to get your needs met?
>
> How did you communicate without your voice?
>
> What did you find the most effective: facial expression or body movements and gestures?
>
> What have you learnt from this activity?
>
> Who you are speaks so loudly I can't hear what you're saying. (Ralph Waldo Emerson, n.d.)

Non-verbal communication has massive cultural variance: what is a sign of affection in some cultures can be an insult in other cultures. Let's consider some of the other ways non-verbal communication can be perceived differently from how it was intended.

Eye contact

The section above acknowledges that eye contact means different things to different people. Age and gender are just two factors that influence its meaning. How long the contact lasts and who instigates it has significance in some cultures and countries. In some Asian cultures, avoiding eye contact communicates respect. In Ghana, a child making eye contact with an adult is seen as a sign of defiance. In North America, making eye contact is taken to convey equality. Eye contact around the world differs tremendously and it is worth taking a moment to consider some examples.

Eye contact recommended

United Kingdom – Eye contact is mainly seen as a sign of trustworthiness and openness. A lack of eye contact could be seen to suggest shiftiness, dishonesty or even lying.
USA – Eye contact shows a commitment to the conversation but should not be held too long or too intensely.
Australia – Eye contact conveys honesty and trust but should not be overdone.
Greece – Eye contact shows interest, honesty and sincerity. A lack of eye contact could well generate a sense of unease.
France – Unbroken eye contact is extremely desirable and to break eye contact could be considered very rude.

Eye contact not recommended

China – Eye contact could suggest anger or disrespect.
Japan – Eye contact is often considered rude. Children are taught to focus on the neck of the person they are talking to in order to soften their gaze.
Vietnam – Eye contact can be a way of expressing attraction, but eye contact with someone of the same gender could well instigate an argument.
Cambodia – Here women are expected to look at the ground when speaking to men and eye contact in general can signal disrespect.

Eye contact sometimes recommended

Iran – Eye contact is not OK between different genders where the gaze needs to be lowered. Likewise, young people should not make eye contact with older people. However, it is OK to make eye contact with friends and family members.
Indonesia – It is not usually OK to make eye contact with people in authority, but it can be OK if it is not prolonged in other conversations.

Kenya – The use of eye contact varies a lot in this vast country. Eye contact is less accepted in rural areas than in cities.

The above examples clearly illustrate what a minefield eye contact can be when communicating. The best way forward is simply to follow the lead of who you are talking with and not to make assumptions or try to guess what is the best thing to do. How do you experience eye contact?

Touch

We have already acknowledged the emotional factors affecting how touch is received, but there are also cultural and geographical considerations. Some examples include:

- It is OK to touch children on the head in North America but is highly inappropriate in Asia, where the head is a sacred part of the body.
- In the USA and the UK, a strong handshake is an acceptable greeting, but in France the equivalent would be kissing both cheeks.

Touch between genders varies widely across countries and cultures. Overall, in a helping relationship, the rule of thumb is simply no touching. However, some professional roles, such as caring and nursing, require a considerable amount of touching. It is down to the skill of the professional to ensure that any physical contact is appropriate to their profession and not just casual acts of contact, even if the intention is that of affection.

How do you experience touch?

Gestures

Again, let's take a moment to consider the possible variables of a simple hand symbol. Touching the thumb with the forefinger to form a circle means:

- Something is acceptable in America
- Money in Japan
- Zero in France
- A rude word in some areas of Eastern Europe.

So many different meanings for a tiny little gesture, and that's just one example among many.

Facial expressions

As for gestures, facial expressions mean a myriad of different things. Winking in Latin America is romantic and often a sexual invitation, but it is just plain rude in China. The Yoruba people in Nigeria use a wink to ask a child to leave the room.

Posture

In helping work, it is suggested that practitioners have an open posture, and an open posture means not sitting with arms or legs crossed. In some Arab countries, someone might not cross their legs to avoid showing the bottom of their shoes because it is considered dirty. An American standing with their hands on their hips would be communicating power and strength, but an Argentinian doing the same thing would suggest anger and a challenge.

This section could go on for hundreds of pages and still not be complete. When using counselling skills, we need to be mindful of difference and diversity and not assume that other people assign the same meaning to non-verbal communication as we do. Rather than make assumptions, we can check things out. *What did that mean to you? Is that OK with you?* Remain curious and open to how different people communicate and watch and learn rather than rushing ahead with a set of preconceived ideas.

Summarising

Summarising is like a bigger version of paraphrasing and reflection. It is generally used at the end of a helping session to acknowledge everything that has been talked about. It helps to link the different things that have been discussed and to acknowledge the different feelings that have been shared. It can also be used mid-way through a session and can be effective to help someone prioritise or focus. For example, 'You have talked about a few different things; your sister, your work, how you feel about other students on your college course and also about wanting to lose weight. Which one of those would you like us to talk about? Which one shall we start with?' Summarising should not be simply a list of what's been said or a verbatim report of what someone has said. It needs to pull all the parts of the conversation together to acknowledge what's been said and to communicate listening and understanding.

A summary near the end of a helping session also helps to prepare for the ending, allowing the pace and emotional intensity to slow down, to ensure the person is ready to leave and face the outside world without feeling too vulnerable or exposed.

Thoughts on offering a summary

Here are some effective ways of summarising:

> We are coming to the end of our time together today and I'd just like to summarise what we've talked about in order to make sure I've heard and understood. You talked about…. Have I got that right?

> You've talked about several different things. Which feels like the most urgent one?

> You started talking about holidays and this reminded you of when you were younger, which put you in touch with some difficult feelings of shame and betrayal; both feelings you find very difficult to manage. We soon need to stop for today and I'm wondering how you can take care and be gentle with yourself for the rest of the day.

> Thank you for sharing with me today, you showed a lot of motivation around starting your new business and making a fresh start. You feel very positive and hopeful and would like our meetings to help you to stay on track and for me to remind you of why you are doing this, if it becomes a struggle at times. Is that what you meant?

> So you feel… and also there were other things you mentioned, such as…. Have I heard that correctly?

> You talked about how hard it is to make a decision. On one hand there's all these things pointing towards saying yes and on the other hand a different set of reasons that suggest you should say no. Sounded like a lot of ambivalence keeping you stuck. Where does that leave you now?

> You spoke about your feelings towards a work colleague and feeling upset about how you have been treated because it reminds you of a very painful time when you were bullied at school. Have I got that right?

Summarising is a belt-and-braces counselling skill. It is at its most valuable when ending a helping session, but is also useful for focusing and for refocusing when the helping session becomes confused or circular.

Learning journal

Responding skills

I am a lot more comfortable learning about responding skills than I am practising them. Before this course, I thought counselling skills was about giving people advice and pointing them in the right direction. Now I know that the skills that I am learning will help people to find their own solutions and ways of healing and moving forward.

If I start giving advice, it makes me the expert and actually disempowers the person I am meant to be helping. On top of that it is very arrogant of me to think I know what is best for someone. If someone is doing something that I think is not good for them, I thought the right thing to do was to try to get them to stop, but I'm learning that this is not altogether helpful. I had an example of this in my personal life recently. A good friend of mine has been drinking far too much after a relationship break-up. I have been using my new skills to listen, but felt I had to do more and tried to persuade her to stop drinking so much. This seemed to be working and she told me how she had cut down and was feeling much better. After a few weeks I saw her very drunk in a pub and her sister told me she was drinking more than ever. When I asked her about it, she said that she had to lie to me to shut me up as I put so much pressure on her to stop. In my attempt to help her I had actually made things worse. By putting pressure on, I had stopped being a support and became the opposite. She felt judged by me and unable to tell me the truth. What she needed was someone just to listen and be there for her. She didn't need me to do anything, she simply needed me to be able to sit with her and understand. This was a big lesson for me, and I hope I can remember it when I get the urge to tell someone what they need to do.

I have been practising paraphrasing in my everyday conversations to try to feel more comfortable with this way of communication. It felt very clumsy at first. I was so busy trying to remember exactly what someone had said in order to paraphrase it back to them using different words that I missed a lot of what they were saying. By the time I'd worked out how to paraphrase something they had said, the conversation had moved on and my carefully constructed paraphrase was no longer relevant. The more I practise, the more relaxed I feel, and the paraphrases I offer feel more genuine and not as wooden and forced. Initially, I thought paraphrasing was a bit of a waste of time and was worried people might think I was patronising them by just repeating back to them what they had said, but I have been pleasantly surprised. The main thing I find is that people tend to open up more and to continue talking more freely after receiving a paraphrase. I think paraphrasing lets someone know you are with them, walking alongside them with understanding and interest.

Using silence is a skill I find difficult. I didn't regard it as a skill until now; quite the opposite. I thought silence was a bad thing that should be filled as quickly as possible. Now, I am beginning to tell the difference between a helpful silence and a horrible silence. The horrible silences are those I just sort of freeze in and don't know what to do and sort of panic inside. Other silences still feel uncomfortable, but it's like I still feel connected to the person I am listening too. It's hard to explain. A horrible silence feels like two separate people sitting in a room. A good silence feels as if the people are thinking about the same thing together. It was good to think about why silence is hard for me. I think I feel uncomfortable because I think I should be doing something, and sitting in silence doing nothing can't possibly help anyone. I should do something, say something, and help in some way. It's hard to believe that offering and sitting with silence is helpful and supportive.

Tutor feedback

Your description of trying to learn the skill of paraphrasing made me laugh out loud. Just as you get the perfect response, the moment passes ... the proverbial horse has bolted.

It is good to hear that you are practising your skills in everyday situations and relationships. A word of caution: practise your skills by all means, but do not take on everyone's needs and problems. Self-care and wellbeing must come first. Be mindful of the need for balanced relationships with give and take. I would be interested to read about your personal patterns of relating. In your personal relationships, do you tend to give more care than you are given? Or vice versa? Who sorts things out and gets things done? I think more will be revealed as the course unfolds.

Silence can be a challenging skill to offer and sit with. It can be uncomfortable for both people, but it offers the gift of reflection and time to get in touch with feelings and memories that may have been hidden under the chatter of everyday life.

Rumi said – the quieter you become, the more you are able to hear.

Silence

It can seem a little strange to think of silence as a counselling skill, but it is an important and helpful skill when used in a sensitive and timely manner. Silence means different things to different people. Some people are comfortable with silence, whereas many find silence very uncomfortable. It is this discomfort that causes helpers to fill the silence with questions, suggestions and advice, etc., all of which are unhelpful.

Activity – Silence inventory

How do you feel about silence?

What are your thoughts and feelings when there is silence in a helping session you are facilitating?

What do you do and say when confronted with silence?

In the space below draw a picture, diagram, mind map or collage of what silence contains for you. What thoughts and feelings are in the silence? What does silence mean to you?

Even when we try hard to sit with silence, there can be an urge to fill it – silence can be very powerful and dynamic.
Silence:

- Can help someone get in touch with their feelings and what's really going on for them
- Can allow time to reflect and gather thoughts together

- Can move the session forward and allow the helpee to bring something into the helping session that had previously been left unsaid
- Challenges the helpee to take responsibility and use the helping session
- Gives time to someone to decide what they want to talk about
- Is an intimate experience and requires trust to stay with it and allow the process to unfold
- Can be louder than the spoken word; feelings can be heard within silence
- Can be experienced as empathic and considerate and also as frightening and anxiety-provoking
- Can be too long and be unhelpful and unproductive; it is not helpful to leave the client floundering without containment and purpose
- Distorts time; 30 seconds of silence can feel like an eternity.

As with all counselling skills, timing is crucial. Helpers need to be mindful of when to use silence and how long the silence should last. Silence needs to allow space for the helpee to reflect and ponder, but not be so much that the helpee becomes overwhelmed and drowns in it.

As George and Cristiani (1995, p. 28) state: 'Silence communicates to the client a sincere and deep acceptance.'

Questions

Questions could be seen as the chilli pepper of counselling skills. They need to be used sparingly, but when used properly they are very valuable and can really enhance a dish and bring about much needed change. A risk of using questions is the temptation to ask a question because you can't think of anything else to do and find just staying with someone's pain and unhappiness too difficult. A question can move someone away from feelings into a more content-based dialogue.

Open and closed questions

Basically, a closed question is one that requires a 'yes' or 'no' answer. They are fact-finding questions and generally seek specific information for a specific reason, e.g. a doctor asking health questions to ascertain what ails someone and what medication they need.

- How old are you?
- Is the pain at the front or back of your chest?
- Do you have a temperature?

- Is there pain when you breathe?
- Have you ever had asthma?
- Have you had a cold recently?

Closed questions tend to be about what the helper wants to know, rather than what the helpee wants to talk about.

Open questions are those that invite someone to talk, to open up and explore an issue, topic or problem. They focus on the helpee's agenda rather than the agenda of the person asking the question. Open questions are a valuable counselling skill as long as they are not overused. An example is a support worker asking someone about their day:

- How are you feeling about what John said?
- You said you want more independence. What could you do to make a start to be more independent?
- What do you like about shopping?
- What don't you like about being in crowds?
- What would you like to talk about today?
- Why did you do that?

'How' questions are often an invitation for someone to talk about their feelings.

'What' questions can elicit further facts and detail about something.

'When' questions are generally to do with the timing of the problem or situation, which can help to contextualise certain thoughts and feelings.

'Where' questions are generally concerned with the setting, environment and situation or place where something happened.

'Why' questions invite deeper information in relation to an event, feeling or situation. Why questions can be difficult to answer. Sometimes we don't know why we do or say certain things and therefore why questions can feel very challenging and cause someone to become defensive or worried and to perhaps try to justify or rationalise, perceiving the question to be a criticism or judgement. Why questions are best avoided, on the whole.

Activity – What type of question

In the table below is a list of questions. First, indicate whether the question is an open or a closed question. Then, in the last column, give an example of the opposite type of question, i.e. if the question given is a closed question, write an equivalent open question. The first example is completed for you.

Table 3.2 Activity – What type of question

Question	Type	Equivalent open or closed question
Do you feel happy about being away from home?	Closed	How are you feeling about going on holiday?
What do you like about snorkelling?		
When do you go to Malta?		
How many times have you had the flu?		
Where is Germany?		
Why do you dislike watching television?		
What would you like to happen on your birthday?		
How did you manage that?		
Do you want a sandwich?		
What is your favourite colour?		
Why do you like to sleep so early?		
Do you like beans?		

As has been already mentioned, there are some risks to asking questions:

1. **Bombardment/grilling** – It is easy to become reliant on asking questions, which can give a sense of being in control, but it is not helpful to the person you are helping/supporting. Instead of being a well-paced helping session, it becomes almost an interrogation. If this happens, the helper leads the session and decides what the helpee needs to talk about. The helping session can simply become question after question after question with no room for the helpee to talk and explore their feelings and situation.
2. **Directive closed questions** – This is a very sneaky way of making suggestions and forcing the helper's opinions on the helpee. For example: 'Don't you think it would be good if you got a job?' 'What do you think of eating healthily instead of all the junk food you eat?' 'Don't you think you'd be better off if you studied more?'
3. **Cultural issues** – People from different cultural backgrounds may respond to questions in different ways. Some cultures favour and find a lot of questions normal and acceptable. Others cultures will interpret questions as being intrusive or even rude. It is important to consider difference and diversity.
4. **Nosey questions** – This is where the helper wants to know something out of curiosity, rather than for the good of the helpee.
5. **Why questions** – These can feel attacking and intrusive and are best avoided: Why did you do that? Why don't you stop using drugs? Why didn't you think of the consequences?

Activity – Questions

For an entire day, aim to ask no questions – with family, friends and colleagues – and take note of how it feels.

How did you find the activity?

Why do you ask questions?

What are the benefits and shortcomings of asking questions?

Did you manage to get through the day without asking any questions?

If so, what were your interactions like?

If not, what types of question did you ask and why did you ask them? How helpful were they?

What feelings did you experience during this activity?

How do you feel about asking questions now?

How do you feel about all these questions?

It can be helpful to have a collection of useful open questions that can help someone to open up and talk. For example:

- What brings you here?
- What would you like to achieve from our time together?
- What things are difficult to cope with in your life right now?
- What is the problem from your point of view?
- How does this problem make you feel?
- What are your thoughts and feelings right now?
- Overall, how would you describe your current situation?
- If you could wave a magic wand, what positive changes would you make happen in your life?
- What do you think it would take to make you feel better, happier and more content?

Other responding skills

Restatement

This is the simplest of responding skills and means to repeat one or two words back to the helpee, to repeat back using the helpee's actual words, which are pertinent and important parts of the conversation.

Helper: I'm so unhappy

Helpee: You're so unhappy

Helper: I want a pair of red shoes

Helpee: Red shoes

Helper: I love him but I don't think I can stay with him

Helpee: Can't stay.

Restatements can facilitate clarification and help someone continue talking by offering a reassurance that you are listening and are walking alongside them. It is important to capture the essence of what is being said and then restate that. It should be used sparingly to avoid the risk of sounding like a parrot and being very irritating.

Self-disclosure

If questions are the chilli pepper of counselling skills, self-disclosure is the Carolina Reaper pepper of counselling skills – only to be used exceedingly sparingly on very rare occasions. Self-disclosure is when the helper talks about their own personal experiences, feelings and thoughts. It is crucial to check the motive for disclosure. It must be for the helpee's benefit and to be helpful to the helpee in some way. The helper must be able to explain why they self-disclosed and why it was useful to the helpee.

When thinking about social workers using counselling skills, Zur (2011) wrote:

Appropriate and clinically driven self-disclosures that are carried out for the clinical benefit of the clients and unavoidable (non-harming) self-disclosure that takes place in the community are considered boundary crossings. Inappropriate self-disclosures, such as self-disclosure that is done for the benefit of the therapist, clinically counter-indicated, burdens the client with unnecessary information or creates a role reversal where a client, inappropriately, takes care of the therapist, are considered a boundary violation. (Zur, 2011, p. 1)

Newman (2007) poses the following self-reflection questions:

- Whose needs are being met? Your needs or the helpee's?
- Have you been clear and defined your role?
- Do you enter into self-disclosure?
- Can you explain why you took a particular course of action?

Self-disclosure can be invaluable in certain situations. Knowing someone has had a similar experience or response can go a long way to addressing shame and isolation. It can break the myth of being 'the only one'. In terms of solutions, sharing with someone what has worked for you can feel very close to advice-giving, and makes the assumption that what works for you, will work for them, which can place undue pressure on someone to follow in your footsteps and then feel like a failure if they are unable to do so.

Before deciding whether or not to use self-disclosure, consider the advantages and disadvantages.

Advantages

- Builds a closer relationship, supporting rapport and trust
- Validates and normalises
- Can provide a sense of equality, challenging the power imbalance
- Helps to provide a sense of belonging, challenging feelings of being alone or being 'the only one'
- Provides a role model.

Disadvantages

- Crosses boundaries and can compromise the professional relationship
- Can change the professional relationship into something more like a friendship
- Can move the focus away from the helpee
- Can lead to role-reversal and confusion, where the helpee can feel sorry for the helper

- Can burden the helpee, who stops talking about their own pain and problems
- Can be experienced as intrusive and suffocating
- Can 'pressure' the helpee into disclosing when they are not ready
- Can leave the helper feeling vulnerable and unable to re-establish the boundaries.

Activity – Self-disclosure

We are all different and no situation is the same. No helping session is the same and there are no set responses and approaches.

What is your opinion on the above statement?

What is your personal opinion on self-disclosure?

Can you think of a situation where self-disclosure might be helpful?

Have you ever shared your experience with someone and had a positive outcome?

Have you ever shared your experience with someone and had a negative outcome?

Has a professional ever self-disclosed to you? What was this like?

If you are considering self-disclosing, PAUSE, and ask yourself why you are doing it.

If you decide to go ahead, be brief and don't go into details or specifics.

Make it clear you are only talking about your own experience and that it isn't advice or guidance, merely your opinion, which is not true for everyone.

Think about whether your disclosure is relevant to the person you are helping.

Think about the consequences. Could it be taken the wrong way? Could it be burdensome? Intrusive? Etc.

Are you comfortable and willing to self-disclose or are you doing it because you feel your experience is all you have to offer?

Immediacy

This is an interesting counselling skill. It is not as famous as paraphrasing, reflecting and using open questions, but it can be very helpful when used at the right time and in the right circumstances. Immediacy is about noticing what is going on in the room between the helper and helpee. It requires courage and honesty as it can mean identifying and talking about difficult and challenging material. Immediacy allows a dialogue about how the helper and helpee feel about each other and the work they are doing together. Immediacy allows for the introduction of hunches and the helper's sense of what is happening. It therefore carries the risk of being wrong and damaging the relationship. Thus, it is important to admit to being wrong and/or mistaken. A gentle interpretation is acceptable but if the helper denies or disagrees, it is not acceptable or helpful to argue or push for an agreement.

Here are some examples of interventions:

You looked away when I spoke about motivation and change and your jaw looked quite clenched. I thought you might be angry with me for pushing a subject you don't want to talk about.

You gave a big sigh just then and I wondered what it's like for you being here. Would you be able to tell me if you thought I was incompetent and a waste of time?

You never really look at me. I know you had a good relationship with your last support worker. Maybe I'm a poor substitute.

I feel quite frustrated and wonder what feelings are present for you.

Immediacy is very much about the here and now and the helping relationship itself. It can point out discrepancies between any cognitive dissonance in the room – when what is said is different from the behaviour shown. Like self-disclosure, it should only be used for the helpee's benefit and to deepen and support the helping relationship. The helpee can feel hurt or attacked when discrepancy is observed, and voices and immediacy should therefore be used sensitively, gently and carefully. Immediacy is most effective when you have been working with someone for some time and have been able to build a trusting and safe helping relationship, where challenge and exploration can be used without introducing a sense of criticism and attack.

According to Egan (1998), immediacy not only clears the air, but is also a valuable learning experience. To be healing rather than harmful, helpers need to have adequate self-awareness to be able to accurately identify their personal feelings, thoughts and behaviours in relation to the client, and the insight to accurately identify the helpee's feelings, thoughts and behaviours towards the helper. The helper then needs the courage and willingness to discuss and explore what's happening in the helping relationship. Immediacy can be a tricky skill to use and is used best in the hands of experienced helpers.

Minimal encouragers

The last counselling skill to be covered is a very simple one – the simplest in fact – and is the practice of minimal encouragement. The techniques used are known as minimal encouragers. Minimal encouragers are the tiny gestures and mannerisms that skilled helpers deploy to encourage someone to talk. They allow the conversation to flow without too much interruption by the helper. They let the helpee know the helper is listening and following what they are saying. They let the helpee know that the helper is with them and ready to hear what they are saying. They show interest without interruption.

Examples of minimal encouragers are:

- 'Yes'
- 'OK'
- Facial expressions
- Hand gestures
- 'Uh huh'
- 'No'
- Shrug
- 'I see what you mean'
- 'Umm'
- Silence, accompanied by positive facial expression, nods or open gestures. (Young, 2005)

Minimal encouragers are powerful skills because of the paradox that they create. In using them, helpers are helpful by being out of the way.

There are other responding skills but the main ones that are covered here provide a tool box for you to use to offer support and care to another person. Like all tools, they need to be used regularly to be of the greatest benefit, and they also need to be looked after and kept carefully, so that they stay effective and useful. The more we practise with any tool, the more adept we will become. The more we understand how a tool works and what it is useful for, the more we will become confident at choosing the correct tool for the job in hand. Some tools work well together and we can explore and practise those combinations with peers, family and friends. At first, keep things simple, do what you know and what has been suggested. A medical student ought not to be practising brain surgery, and the same is true for using counselling skills.

FOUR

Skills practice for counselling skills and helping sessions

Counselling skills training will provide ample opportunity to practise newly learnt skills and qualities. Skills practice sessions will also focus on the helping session and your ability to facilitate the beginning, middle and end of the session. Skills practice sessions generally take place in triads. Triads consist of three roles:

- Helper
- Helpee
- Observer.

The helper and helpee engage in a helping session and the observer gives the helper feedback on how they managed the helping session. The observer can be a peer or tutor or both. Skills practice can help improve how we work with others in a number of different ways. Feedback from others holds a mirror up for us to see things we may not have been aware of.

Learning journal

I have been dreading this week. The first week of triads. I had never head of the word 'triad' before this week, but it simply means three people working together. Today we were practising being in a helping session. The three roles are the helper, the helpee and the observer. In other words, two people work together and one watches and gives feedback. I was OK being the helpee – I can talk for England if I'm not the one being observed.

I found the observer role difficult. I don't like giving feedback; partly because I don't want to come across as judgemental, and also because I don't feel qualified to give feedback as I know so little myself. I am OK giving nice feedback and telling people what they have done well, but I find pointing out what I think someone hasn't done well is really hard. This isn't surprising to me because I find it difficult in all areas of life to tell someone what I don't like about what they are doing. I do realise that it's important to give constructive and honest feedback, though. I don't want to be told that I'm completely useless, but I do want to know what I do well and where I need to improve. If I only get positive feedback, I'll go on my merry way thinking things are OK when they're not, and plus I won't learn anything. Knowing this helps me to push through my fear and to give feedback as honestly as I can. When I was observing D today, I noticed he sort of ignored H when she was speaking about how hurt she was about how her teenage son treated her. D reflected back a couple of times that it sounded as if H was angry about how she was being treated. This isn't what H had said, and in my feedback I said that I had noticed that D hadn't picked up on H's hurt. I also acknowledged that the session had started well and that the summary at the end was timely and allowed the session to end safely. I felt quite guilty after I'd given my feedback as D went very quiet and didn't really say anything.

In the closing circle at the end of the day, he mentioned the skills practice and said he was grateful for the feedback because he realised his own 'stuff' had come into the helping session. He had been (in his words) hard work as a teenager, and had been pretty horrible to his mum on many occasions. He remembered her being angry, but it was painful for him to remember how much he had actually hurt his mother, which is why he had reflected anger in the helping session but ignored H's pain, which had put him in touch with his own mother's pain. This example helped my confidence and I was glad I'd taken a risk and been honest about what I'd observed. I like the analogy of sausage roll feedback... the sausage is the challenging or negative feedback and the pastry is the positive feedback. It is important to cover the challenging feedback completely but still leave bits peeking out, so it doesn't get lost. I really like sausage rolls, and what I like to do is eat the sausage first and leave all the pastry until last. I wonder what that says about me.

The hardest part of triad work is when I'm in the role of helper and have to be observed facilitating a helping session using my counselling skills. It feels as if I am under a huge magnifying glass and

I feel very small and awkward, even my words trip over each other and I feel clumsy. My head is so full of all the things I shouldn't say and mustn't say that I find it hard to say anything. I know that silence can be helpful, but not the horrible 'Oh my god, what can I say?' silences where I feel like a rabbit in headlights. I find myself just saying '…and how does that feel?' over and over again like a parrot. It feels so false and like speaking in a foreign language.

It's being observed I hate. I feel judged and that makes me feel ashamed. It's even worse when there is tutor observation. I really want to do well and show that I am capable, but instead I sit there like a stuffed dummy with a nodding head.

Tutor feedback

The thought of a stuffed dummy with a nodding head made me smile, but I also read how anxiety-provoking skills practice is.

You find giving feedback hard but are aware of what your difficulties are in this area and have been able to move past your own fears in order to help someone improve their use of skills. By offering only positive and pleasant feedback, feelings won't get hurt and you won't feel guilty or frightened of potential consequences or conflicts. Offering pleasant feedback only helps you it does not help the person receiving the feedback. Giving honest and real feedback really values yourself and the other person. It shows that you esteem them enough to risk them feeling uncomfortable and even not liking you.

It is difficult being the helper and knowing someone is watching your every move and listening to every word. We will look at ways of hopefully supporting triad work so that it is not so terrifying.

I like your analogy of 'sausage roll' feedback. Rolling up the challenging feedback in what was done well is a good idea. By the sound of it, eating a sausage roll will never be the same for you again. Perhaps you are a great lover of pastry who gets the sausage out of the way first in order to savour the delicious pastry; or is it the other way around?

What suits you best in life? To get the horrible out of the way first and save the best until last, or to eat the delicious first and then take on the horrible?

When practising skills and giving feedback, it is helpful to use a feedback form that identifies how a helping session is ideally structured. The feedback sheet in Table 4.1 may be helpful.

Table 4.1   Observer feedback to helper

Beginning the session		
Did the helper	**Y/N**	**Describe with example(s)**
Welcome the helpee		
Explain what is on offer		
Outline limits of ability and role		
Describe confidentiality and its limits		
Inform the helpee of the time boundaries		
Begin to build rapport		
Invite the helpee to talk		

The body (middle) of the session		
Did the helper	**Y/N**	**Describe with example(s)**
Keep the focus on the helpee		
Have appropriate body language:		
• Open posture		
• Respectful spacing		
• Lean towards the helpee		
• Be relaxed		
• Appropriate eye contact		
Use minimal encouragers		
Show interest		
Use responding skills:		
• Paraphrasing		
• Restating		
• Summarising		
Offer empathic understanding and stay with uncomfortable feelings		
Use questions when necessary:		
• Open		
• Closed		
Sit with silence		
Use immediacy effectively		
Use self-disclosure to support the helpee		
Show:		
• Respect		
• Kindness		
• Consideration		
Be responsive to the change process		
Maintain professional boundaries throughout the session		

(Continued)

Table 4.1   (Continued)

Ending the session

Did the helper	Y/N	Describe with example(s)
End the session safely		
Inform the helpee that the session is coming to an end		
Maintain the time boundary		
Summarise the session		
Check helpee is safe to end		
Let helpee know what happens next and what options there are		
Offer signposting options or support referral if appropriate		
Agree date and time of next meeting if applicable.		

Contraindications and areas needing work

Did the helper	Y/N	Describe with example(s)
Ask too many questions		
Follow their own agenda		
Give advice or make suggestions		
Placate or sympathise		
Judge		
Interrupt		
Talk over the helpee		
Make assumptions		
Rush		
Take offence and become defensive		
Fill silences		
Use self-disclosure inappropriately, making the session about themselves		
Talk too much		
Overpower the helpee		

Observer feedback to helper

In skills practice sessions, the helping role is often seen to be the most important, but actually the role of observer is vitally important. The observer needs to evidence skills and qualities around giving constructive feedback. Giving honest and helpful feedback requires candour and

Table 4.2   Observer inventory sheet

	Y/N	Describe with example(s)
Did you give the helper feedback that was:		
• Honest		
• Specific		
• Confident		
• Balanced		
• SMART		
• Constructive		
• Courageous		
If not... why not?		
Are you able to discern between 'good' and 'bad' practice?		
How do you feel about feeding back on areas that need improvement?		
What are your fears about giving feedback that might be difficult for someone to hear and receive?		

courage, and sensitivity is need when offering challenging feedback that could be received with discomfort and even pain. The observer inventory sheet in Table 4.2 will enable the observer to identify and reflect on the quality and effectiveness of the feedback offered.

Giving and receiving feedback

Feedback can be a difficult and painful area, both for the person giving feedback and for the person receiving it.

Some of the reasons why giving feedback can be difficult include fears around:

- Hurting someone
- Being hurt
- Invoking an angry or defensive response
- Not being liked
- Reprisals
- Being wrong.

Some of the reasons why receiving feedback can be difficult include:

- Feeling judged
- Feeling inadequate

- Disagreeing with feedback
- Feeling exposed
- Feeling not good enough
- Feeling shamed
- Feeling hurt
- Feeling vulnerable
- Feeling attacked
- Feeling misunderstood.

An unfortunate truth is that we tend to remember the negative feedback for far longer than we do the positive feedback. This is called negativity bias and means that receiving criticism has a greater impact on us than receiving praise. Therefore, we need to find a way of offering and receiving feedback that can be heard and digested without causing too much distress. It is important that feedback is honest or it becomes a complete waste of time. Using counselling skills benefits greatly from honest and specific feedback. We can be blind to some of our behaviours, and having them brought to our attention can help us to build self-awareness and grow in competence and ability. Feedback that is offered in a harsh and critical way can bring about the very thing it is trying to prevent. Someone who feels harshly criticised could become defensive or lose confidence, and this could impact on their ability to use counselling skills ethically and safely. Constructive feedback aims to do just that, to construct and build ability and competence. It therefore needs to acknowledge both what is done well and what areas need improvement.

To be palatable and digestible, the positive feedback should outweigh the negative feedback. The positive feedback can act like a cushion against the sting of criticism which can be a by-product of negative feedback, offering areas for growth and improvement. The feedback sandwich, or constructive criticism sandwich, offers a way to give feedback that is tasty and digestible with little risk of emotional heartburn and indigestion. In this model, the positive feedback is offered first and last. And the area for improvement is sandwiched between the positive feedback.

First slice of bread: Something the helpee did well
Sandwich filler: Something the helpee could improve on
Last slice of bread: Something else the helpee did well

In his famous verse drama, *Murder in the Cathedral*, T. S. Eliot wrote:

The last temptation, the greatest treason
To do the right deeds, for all the wrong reasons

Table 4.3   Appropriate forms of feedback

Wrong reasons for giving feedback	Right reasons for giving feedback
To condemn	Commitment to safe and ethical work
To affirm own personal opinions	Concern for the person and their work
To attack	Responsibility
When in a bad mood and unable to put own feelings to one side	To guide and support
	From care
To look good	To enhance someone's skills
Superiority	To help
To please a third party	To share knowledge
To feel powerful	To build ability and competence

It can be helpful to remember this quote when offering construc-tive feedback. It needs to come from the 'right' place, and to be a supportive tool rather than a weapon of control and manipulation. Table 4.3 provides some of the right and wrong reasons for giving feedback.

Tips for giving and receiving constructive feedback

Giving feedback

- Be honest and genuine
- Own the feedback – begin with, 'I', e.g. I feel…, I saw…, I might be wrong but…
- Start with the positive – what the person did well, what skills they used effectively
- Be specific and give actual examples where possible
- Focus on behaviour (what can be changed) rather than personality (which can't be changed)
- Offer alternatives and suggestions for change and improvement
- End with a positive
- Remember to give SMART feedback
  - Specific
  - Measurable
  - Achievable
  - Realistic
  - Time boundaried
- Offer feedback in the feedback sandwich – some positive feedback, an area for improvement, more positive feedback.

Receiving feedback

- Listen even if the feedback is uncomfortable
- Listen even if you disagree
- Listen even when you want to argue or explain
- Listen
- Clarify understanding
- Check you have heard correctly
- Check with others for accuracy
- Ask questions
- Take time to digest and reflect
- Respond rather than react to feedback
- Thank the person for the feedback and the opportunity to grow and learn (even if you would rather eat your own head than do so!!)
- Listen
- Listen
- Listen.

For all of us, hearing negative feedback can sound like a criticism or judgement, and in many ways that is what it is. It is natural to feel and to act defensively and to be resistant in these instances. It can be helpful to explore how to manage or respond to this resistance. For some of us, we are all too accustomed to being criticised and judged, and we will simply accept all the negative feedback without checking whether it is accurate. Listen to feedback and reflect on whether it belongs to you. Treat it like trying on a new coat. If it fits – wear it. If it doesn't – hang it back on the peg.

Activity – Offering constructive feedback

Read the following accounts from people using counselling skills in their professional role and give each person constructive feedback on:

What they did well

Areas for growth.

Situation: Rehab for substance misuse

Role: Keyworker

I met with C and A today – I asked them if they'd been involved with the group relapse. They were giggly and I think they found it all really exciting. I could feel myself getting cross with their attitude. I was thinking, you are both bright, articulate people – you are better than this – why don't you behave differently? Don't you want to recover? People's lives are at risk and they seemed to think it was funny. I like the pair of them enormously, they are both witty and intelligent, and they have a good standard of education and are articulate and well spoken.

I was so disappointed with their behaviour and rather than asking how they were, I found myself saying I was really disappointed with them and that I expected more. C started sniggering and I found myself getting really cross, asking if he thought it was a joke and that he was close to be kicked out. Thinking about it now. I feel quite mortified. I realised that I had expectations of them because of their backgrounds – the rest of the residents are mainly ex-offenders, and some have not had been able to maintain any education. I think this fails both groups – they didn't get their needs met and I behaved like a critical mum would have. I think I have really damaged my relationship with both of them. What's really worrying is – do I have lower expectations of the others?

A said she was bored but had been feeling low recently with the same old same old, and the relapse had saved her from suicidal thoughts. I was feeling cross by this stage and decided she was being manipulative. I think she feels sorry for herself a lot. So rather than offering more support, I said nothing. I feel really torn between the whole tough-love scenario and offering support, but on reflection, I think I was using tough-love as a kind of punishment. I think this whole situation has opened a really unpleasant aspect of myself. I really felt like I was being a cross and strict parent with absolutely no empathy. I was really dismissive.

I'm not sure how to move forward with this.

Situation: Women's Centre

Role: Group worker

I really messed up today. We had our first women's group and it was marvellous. The women were opening up and there was lots of great sharing. I did an exercise where partners stared into each other's eyes – to understand how intimacy might feel. Some members of the group felt really awkward with it and I used my skills to facilitate a safe space where the women could be as engaged as much or as little as they wanted to.

The women went on to discuss differing issues and one very young, but very large black woman (E) revealed that her mum had used her as a dominatrix. It took me by surprise and I actually laughed in shock. I apologised immediately and said it was a shock reaction. She looked hurt. I said 'You are so young, that's so awful'. I really wanted to rescue her (and myself) from my awful reaction. The group took over and offered her support. No one had a pop at me, but I still felt miserable – I still do. I am overwhelmed at how loving the group is. One older former sex worker was really skilled – showing compassion and a level of (irreverent) identification that had the whole group in stitches. It was a comment about 'punters', which was actually rather demeaning, but it definitely did the trick. By this stage we were very close to finishing – I had not been watching the clock as it felt somehow dismissive of what was happening. We were in the lounge with a locked door and I decided to prolong the group, capitalising on the privacy and space. Everyone was really pleased about this but within 10 minutes inertia kicked in and it really felt like we had exhausted the group. So, it came to a limping halt.

Later I found that my colleague had complained that I ran over time, so I had to discuss this with my boss. He said running over was a big no-no, and for the first time ever I felt I had really done something wrong – he is normally very casual about my perceived failings. I didn't tell him about my shock reaction. I couldn't bear the judgement and condemnation. I am really struck by how upset his disapproval of my conduct has made me. I think I have him on a pedestal, which probably isn't healthy, but he really knows so much. I also find myself getting cross with my co-worker. Our contracts are for 12 months and there is only one post going forward. She has said she really wants it. She is assertive, but I don't rate her and cannot challenge her. I have just realised that it is easier to feel cross about her than it is to feel the awfulness of my mass failing today.

As Dale Carnegie reminds us:
Abilities wither under criticism, they blossom under encouragement.
(Carnegie, 1998, p. 220)

FIVE

Empathy

Empathy is a very important quality. In simple terms, it means to understand someone, to see the world through their eyes, to feel through their heart. When looking at someone's situation, empathy is about understanding that situation from their viewpoint. Generally, when we make a judgement or have an opinion about something, we are using our values, past experiences and beliefs to make that judgement. When using empathy, we need to put all that to one side and look at the situation with the other person's values, past experiences and beliefs. Empathy seeks not to be understood; it seeks to understand. We can use our own self-awareness and a full range of counselling skills, values and qualities to truly understand someone and their world in as deep a way as we can. In many ways we need to learn to suspend disbelief and belief in order to see someone clearly without the blinkers of our own experience. Communicating empathic understanding allows someone to feel accepted, supported and understood.

Empathy is not about feeling sorry for someone, it is not about 'Oh you poor thing'. Empathy is not done to someone; it is done with someone. It is hard to truly empathise and requires scrupulous self-honesty, willingness and open-mindedness. Empathy also requires enormous amounts of effort, concentration and discipline.

If we had a secure childhood with enough to eat, warm home and clothes to wear, we might struggle to understand why someone steals food and even hides food. If we have never been hungry, this could make no sense. If we step outside our experiences and imagine what was going on for the person who steals and hides food, we will go on to learn that the person is from a family of nine. Their father was an alcoholic and their mother had three cleaning jobs to try to make ends meet. There was never enough. Never enough money, never enough love, never enough food. The person had a strong sense of deprivation and fear that they would be left hungry, without the means to feed themselves. It then becomes easier to understand why the person steals and hides food. While we were looking through our own eyes of having enough, it was hard to understand how desperately the person was trying to make up for the lack in their past. Once we saw the situation through the eyes of a starving child, we could not help but truly understand and feel compassion and tenderness for someone trying to make sure they would be safe and OK.

Attunement

Attunement is similar to empathy but goes a little step further. It refers to the reactiveness we have to another person. It is the part of the process by which we form relationships. It refers to the helper's ability to pick up on the nuances of the helpee's presence and conversation, and then to respond in a way that lets the helpee know that they have been heard and seen; that the helper 'gets them'.

A definition of attunement is:

> a kinaesthetic and emotional sensing of others knowing their rhythm, affect and experience by metaphorically being in their skin, and going beyond empathy to create a two-person experience of unbroken feeling connectedness by providing a reciprocal affect and/or resonating response. (Erksine, 1998, p. 236)

Attunement means literally the ability to tune-in and relates to how connected we feel to someone and how we communicate that sense of connectivity to them. Once we are 'in-tune', we will be able to offer the helpee appropriate and effective counselling skills, techniques and interventions. It is worth acknowledging the importance of being attuned to ourselves. Perhaps attunement in relationships is like playing a musical instrument. If the musical instruments are 'in tune', they make a harmonious and pleasing sound. If they are 'out of tune', the sound can be grating, unpleasant and hard to hear. It is the same with relationships. When we are attuned, there is harmony.

Blocks to empathy

For all of us, there are things we struggle to empathise with and understand. We need to identify what these are in order to understand their roots and also to clarify what we are able to work with. There could be some things we can't understand and there could also be things we don't want to understand. There could be things that we find repulsive or disgusting and we don't want to explore them and find understanding. There could be things we understand but still feel repulsed by, things we simply do not like and don't want to talk about and explore with someone.

Activity – Reflection on empathy

In the table below are some statements. For each one, answer the following questions:

Are you able to understand and empathise?

What thoughts and feelings do you have in relation to each statement?

Have you ever been in a similar situation?

Which person were you in the scenario – the person causing harm or the person being harmed?

Has a loved one been in a similar situation?

Which person were they in the scenario – the person causing harm or the person being harmed?

How does this activity help you to understand empathy better?

A carer stealing from disabled people in order to play online bingo	A young man stealing money from his grandmother's handbag as she makes him a cup of tea and a sandwich	Someone tampering with an ex-lover's car, to cause a crash, as an act of revenge
A heavily pregnant woman is prostituting herself to pay for drugs	Someone who is drunk driving at over 85 miles per hour	Someone having unprotected sex with someone while knowing they are HIV positive
A mortuary attendant having sex with corpses	Someone forcing a child to perform oral sex and threatening to kill their sibling if they don't	Someone bullying and ridiculing someone until their victim suicides

(Continued)

(Continued)

A woman having sex with her sister's partner	Someone murdering for money and cutting up the body to hide it in different places	Someone who worked in a concentration camp
Someone punching themselves in the face in front of their children	A surgeon performing unnecessary surgeries	Someone burgling a house and taking jewellery and photographs and personal items
A racist	A father sexually abusing his son and daughter	Someone forcing their partner into prostitution to pay for the bills
A woman watching her boyfriend rape a 3-year-old child	Someone putting cigarettes out on a child's face and arms	Someone screaming at their children that they hate them, that they are disgusting and should never be
Someone injecting drugs into their groin	A rapist	Someone performing an illegal abortion

It is OK not to understand or want to understand everything. It is OK not to have global empathic understanding. If we simply do not want to understand certain issues, that's fine too. What our self-awareness and insight will give us is choice. Working with certain issues or people might be very painful and trigger painful memories. We do not have to work with these issues if we don't want to.

Self-awareness allows us to know what our personal and professional limits of ability are. It helps to show us what we are qualified to work with on a professional level and also the things we feel able to work with on a personal level. What is important is to be aware of what our personal blocks to empathy are and how we want to manage them. If there are some areas we want to challenge and overcome in order to find and offer empathic understanding, that's fine. Self-awareness and empathy are inexorably intertwined. If we have experienced some of the scenarios in the activity above, our empathic understanding will almost certainly have been affected. We could be the perpetrator or the victim. If we have behaved in an abusive and harmful way, we could have insight into what drove that behaviour, why we did what we did. That insight and understanding could shine a light of empathy onto someone else's 'bad' behaviour. Conversely, if we deny or disavow our own behaviour, we might find it impossible to accept it in someone else. Of course, if we have been on the receiving end of someone else's abusive or harmful behaviour, the awfulness of the experience and subsequent hurt and pain could limit our ability to want or desire to empathise.

Personal and cultural differences can impact on how we empathise. What is acceptable to some people and some cultures is abhorrent in others, and it can be all too easy to expect others to abide with our own beliefs and values. Being aware of and acknowledging differences and diversity promotes cultural empathy. Cultural empathy simply means to consider, understand and appreciate the feelings, thoughts and behaviours of members of a group with a different cultural background from our own.

For example, someone seeing a woman wearing a hijab or burqa could assume that she is oppressed, devalued and probably controlled by her culture, religion and husband. Someone practising cultural empathy might also consider that the hijab or burqa is the woman's choice and a way of honouring her religion and culture. There is not an automatic assumption of gender injustice. Of course, as with all things, we won't know the woman's reality until we talk with her and build a safe and trusting relationship.

In order to use counselling skills to communicate empathic understanding in a helping situation, it can be helpful to:

- Identify differences and similarities
- Understand the helpee's social environment
- Learn about the helpee's culture and background if possible
- Use culturally appropriate communication skills
- Be mindful of any personal prejudices and stereotypes in relation to certain cultures
- Accept the helpee's values and beliefs regardless of whether they are the same as yours
- Investigate and offer additional information and signposting to helpees who feel underprivileged and/or discriminated against
- Be aware of the psychosocial adjustments that may have had to be made by helpees who have moved from another country.

Learning journal

Empathy

In general, I think I am an empathic person. I find it quite easy to understand most things. A good friend of mine said I'm too understanding and let people get away with blue murder. I've made a lot of mistakes in my life and done many things I'm not proud of, things I'd rather not have done. I hope I'm not making excuses for myself but I did the best I could at the time. I know I hurt people and I hurt my children by being absent and bad tempered. I feel guilty about those times but they do help me to empathise with people who have done and said 'bad' things or behaved in hurtful ways. There is a saying I like which says, 'When I'm behaving at my worst, it's when I need loving the most'. I think this is true. When I'm swearing and shouting and out of control, it is almost always because I feel overwhelmed, unable to cope, scared and alone. I try to see other people's behaviour through that lens. I have learnt that when we judge, we can't empathise and truly understand and accept someone else. These are blocks to empathy. I have old prejudices that I'm able to understand, challenge and work through. For example, when I was naughty as a child, my mother would tell me that the men in the white coats would come and take me away.

I have current blocks to empathy that I understand but can't challenge and work through. If I'm honest, I don't want to understand. I can't empathise with paedophiles. I do know that bad experiences can cause people to do bad things and I also know that good people can do bad things, but I just wouldn't want to listen to and support someone who does such awful things to vulnerable children. I also have a block to empathy for married men who are unfaithful. I know that this is because it happened to me and was one of the most painful and humiliating experiences of my life. Everyone knew my husband was seeing someone else except me. Even when he told me about it, I still wanted him to stay, but he chose to leave and be with the other woman. I cannot imagine a time when I would be able to listen to and offer support to someone who was having an affair and wanted to leave the marriage, without being taken back to the pain of my experience.

I don't think I'm racist but growing up, there were a lot of stereotypes applied to different races and cultures. Whole races were considered mean or stupid or greedy or cruel or violent, and although I know that such labels cannot possibly apply to whole groups of people, the old messages are still there at times. What I do find difficult is responding to other people being racist. I don't feel brave enough to challenge someone, but then I feel guilty that I had in some way colluded. Last week I was in the supermarket and someone made a very derogatory comment to me about Chinese people and how they should take their ways back to their own country as they weren't welcomed here. They used really vulgar language and I felt uncomfortable and also angry, but all I did was half nod and half smile and made my escape. I felt as guilty as if it had been me who had made the horrible comment.

Tutor feedback

Thank you for your thoughts on empathy and making judgements. You write really well about your blocks to empathy and who you are and are not willing to listen to and offer support. You wrote about your fears about the topic and worrying about what people might think of you if you got something wrong. In several of your journal entries you have written about how important other people's opinion of you is. It would be interesting to read more about this. Is it a need for approval or a fear or conflict or being disliked, or something else entirely?

You raise an important question. Is it possible to be too empathic? I think the answer is... yes, but only if we allow ourselves to be hurt by doing so. If someone loses control and lashes out, hitting us, in rage and savage emotions, we might well be able to understand and empathise with that behaviour. We know how good people do bad things and understand that when someone is overwhelmed by strong feelings they can act out and behave in violent and hurtful ways. Yes, we can understand, but that doesn't mean it is OK to stay put and be hit again. We can understand and accept without colluding with hurtful and harmful behaviours.

You wrote: 'They used really vulgar language and I felt uncomfortable and also angry, but all I did was half nod and half smile and made my escape. I felt as guilty as if it had been me who had made the horrible comment.' *Someone acted badly but it was you who felt guilty. Is this a pattern you can recognise elsewhere in your life?*

Activity – Empathy

Below are some quotes on empathy. Choose three of your favourite ones and explain why they appeal to you. Are there any you disagree with?

To see with the eyes of another, to hear with the ears of another, to feel with the heart of another. For the time being, this seems to me an admissible definition of what we call social feeling. (Alfred Adler, 2002, p. 64)

You can only understand people if you feel them in yourself. (John Steinbeck, 2002, p. 391)

We think we listen, but very rarely do we listen with real understanding, true empathy. Yet listening, of this very special kind, is one of the most potent forces for change that I know. (Carl Rogers, 1980, p. 116)

The empathic understanding of the experience of other human beings is as basic an endowment of man as his vision, hearing, touch, taste and smell. (Heinz Kohut, 2012, p. 144)

If we can share our story with someone who responds with empathy and understanding, shame can't survive. (Brené Brown, 2012, p. 68)

If it is not tempered by compassion, and empathy, reason can lead men and women into a moral void. (K. Armstrong, 2010, p. 52)

To embrace suffering culminates in greater empathy, the capacity to feel what it is like for the other to suffer, which is the ground for unsentimental compassion and love. (S. Batchelor, 2010, p. 165)

Among all the creatures of creation, the gods favour us: We are the only ones who can empathize with their problems. (D. Eagleman, 2009, p. 78)

I believe empathy is the most essential quality of civilization. (R. Ebert, 2010, p. 1500)

Empathy is the fifth component of emotional intelligence. ... Respect is a stepping stone to Empathy. (S. Erakat, 2006, p. 255)

This is what differentiates sympathy from empathy. No matter how much I care for you, it's not until I recognize me in you and you in me that the veil of gauze is lifted on the world. (J. Galaxy, 2012, p. 104)

What dooms our best efforts to cultivate empathy and compassion is always, of course, other people. (T. Kreider, 2013, p. 59)

When your own life is threatened, your sense of empathy is blunted by a terrible, selfish hunger for survival. (Y. Martel, 2003, p. 132)

One of his greatest talents was empathy; no sadist can aspire to perfection without that diagnostic ability. (V. Vinge, 2010, p. 454)

Cognitive empathy must play a role when a lack of emotional empathy exists because of racial, ethnic, religious, or physical differences. (H. Riess, 2017, pp. 74–7)

Vulnerability is the birthplace of love, belonging, joy, courage, empathy, and creativity. It is the source of hope, empathy, accountability, and authenticity. If we want greater clarity in our purpose or deeper and more meaningful spiritual lives, vulnerability is the path. (B. Brown, 2012, p. 37)

If there is one lesson that I have learned during my life as an analyst, it is the lesson that what my patients tell me is likely to be true – that many times when I believed that I was right and my patients were wrong, it turned out, though often only after a prolonged search, that my rightness was superficial whereas their rightness was profound. (H. Kohut, 2009, p. 93)

Empathic listening takes time, but it doesn't take anywhere near as much time as it takes to back up and correct misunderstandings when you're already miles down the road; to redo; to live with unexpressed and unsolved problems; to deal with the results of not giving people psychological air. (S. R. Covey, 2004, p. 253)

Life is the first gift, love is the second, and understanding the third. (M. Piercy, 2016, p. 685)

Learning is a result of listening, which in turn leads to even better listening and attentiveness to the other person. In other words, to learn from the child, we must have empathy, and empathy grows as we learn. (A. Miller, 2002, p. 101)

Empathy may be the single most important quality that must be nurtured to give peace a fighting chance. (A. Roy, 2004, p. 39)

Yet, taught by time, my heart has learned to glow for other's good, and melt at other's woe. (Homer, 2008, p. 146)

Peace requires something far more difficult than revenge or merely turning the other cheek; it requires empathizing with the fears and unmet needs that provide the impetus for people to attack each other. Being aware of these feelings and needs, people lose their desire to attack back because they can see the human ignorance leading to these attacks; instead, their goal becomes providing the empathic connection and education that will enable them to transcend their violence and engage in cooperative relationships. (M. B. Rosenberg, 2005, p. 129)

Peace cannot be kept by force; it can only be achieved by understanding. (Albert Einstein, 2010, p. 252)

The core conditions

In 1957, Carl Rogers identified six necessary and sufficient conditions to facilitate change and these are explained in full in Chapter 9 (Rogers, 1957, pp. 95–6).

In counselling and helping work, the term *core conditions* is widely used. Interestingly, the term *core conditions* was not used by Carl Rogers, but is now used to refer to conditions 3, 4 and 5 of his six necessary and sufficient conditions. These are:

3. The counsellor is congruent (genuine).
4. The counsellor experiences unconditional positive regard (UPR) non-judgemental warmth and acceptance – towards the client.
5. The counsellor feels empathy towards the client.

These conditions are over 60 years old and yet they seem to have stood the test of time and are still a bedrock of counselling and a range of health and social care roles. They can also be referred to as the *facilitative conditions* or *therapist's conditions*. Empathy is one of the core conditions and is therefore essential to the process of change and healing.

Communicating empathic understanding

- Actively listen to the person – challenging any blocks to listening which get in the way of really hearing what someone is saying
- Use minimal encouragers and an open body language to encourage someone to tell their story
- Mirror the person's body language and facial expression but in a natural and gentle way
- Imagine what it would be like to be in their position
- Don't feel bad for them, or patronise or express sympathy
- Work hard to understand them
- Challenge any personal prejudices and judgements that get in the way of understanding
- Use paraphrasing and reflecting to check understanding and encourage the person to continue talking
- Summarise your understanding to let them know you empathise.

Empathy is often thought to be simply acknowledging how someone feels but Rogers' conception of empathy is different and more complex than simply responding to feelings. He said:

Being empathic is to perceive the internal frame of reference of another with accuracy and with the emotional components and meanings which pertain thereto. ... It means to sense the hurt or the pleasure of another as he senses it and to perceive the causes thereof as he perceives them. (Rogers, 1980, p. 140)

Here are a few examples of empathic responding:

You feel anxious because you are giving a presentation at work.
You feel depressed because your relationship has ended.
You feel angry because you did not receive the raise you expected.

Reflective listening may not reflect both feeling and content. Here are a few reflective statements that are not empathic responses:

I hear you are giving a presentation at work.
You feel that your relationship could have continued.
You feel that your boss was not fair in her decision.

Note: None of the above three statements reflects 'feeling', which is part of a true empathic response.

Another potential response is called solicitation. Solicitation responses are those the therapist makes that invite the client to explore further. Examples include:

Tell me more about what is making you anxious.
You said the relationship was traumatic. What made it traumatic for you?
Describe how you and your boss interacted.

Each of these responses invites the client to explore their feelings and situation further.

Identification

In its simplest terms, to identify means to recognise similarities between ourselves and others. The *American Heritage Dictionary of the English Language* (2016), defines identification as:

A person's association with or assumption of the qualities, characteristics, or views of another person or group.

Identification, although not empathy, can be extremely valuable. It can be extremely painful for someone to believe they are the only one to feel the way they do, the only one to react and behave the way they do, the only one to have been abused, the only one to have been treated in certain ways. It can be a huge relief to find out that others have had similar experiences, that they are not unique, weird or mad. Identification can strip away stigma and isolation. In helping work, it should be used with caution. Generally self-disclosure is required for identification to take place and this should be used carefully and sensitively and only if it is in the best interests of the helpee. When a helper identifies with the helpee, there is a risk of assumptions being made. The helper could jump to conclusions and think they understand how the helpee is without actually talking and listening to the helpee in order to enter their unique world. Experiences may be the same or similar, but this does not mean that the associated thoughts, feelings, behaviours, perceptions and reasons are the same. The statements below may shed some light on this.

1. I absolutely understand, the same thing happened to me

Although the same thing happened, how the person experienced it will almost definitely be different. Your response, thoughts and feelings in response to the experience could be totally different from someone else's. How we perceive and respond is based on hugely complex interactions between many factors that include culture, upbringing and family of origin, age, gender, personality, history of relationships, race, religion and personal identification. This list is far from exhaustive but clearly highlights that we are all unique individuals and as such can't assume that we experience similar events in a similar way.

2. I know exactly what you mean, I had three children too

As above, we have no idea of the interplay surrounding having three children. What is the person's social situation, financial situation and family situation? How old are the children? How does the person feel about the children? Does the person have support? Are there cultural considerations? What gender are they? Just those few questions quickly highlight how ridiculous it would be to assume that everyone with three children is having the same experience.

3. I'm frightened of spiders too and know why you are frightened of them

We have no idea why the person is frightened or even what fear means and how fear is experienced by them. We don't know the extent of the fear or how the person reacts or responds to their fear. We certainly don't know enough to make such an assumption as this.

Compassion

A chapter on empathy would not be complete without mentioning compassion. The literal meaning of compassion is to *suffer together*. It is not the same as empathy, but the concepts are most certainly related.

Gu et al. (2017) identified five elements to compassion:

1. Recognising suffering
2. Understanding the universality of suffering in human experience
3. Feeling moved by the person suffering and emotionally connecting with their distress
4. Tolerating uncomfortable feelings aroused (e.g. fear, distress) so that we remain open to and accepting of the person suffering
5. Acting or being motivated to act to alleviate suffering

Buddhism considers compassion as loving kindness and something to be used to alleviate the suffering of others. Compassion acknowledges and honours both our own suffering and the suffering of others and aims to arrive at a place of acceptance for both. So, interestingly, compassion draws on both Eastern and Western Philosophies. The risk of compassion could be over-identifying with the helpee and becoming emotionally tangled.

The New Quotable Einstein by Alice Calaprice (2005, p. 206) recalls a pertinent comment by Albert Einstein:

> A human being is a part of the whole, called by us 'Universe,' a part limited in time and space. He experiences himself, his thoughts and feelings as something separate from the rest – a kind of optical delusion of his consciousness. The striving to free oneself from this delusion is the one issue of true religion. Not to nourish it but to try to overcome it is the way to reach the attainable measure of peace of mind.

To summarise, empathy is the heart of counselling skills. It works hard to enter someone's world carefully and sensitively. Its purpose is acceptance and understanding. Empathy is kind.

SIX

Equality, diversity, discrimination and inclusion

Be the change that you wish to see in the world. (Mahatma Gandhi, n.d.)

The previous chapter highlighted the enormous value of the quality of empathy. It also highlighted that empathy cannot exist where there is judgement and a lack of understanding and acceptance. Empathy means to step into someone else's world and shoes, feeling through their heart and seeing through their eyes. In order to do this, we need first to be aware that other people are different from us. If we can't do that, we will simply imagine how we would feel in their situation and this is not empathy. We are all different. Even 'identical twins' are each different and unique. We also have different experiences and perceptions of life, experience, health and wellbeing. No matter how many similarities there may be, each person is unique and has a unique experience and viewpoint on life, relationships and themselves. The differences may be visible or invisible but they will be there. Table 6.1 lists just a few examples of 'differences'.

It is interesting to note that there are as many, if not more, unseen differences, which emphasises the need to use counselling skills to form a relationship that supports someone to open up about who they are and how they feel, so we can truly get to know them and not simply make guesses and assumptions. In order to use counselling skills in an effective, heartfelt way, we need to understand our own relationship with difference or diversity and become aware of all the ways we judge, discriminate, devalue, exclude and cause harm from prejudice, ignorance, fear and a whole host of other things that cause separation

Table 6.1   Visible and invisible differences

Visible differences	Invisible differences
Disabilities that can be seen	Disabilities that can't be seen
Colour / race	Taste and preference / likes and dislikes
Age	Feelings
Language	Sexuality
Dialect / accent	Religion and spirituality
Physical appearance, e.g. size	Values and beliefs
Gender	Family background / upbringing

Activity – Differences

You are invited to complete Table 6.1 by considering all the ways we are different, diverse and unique.

from others. When using counselling skills, it is all too easy to assume we know who someone is and what they need, without taking the time to find out.

The word 'diversity' can stir up some challenging feelings. For some people, the desire not to be judgemental can result in differences being ignored. There can be a fear of doing or saying the wrong thing and causing offence without meaning to, which results in not being able to make a real connection. Denying differences is like denying the person and ignoring who they are. By ignoring and not mentioning the fact that someone, for example, has a disability will not make the disability go away. Difference and diversity are about acknowledging, understanding and communication with curiosity and acceptance. It is saying to someone: 'What is it like to be you, here and now?' It is saying: 'I would like to understand what it is like to be you, here and now.' To begin the journey into being non-judgemental, understanding and accepting, there is a need to understand the terminology and language related to this issue and to take the time to reflect on our own person relationship with difference and diversity.

Discrimination

Discrimination means to exclude people because of their differences. Discrimination is often based on a person's negative attitude towards others. Various things can cause negative attitudes towards others, for example:

- Stereotyping
- Intersectionality
- Prejudice
- Assumptions.

Stereotyping

Stereotyping means to label entire groups of people with the same attributes. The definition of a stereotype is:

A fixed, over-generalised belief about a particular group or class of people. (Cardwell, 1996, p. 234)

For example, a 'Hells Angel' biker dresses in leather.

One *advantage* of a stereotype is that it enables us to respond rapidly to situations because we may have had a similar experience before. One *disadvantage* is that it makes us ignore differences between individuals; therefore, we think things about people that might not be true (i.e. we make generalisations).

As I am writing this, I have a whole host of stereotypes in my head that I have heard over the years. I am loath to write them down as they are mostly insulting and derogatory towards various groups of people. Most stereotypes follow the format:

All... are ...

An example might be:

All people who wear glasses are clever.

Stereotypes also exist in health and social care settings. Certain groups can be labelled as 'difficult' and/or demanding and this can impact on the care they receive. Once someone is labelled as 'difficult', this label can be handed on to new carers and support workers, who then meet the person with a preconceived expectation and may well act differently

---

Activity – Stereotypes

Take some time to reflect on the stereotypes you have heard and think about whether you believe them.

Also take the time to think about whether you would be comfortable writing them down and/or speaking them out loud.

---

towards them because they are expecting conflict or difficulties. This can be especially true in mental health services. Borderline Personality Disorder (BPD), also known as Emotional Instability Disorder, was once thought of as something that was not treatable. It is a horrendous label which suggests that for people with this diagnosis there is no help. BPD is linked closely to emotional instability and often people with a BPD diagnosis have a history of severe trauma and abuse. There is treatment for BPD today, but the old stigma and stereotype can still persist. The stereotype itself is, in my opinion, a way of perpetuating the instability, emotionality and irrationality associated with the disorder as the professionals involved risk responding to the label of 'difficult and demanding', rather than seeing a unique individual in terrible pain and distress, and who lacks the ability to manage their feelings and environment – somewhat like a tiny child.

Activity – Recognising stereotypes and discrimination

The below account is from a young woman called Rose. Once you have read her experience, comment on the questions it raises.

My name is Rose, I am mixed race and 21 years old. I take a lot of medication to stabilise my mood and for psychosis. Basically, I've had a crap life. My mum has mental health problems and my dad sexually abused me from when I was 3, maybe younger. I came into services when I was 12 years old. I was self-harming myself pretty badly by then. Being part of child mental health services wasn't too bad – I generally got the feeling they wanted to help me. I was admitted to hospital a few times for months on end and quite a few times I was restrained and held down by several people and injected with some sort of sedative – this was because I think I was having flashbacks to the abuse and just freaked out.

When I was 18 years old, they moved me into adult services and as time has gone on things have felt really different and I feel blamed and judged nearly all the time. On my first admission to an adult ward, I felt ignored and judged, and when I tried to say this, it was suggested that I was making it up due to my illness. I wasn't making it up. I know when someone is patronising or ignoring me. I was told to take responsibility in an adult way, but had to ask to go outside for a cigarette and would sometimes have to wait over an hour for someone to unlock the door. Told to be an adult, but treated like a child. I felt they hated me and saw me as a time waster, stopping all the people who were really ill from getting help. Both in and out of hospital I know I am difficult; I was just all over the place, my moods seemed so extreme.

I felt so terrified most of the time and would reach out and ring the crisis team for help, but they couldn't wait to get me off the phone. I felt wretched all the time and nobody seemed to understand. They kept telling me to stop being attention-seeking and take some responsibility for myself. But I just felt like exploding all the time. The more they didn't like me and ignored me, the more I needed help and wanted to hurt myself, and the more they said I was attention-seeking. I didn't wash or look after myself, but I didn't know why. I just knew I was desperate and alone and trying my best but no one seemed interested. I tried to kill myself several times and was taken to A and E, but they just discharged me after a couple of hours and I was left on the street with no way of even getting home. I hadn't even been told I had been diagnosed as having a personality disorder – I don't know if they treated me the way they did because of how I behaved or because they had been told my diagnosis. I just know it was a shit time and no one seemed happy – me or them.

What stereotypes do you think might have been applied to Rose?

What sort of discrimination could result from this stereotyping?

If you were working with Rose, what sort of things could you do to ensure she is not being discriminated against within services?

Intersectionality

The Oxford Dictionary states:

Intersectionality, n.
The interconnected nature of social categorizations such as race, class, and gender, regarded as creating overlapping and

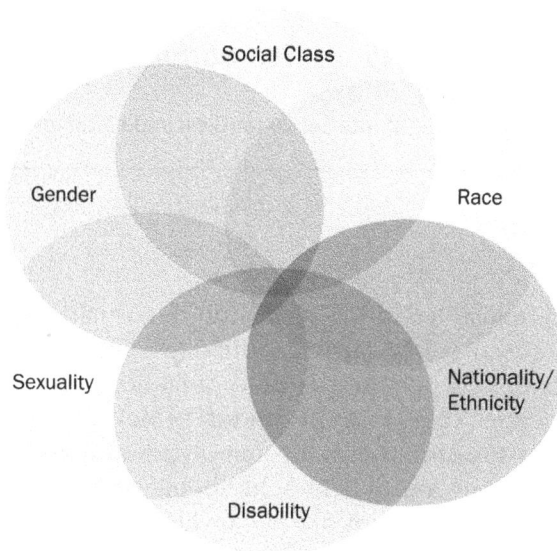

Figure 6.1   Intersectionality (created by Jakobi Oware)

Source: Reproduced under CC BY-NC-SA.

interdependent systems of discrimination or disadvantage; a theoretical approach based on such a premise.

Intersectionality is therefore a framework for understanding how different aspects of someone's identity combine to produce unique modes of discrimination and privilege (see Figure 6.1). It identifies advantages and disadvantages that are felt by people due to a combination of factors.

In simple terms, intersectionality refers to how some people are discriminated for more than one characteristic and that people can be disadvantaged by multiple areas of oppression, e.g. race, class, age, gender identity, religion or lack of, age, sexual orientation, etc. For example:

> A woman earns less than a man.
> A black woman earns less than a white woman who earns less than a man.
> A trans black woman earns less than a white woman who earns less than a man.

This is quite a simplistic example but it shows that when there are multiple areas of potential discrimination, the impact on the person is greater.

Activity – Intersectionality

In the activity above, how might intersectionality be impacting on Rose's experience?

Prejudice

Prejudice is an unjustified or incorrect attitude (usually negative) towards an individual based solely on the individual's membership of a social group. For example, a person may hold prejudiced views towards a certain race or gender (e.g. a sexist attitude) (McLeod, 2008). There is a relationship and similarity between stereotypes and prejudice. Basically, as stated, stereotypes are beliefs held about certain groups of people. Prejudice is how those groups are negatively assessed. Prejudice has an emotional component and response, whereas stereotyping is more of an intellectual exercise. We are prejudiced when we make judgements about individual members of a stereotyped group and, from that judgement, decide whether someone is acceptable or not acceptable. On a simplistic level, prejudice is to pre-judge. It is to make a decision before we have any of the information we need to make a fair and accurate appraisal.

> If we are homophobic, we are prejudiced against all gay people, before we have even met them.
> If we are an Anti-Semite, we are prejudiced against all Jewish people, before we have even met them.
> If we are a xenophobe, we are prejudiced against all people from other countries, before we have even met them.

Assumptions

An assumption is the act of supposing something or taking it for granted without proof. When using counselling skills, it is all too easy to assume we know things without evidence and information to back up our knowledge. Assumption kills curiosity and stops us from wanting to know and understand more. If we know something, why would we keep looking for it? Sometimes assumptions can be accurate and sometimes they are not, and that is too much of a gamble to take with someone's life. If we do think we know something, it is important to check it out for accuracy rather than running with the assumption. When using counselling skills, we need to keep reminding ourselves about the distinction between facts and assumptions, to ask questions if needed and to keep the conversation open and flowing. Part of using counselling skills may also be to challenge someone else's assumptions. Someone may assume a friend doesn't like them because they haven't phoned. This may be true, but there could also be many other reasons why the friend hasn't phoned. Counselling skills can gently challenge the assumption, explore the feelings it has evoked and look for ways to find resolution.

> Some everyday assumptions might be:
> Most people have a better life than I do
> I am right and anyone who disagrees is stupid
> I will wake up tomorrow
> My partner will be faithful
> Things will work out OK
> The grass is greener on the other side
> I can get a lover as long as I am attractive and pleasant and nice
> It won't happen to me
> Being rich will make me happy
> Everything happens for a reason
> Everyone is having an affair or cheating
> Good times are just around the corner
> There is life after death.

The most important thing to take from this chapter is to understand why we judge, the origins of personal and societal stereotypes and prejudice, and the willingness to challenge and move past them in order to be able to communicate and support someone without the blinkers of judgement and assumptions. In terms of offering care and support, the goal is to be inclusive and to work hard to make sure that difference is not a reason for refusing care and support.

Inclusion

Inclusion means being included within either a group or society as a whole. Inclusion doesn't simply mean an open-door policy. Inviting someone in a wheelchair to a support group that takes place on the third floor of a building that has no lift is not being inclusive. Inviting a deaf person to a motivational talk without the provision of sign language and placing them too far back from the stage to read lips is not being inclusive. A care worker telling someone what to do and doing everything for them may seem appropriate for someone with complex needs, but actually everyone has the right to have a say and take part in their care and life, no matter how small or seemingly insignificant. When using counselling skills, it is vital to include the person being supported. When working with someone who has a hoarding disorder, who is just about to lose their child and their home due to the state of that home, it can seem very helpful and necessary to just clean up the house, but this would not be useful. The person with the disorder needs to be included in the process for it to be meaningful and helpful in the long term.

Inclusivity covers more than just premises and improving access; among many other things, it can include times and dates, language, gender, disability, ability, age and whether parents can bring their children with them. The list is long and careful consideration is needed to ensure that no one seeking help and support is excluded. It is important to understand someone's differences so that they can be included and treated equally and fairly. Those using counselling skills must take care to ensure the work is inclusive and that everyone has the opportunity to take part when they want to.

Noah's Ark

When I think of inclusivity, I think of the story of Noah's Ark. All animals, beasts, insects and birds of the earth and sky were welcome and able to board Noah's Ark. The entrance was big enough and wide enough for all and there was somewhere for all to live and sleep. No creature was left out. No creature was the wrong colour, shape, size or demeanour to be excluded. They were all different but all were of equal value. They must have had to find a way to exist together ... and certainly not to eat each other!

Figure 6.2   The animals go in two by two – hoorah, hoorah!

Source: George F. Cram, 1882

Activity – Create your own Noah's Ark

Design a modern-day Noah's Ark for people – all types of people, all sizes, colours, abilities, personalities, shapes and genders.

Design the inside and also the entrance way.

Where would people sleep, cook, eat, socialise, play, work, etc.?

How would you assign the jobs that needing doing and to whom?

Unlike real life, you have unlimited space and an unlimited budget.

Please draw your **Ark of Life**.

Many of us understand the pain of being excluded, of not being picked for a school sports team or not being invited to a party, of being left out and not belonging.

Learning journal

The topic 'difference and diversity' was covered today. I feel a lot of fear around this subject. I feel scared of getting things wrong and saying the wrong thing. I don't want people to think I'm racist or homophobic because I use the wrong term or word.

I don't think I'm racist but growing up, there were a lot of stereotypes applied to difference races and cultures. Whole races were considered mean or stupid or greedy or cruel or violent, and although I know that such labels cannot possible apply to whole groups of people, the old messages are still there at times. What I do find difficult is responding to other people who are being racist. I still don't feel brave enough to challenge someone, but then I feel guilty that I have in some way colluded with them. I've written about this in a previous journal entry and it remains a real problem for me. Last week I was in the supermarket and someone made a very derogatory comment to me about certain people who should take their ways back to their own country as they weren't welcomed here. I felt uncomfortable and also angry, but all I did was half nod and half smile and made my escape. I still feel as guilty as if it had been me who had made the horrible comment.

In the skills practice sessions, I know we are meant to acknowledge and work with the differences and similarities between us, but my default position is to pretend I haven't noticed any differences, even when they are glaringly obvious. In last week's skills practice session, I was working with a peer who is a black woman and quite a lot older than I am. I mentioned the age difference between us but just could not bring up the difference in race. Even writing this, I don't know whether to write – race or colour or culture. So, the most obvious difference between us – I am white and she is black – was ignored.

Another thing I do which really annoys me is that I am overly nice and jolly to people I see who have a physical disability. Because I feel uncomfortable, I act stupidly and then I feel guilty about that.

Tutor feedback

Thank you for your honesty. You have a lot of guilt.

You give a good overview of your fears and discomfort around difference and diversity. I appreciate all that you wrote and agree that words can wound and hurt, but the attitude and intention behind the words is the power that has the strength to harm or heal. The skills session with your peer, as you acknowledge, would have been so much richer by not only acknowledging the differences between you but also acknowledging your difficulty in talking about it.

I agree, it is difficult to challenge other people's prejudice and hatred towards certain groups, and in some cases it risks the bad feeling turning onto you, but, as you say, you felt as guilty as if you had made the horrible comment. If you had been able, what would you have wanted to say and do in that situation? As stated, you have given a good overview and identified some challenges. I would now invite you to reflect on your personal prejudices and discomfort around the topic of diversity. What feelings are there? What prejudices persist even after challenge? What role does fear play?

Working and living to ensure equality of opportunity and a fair society is not just a nice thing to do. Being judgemental is not confined to the worlds of counselling, care, support and helping others. It is the law.

The Equalities Act 2010

The Equalities Act was introduced in the United Kingdom in 2010. It provides a legal framework of anti-discrimination and promotes equality of opportunity for all. It is an umbrella of protection from unfair treatment and promotes a just and equal society. The Equalities Act works by offering legal protection against discrimination or unfair treatment for certain personal characteristics which are vulnerable to discrimination. These personal characteristics are called 'protected characteristics' and it is against the law to discriminate against anyone because of:

- Age
- Disability
- Race, including colour, nationality, ethnic or national origin
- Being pregnant or on maternity leave
- Gender reassignment
- Being married or in a civil partnership
- Religion or belief
- Sex
- Sexual orientation.

The law protects those with these protected characteristics:

- At work
- In education
- As a consumer
- When using public services
- When buying or renting a property
- As a member or guest of a private club or association.

The Equalities Act is not inclusive to those within the 'protected characteristics'. The law also offers protection from discrimination for those associated with someone who has a 'protected characteristic', for example friends, family members, partners. The law also protects anyone who complains about discrimination or supports someone else's complaint.

Perception

There is something else that can get in the way of being non-judgemental and that is our own feelings and perceptions. Some days I am an incredibly loving and understanding person – on other days, I don't like

A tale of perception

Version 1

I woke up this morning, feeling warm and cosy. I laid in bed for a few minutes listening to the birds singing outside the window, enjoying the different sounds and how they just sing their hearts out into the world. I could hear the world waking up and stretched and yawned and got up ready to meet the day. I have a duvet cover and pillows with butterflies on and it always makes me smile when I make the bed. I went into the bathroom and noticed how sleepy I looked in the mirror. I splashed my face with water to wake up. Having a shower brought me completely to life and I felt refreshed and clean afterwards. I bought a new dress last week and decided to wear it for the first time. It fits like a glove. I walked into the kitchen and made myself tea and toast, which I really enjoyed. I put a big dollop of peanut butter on my toast, yummy. I stacked the dishwasher and wiped the sides quickly, and had a few minutes to play with my dog Benjy before I went to work. He's a beautiful golden labrador and I just adore him; he's like an actual person and I'm sure he talks to me.

As I left the house, I noticed my neighbour and waved a hello. He was trimming the honeysuckle that grows along the fence between us. He trims my side too and I must remember to buy him a little present as a thank you. The farmer from across the way was trying to reverse his tractor up the track opposite my house. I know how difficult that can be and stopped to help guide him. He told me his daughter has given birth to twins and he now has 11 grandchildren. 11!! He invited me to a little get-together in the village later in the week. I'm grateful to be part of a close-knit community. There was quite a lot of traffic on the way to work, but the time passed listening to a really funny programme on Radio 2. The nursery kids were on their way in and its lovely to see them making a long caterpillar, all holding hands with a teacher at the front and back to make sure no one gets lost. I was a few minutes late for work but I can easily make that up at lunchtime, and I work for a decent company so it's not a problem. I had a chat with colleagues while my computer warmed up and then noticed an email from my boss asking to meet later. I felt excited. I've applied for a promotion and wonder if it's about that. Well, I'll soon find out! John from finance was laughing in the kitchen. He's got a big booming laugh which is infectious and made me smile even though I didn't know what was funny.

I've only been awake an hour and a half and such a lot has already happened. Hopefully the rest of the day will be as good.

anything or anybody, myself included. The story here illustrates this. The story hopefully portrays how personal thoughts and feelings can affect how we see and feel about a situation and how in turn that perception can impact on how we care for and support others when using counselling skills.

A tale of perception

Version 2

I woke up this morning, feeling sweaty and suffocated by the duvet. I laid in bed for a few minutes, and my head was already going a million miles an hour, full of all the things I should do and reminding me of what a mess my life is. The birds were squawking as if they were being tortured outside the window and the noise felt like sandpaper on my brain. I could hear the dustman and the traffic, and some idiot was bellowing on the building site which made me get up as there was no peace to be found in my bedroom. The sheet had come off the bed and I got even sweatier and became more bad-tempered as I tried to manhandle it back on. I went into the bathroom. I looked in the mirror and couldn't believe what I saw. I looked like an old crone and wondered how I even dared go outside with a face like mine. Having a shower nearly gave me a heart attack. The shower ran cold and I nearly drowned myself trying to sort the temperature out. Nasty thing. I got in and out as quick as possible. I put on a new dress I bought last week and was horrified. I looked like a space-hopper squashed into a condom. Disgusting! I make myself feel sick. I took it off and put on leggings and a baggy top, angry with myself for being a fat, ugly, greedy monster.

I walked into the kitchen and made myself tea and toast, which stuck in my throat as I'm far too fat already and should eat fruit rather than toast and a big dollop of peanut butter. It serves me right for being a greedy pig. My dog Benjy heard me and ran in. He wanted a walk but he'll have to wait, which makes me feel guilty for not getting up in time. He jumped up at me and covered me in hairs and I'm too late to change. I shouted at him and pushed him away. I don't even know why I got a dog, I don't like them and they're too much responsibility.

As I left the house, I noticed my neighbour trimming the honeysuckle that grows along the fence we share. He trims my side too, but why doesn't he just mind his own business? He makes me feel guilty and annoyed. Do-gooder! He should stay on his side. So what if the honeysuckle is untidy. I really don't like him and having to pretend to be nice. I waved but couldn't summon up a smile and now am annoyed I even waved as I didn't want to.

Great! The farmer from across the way was trying to reverse his tractor up the track opposite my house. Who made him King of the Road – idiot, entitled buffoon. His stupid daughter has produced yet more offspring and there's a get-together in the village later in the week. I'd rather eat my own head than have anything to do with someone like that. I hope the tractor gets stuck in the mud for a week. There was a ton of traffic on the way to work and I wanted to scream with frustration at the people driving like snails. I was very tempted to just drive into one of them. Some people should stick to walking – morons. Then the nursery kids caused another hold-up crossing the road in a huge great procession – come on, come on, come on, hurry up! Of course I was late for work, and not one person asked if I was OK. Horrible job anyway. My colleagues were chatting together – don't mind me – ignorant people. The first email on my computer was from my boss asking to meet later. What the heck does she want? How does she even know I'm late? What have I done wrong? She can stick the job up her bum if she thinks she can intimidate me. Stuck up bitch. Big John from finance was laughing in the kitchen. What's so funny? He better not be laughing at me.

I've only been awake an hour and a half and already I've lost the will to live.

Both of the above examples are by the same person about the same day. Nothing changed or is different apart from the person's perception. Perception plays a huge part in how we view the world and also how we perceive and judge others.

If I feel bad about myself, I tend to struggle to see anything good in people and the world.

If I feel good about myself, I tend to see goodness in people and in the world.

How judgemental I am about others is often dependent on how I feel about myself. This suggests that when I point the finger at someone else, three fingers point back at me. Some of us have a kind of radio in our head that gets stuck on a certain channel called 'Crap FM'. When we wake up in the morning, Crap FM switches on and we are deafened by the same old song.

You're crap and you know you are. You're crap and you know you are...

If you are the kind of person who has Crap FM in your head, it is important to remember to turn it off every morning.

SEVEN

Helping relationships and sessions

A helping session refers to any interaction where counselling skills are used. The length, structure and content of a helping session is dependent on the role and setting. Counselling skills can be used in many different professional roles and in many different settings. Therefore, a helping interaction can take many forms. Other names for a helping session include:

- Support session
- Listening space
- Counselling skills session
- Keywork session.

Because helping sessions take many forms and are often part of another professional role, the terminology is difficult to summarise. It can be easily understood as time spent supporting another using counselling skills.

The helping relationship or working alliance

A helping relationship is formed when two people come together to focus on the needs of one of those people. Another term for a helping relationship is *working alliance*. Bordin (1979) conceptualised the working alliance as consisting of three parts: tasks, goals, and bond. Tasks are what the helper and helpee agree need to be done to reach the helpee's goals or hopes, based on their presenting concerns. The bond forms from trust and confidence that the tasks will bring the helpee closer to their goals. Other terms include helping alliance, therapeutic relationship and support dyad, all of which suggest two people 'on the same side', working together towards a desired outcome, one person assisting another.

This relationship, as with helping work itself, varies widely. It could be a GP who has built up a relationship over many years or an interaction lasting a few minutes with a housing officer. In addition, the support offered can be very different. A police officer and a support worker would both be able to use counselling skills to form a working alliance, but the nature of the relationship and support offered would be very different. Some roles where counselling skills are used to help and support someone include:

- Nurse and patient
- Social worker and client
- Carer and resident
- Rehab and service user
- Prison officer and prisoner
- Teacher and student.

These name just a few as the actual list is almost endless. Notice that there are many different names to depict the helper and helpee roles.

Activity – What makes a safe and trustworthy helper?

Write down all the professional and voluntary roles that you think would be enhanced by adding counselling skills.

Why do you think that counselling skills would improve the service offered by the roles you identified?

As you identify each role, consider whether you personally have been helped by any of these professionals?

What was the relationship like?

What did you find helpful and what was unhelpful?

Think of a time in your life when you have felt frightened, in pain and alone, a time you might have been badly hurt by someone, or a time when you did something you feel very ashamed of, a time of despair and hopelessness.

What did you need at that time?

What sort of support was available?

Were you able and willing to reach out for support? If not why not?

What skills and qualities would someone need to help you in those darkest of times?

Were you able to talk openly and honestly about your feelings, your problems and your struggles?

If not, what stopped you?

Relationship is a human being's feeling or sense of emotional bonding with another. It leaps into being like an electric current, or it emerges and develops cautiously when emotion is aroused by and invested in someone or something and that someone or something 'connects back' responsively. We feel 'related' when we feel at one with another (person or object) in some heartfelt way. (Perlman, 1979, p. 23)

As we can see, many professionals use counselling skills within their role to facilitate formal and less formal interactions. As well as using counselling skills to help someone, professionals may help in other ways too, for example helping with form filling, helping with personal physical needs, helping with housework, helping with homework, helping with transport, etc. In some ways, these helping interactions, which can be less structured and more spontaneous than formal sessions, can be harder to facilitate. In a more formal helping session, there are clear boundaries and a structure that facilitates a safe space.

An informal interaction could be five minutes in a hallway, in a sports arena, or on a country walk. Counselling skills can be employed at these times to listen and respond effectively, but they might not have the focus and meaning of planned, expected and structured helping sessions. These interactions do not lose value because of their *ad hoc* or 'by chance' nature. Many of us can recall a time when a comment or brief encounter has been life-changing, when someone took the time to really see and hear us and to let us know we were heard and understood and accepted. Some of those tiny interactions are priceless and there are some of those moments I recall in my own personal experience that will live in my heart forever.

In *The Art of Helping Others* (2008), Smith and Smith observed that helping work takes many forms and can take place almost anywhere in a myriad of different contexts:

The helping we explore here is characterized and driven by conversation; explores and enlarges experience; and takes place in a wide variety of settings (many not of the helper's making). However, describing the role exclusively in terms of counselling or teaching or educating narrows things down too much for us. Making sense of what these people are actually doing and expressing entails drawing upon various traditions of thinking and acting. This form of helping involves listening and exploring issues and problems with people; and teaching and giving advice; and providing direct assistance; and being seen as people of integrity. (Smith & Smith, 2008, p. 14)

Learning journal

Last week, we were asked to think of a time in our life when we felt frightened, in pain and alone, a time of being badly hurt by someone or a time we did something shameful, a time of despair and hopelessness, and to think about what we needed then and where we could go to for help.

I immediately thought of when I suffered from post-natal depression several years ago. I was so happy to be pregnant, but soon after my son was born I felt a horrible cloud descend on me. I felt I was literally dragging myself around and everything was a huge effort, even my son. I had no love or even affection for him and there were times, although I'm not proud of it, when I actually thought I hated him. I didn't wash or look after myself and I just wanted to crawl into a corner, curl into a ball and close my eyes forever. I did think of ending my life. I was either in tears or numb. I had no idea what I needed or what would help. I was completely lost. I do know what didn't help, though. My partner tried to help but couldn't understand and would try to cheer me up and then get cross when I didn't cheer up. Some of the comments from family and friends were:

You've got a lovely baby

What's wrong with you?

Come on, cheer up now

You've got more than most people

Make a gratitude list

I don't know what to do with you

Don't you love me?

What have I done wrong?

Hasn't this gone on for long enough now?

It's not all about you, you know, other people are hurting too.

My health visitor was like an angel in the middle of it all. What did she do? She listened. She listened when I was able to talk and she listened when I wasn't able to talk. She also explained to me what post-natal depression was and what treatments were available, but she didn't try to force me into anything. She helped with practicalities and, most importantly, she didn't judge me or try to talk me out of how I was feeling. It's hard to explain what she did exactly, but her visits were like an oasis in a desert. It probably helped me so much because it wasn't *what* she did that helped me; it was *how* she was with me that helped. She never talked down to me, whereas many of my friends and family spoke to me like I was a child. Also, she didn't go on about the baby – and at that time I thought of him as THE baby, rather than my baby.

Slowly I started to talk to her about how I was feeling and I did make the decision to see my GP and take anti-depressants, but the decision was mine and she supported me to make my own decision and met with me to talk about if and how they were helping, or not. As I recovered, she made fewer visits, but not until I felt ready. At no point did she tell me what I had to do or tried to push me when I wasn't ready. When I did go to see my doctor, he was pleasant and helpful but in a different way. He asked a lot of questions and it felt like a problem that needed solving. I can't remember my health visitor asking any questions. Overall, she was kind and it felt like genuine kindness. I think kindness is not highlighted enough in helping and support work. Counselling skills are massively enhanced when kindness is added, in my opinion. In fact, when I look back on my life, the times that stand out most are when people have been kind.

It is now many years later, but when I think of her I feel warm inside. I really hope I can be like she was with someone who is in despair. She was simply a gentle but strong companion in the most awful of storms.

Tutor feedback

There is little I can add as your journal entry more than adequately describes how you were supported through a difficult and dark time. Do you have people like your health visitor in your life today? What relationships do you have that offer support and acceptance? Are you a gentle but strong companion to anyone in your life?

I agree with you about kindness, it can be life-changing. To coin a phrase 'kindness is not weakness'. Kindness doesn't mean overstepping boundaries, rescuing or placating. Kindness is considerate, warm and gentle. Kindness shows care and concern and requires courage and strength. Also, kindness is considered a virtue and does not expect or need praise or reward of any kind. Kindness comes from an open and generous heart.

I'd like to add... when I think of your health visitor, I get a warm feeling too.

As previously mentioned, the reasons and purpose for undertaking a counselling skills course are varied. Many people take a counselling skills course as a first step to becoming a counsellor. Other people undertake the training to learn skills that will enhance how they relate with others. It can be easy to get lost or confused trying to understand the nature and personality of all the types of helping relationship, alliance and interactions, which can cloud the real importance of the work, which is to be there, in a meaningful way for someone in need. Therefore, we can walk a path between the different meanings and purposes and stay focused on how we can help and support someone who is finding life hard, for whatever reasons. Despite the many factors impinging on what type of relationship is formed, the underlying message is unchanged: using counselling skills to focus on the person's wants, needs and abilities, within a safe, respectful and ethical working alliance.

Value of the helping relationship

Many of us suffer from something I like to call 'people rabies'. We really want to be close with people and be supported and cared for, but there is a huge resistance to that and we can be very isolated and withdrawn, unable to reach out for the care and support we so desperately need.

As with rabies, the animal is terribly thirsty and yet terrified of water. This analogy helps me to remember that for some people being in a relationship is very frightening and painful, but that doesn't automatically mean they don't want it.

The helping relationship itself is the most important ingredient to helping and supporting someone using counselling skills. There are many things we can do to form a safe and caring relationship with someone. Good intentions are important, but they must be underpinned with understanding, self-awareness and willingness. Bellowing at someone that we are there to help them, and insisting that they be helped, may not be that helpful. Although that may seem to be a silly thing to write, many professionals can feel personally attacked if their expertise and help is not enough to bring about change. Helping work is not about coercion, control and force. We do not know what people have faced or what journey they have been on, and we simply do not have the right to inflict our opinions and expectations on them. If someone is not behaving in a way we think they should, the fault lies with us and not with them. If someone we are helping does well, we might enjoy basking in the warmth of that success. If someone isn't doing well, we may feel cross and inadequate, with the risk of taking our frustrations out on the person we are meant to be helping.

David Ellerman (2001) has argued for five principles ('doers' refer to the helpee, the person being helped or supported):

- Help must start from the present situation of the doers
- Helpers must see the situation through the eyes of the doers
- Help cannot be imposed on the doers, as that directly violates their autonomy
- Nor can doers receive help as a benevolent gift, as that creates dependency
- Doers must be in the driver's seat.

The helping relationship

Activity – The helping relationship

Below is a list of helpful attributes related to forming and maintaining a helping relationship. Rate each one out of 10 and then provide a rationale for the score you gave.

Skill or quality	Rating out of 10	Reason
Trust		
Patience		
Care		
Understanding		
Acceptance		
Tolerance		
Being non-judgemental		
Kindness		
Self-awareness		
Hope		
Open-mindedness		
Willingness		
Honesty		
Reliability		
Punctuality		
Fairness		
Resilience		
Motivation		
Courage		
Commitment		
Passion		
Integrity		
Boundaried		
Confidence		
Being a good listener		
Skilful communication		
Resourcefulness		
Good sense of humour		
Being ethical		
Compassion		
Wisdom		

Once you have completed the activity above, go back over the skills and qualities and consider how you would know that each skill or quality was present? For example:

How would you know if someone was trustworthy?
How would you know if someone was accepting?
How would you know if someone cared?

All of the above are important ingredients that are required to form and maintain a helping relationship. It might be helpful to choose one a day to reflect on and consider how you fare with that quality. Is it something you have naturally or something you need to work on to acquire?

Skills are generally things we learn outside ourselves and qualities are things that we have inside ourselves. Both can grow and flourish. Once we are able to form a safe and trusting relationship with someone, the reason for the relationship can become clear and the work itself can blossom and grow. The relationship is not about being an expert and telling someone what to do. It is not about being powerful and authoritarian. It is not about being better and more capable. It is about two fallible and imperfect human beings coming together with all their peculiarities and fears and then finding a way forward, together. It is about forming a relationship that is conducive to change and growth, but is never coercive.

Only when we know and find some acceptance for our own fears, insecurities, woundedness and struggles are we able to understand and accept these aspects in another. Change and development are written about in thousands upon thousands of books, with tips and techniques for facilitating change and movement. In my opinion, it is only when we look at ourselves and how hard it is to change, move on, let go and live that we are able to truly appreciate how difficult they can be. I can't recall a day in my life when I have woken up and thought to myself…

'I know I'm going to mess up totally today. I'm going to be bad-tempered and judgemental. I'm going to eat cake for most of the day despite being on a diet and hating my weight. I'm going to make a fool of myself in work meetings and talk over people and insist my way is the only way. I'm going to cry alone in my car because I don't like myself and can't believe that anyone else likes me either. I'm going to lie to get myself out of trouble and feel sorry for myself because no one is coming to rescue me. I'm going to despair of ever getting it right and be unable to find a positive thought or any hope anywhere inside me.'

I never wake up planning to have a day like that but sometimes I do. Sometimes we all do. It is important we remember that when working with others. We all struggle, we all hurt and some days are dark and hopeless. That doesn't make us bad or weak people. Conversely, it is those experiences and that self-knowledge that will help us to form strong helping relationships. Once we know our own vulnerabilities and darkness, it becomes impossible to blame and judge someone for sitting in their vulnerability and darkness. What we can do is to sit in the darkness with them with the knowledge that dawn will come. It's not up to us to try to force or hurry the dawn. There is no need for that. It is not our job, nor is it possible. We only need to wait, with understanding, compassion and knowledge of how dark and long some nights can be. That is enough.

> Often it is not just the knowledge they pass on or the advice they give that makes them special. Rather it is how they are with us, and we with them. We can feel valued and animated and, in turn, value them. Out of this meeting comes insight. (Smith & Smith, 2008, p. 57)

The helping session

The best way of ensuring the helping relationship is safe and strong is by ensuring that the helping session(s) are safe and strong. There are several theories around structuring a helping session (see Chapter 3) but to start, we can think about a helping session having a beginning, a middle and an end and what each part consists of. Skills practice (see Chapter 4) weaves throughout the learning and is generally fashioned around facilitating helping session.

Beginning a helping session/helping relationship

When meeting someone for the first time, there will be a lot of unknowns, the main one being that you are complete strangers. If I go somewhere, I like to know how things work, what I have to do, what will happen. If I go to a concert hall or a theatre, I like a programme to tell me what will happen and in what order. The person you are supporting may have expectations that aren't part of your role, and only by explaining what you can offer is the person able to understand what is on offer and if it is something they want. A helping session needs to have boundaries. Boundaries are the limits, or even the ground rules of the session. Boundaries are in place to keep both helper and helpee safe and will be covered in greater depth in Chapter 8.

> Boundaries are the limits that allow for a safe connection based on the client's needs. (Peterson, 1992, p. 74)

In many ways, the boundaries of a counselling session are easier to define and maintain than the boundaries of a helping relationship.

The helping relationship will have another role, which includes, but is not solely about, counselling skills. A nurse, for example, may be looking at physical needs as well as using counselling skills to offer emotional support. This could include toileting and intimate acts that need to be facilitated with care and respect for the person's dignity. Most counselling sessions take place in a designated room, but many helping interactions occur in the person's home. Although boundaries may vary across settings and roles, there are some basic boundaries that need to be in place before starting work with someone. These need to be covered at the very beginning.

Limits of ability

You need to let the person know who you are and what you can offer them.

> Hi Gary, My name is Hope and I am your helper for today. Before we start, I would like to let you know that I am a support worker with Caring UK. I am not a medical professional or counsellor, but I do have some training in counselling skills and can hopefully offer a listening ear and understanding. Hopefully, we can get to know each other a little today and you can decide if you'd like to carry on meeting with me. How does that sound?

Time

It is important to let someone know how long the session is. If not, you could end up being there far longer than you had planned and feeling unable to stop the person and end the session. Or, the person might feel shut down and even abandoned if you end suddenly without any warning.

> Hi Gary, we have 20 minutes today for you to talk about whatever you would like to.
>
> Gary, we are near the end of our 20 minutes today and have just a couple of minutes left before we end.

Confidentiality

It is vital that the person knows what is and what isn't confidential. Even in counselling, confidentiality is not absolute; there are always limits to confidentiality. These are mainly around safety and safeguarding issues and there are also legal limits, for example drug trafficking and terrorism. (Confidentiality is covered in greater detail in Chapter 8.) In helping work, there may be other limits to confidentiality, for example, you may work as part of a team which sits under an umbrella of confidentiality. This means that what the person tells you is confidential to the team rather than just you. Whatever the role and setting, the person needs to know the limits and extent of the confidentiality you can offer them. They can then decide what they feel safe to discuss. If they think that everything will be kept between you and them, they may open up about tender and painful issues and feel terribly betrayed if they later find out that you have told other professionals or even family members.

> Gary, I'd like to talk with you about confidentiality. Everything we talk about does stay between the two of us but there are some exceptions to that. There are some legal exceptions, which are…, and there are some safety boundaries, which are…. How does all that sound to you? Do you have any questions about confidentiality?

The body of the session

The main part of the session will be focused on what the person wants and needs from your time together. The wants and needs will vary from person to person, setting to setting. The person may have a goal they wish to reach or a problem they wish to solve. Some people will just want someone to listen to them without judgement. Some people will want to make a change in their life and others will want to make a change inside themselves, to build confidence or self-esteem, for example. Some people will want to share their feelings and others will want to share their thoughts. Some people will want to tell you how much they've been hurt and some people will want to tell you how they have hurt others. It does not matter what is the reason for the helping session. Your role is to facilitate a safe space where someone can talk about whatever they want to, where you use your listening and responding skills to ensure the session is helpful, and where your skills and qualities offer understanding and acceptance with kindness and compassion.

The end of the session

Endings can be difficult and painful. Even a short helping session can be painful if the ending is not managed sensitively. It is important that the time boundary is maintained. If you have told someone you have a certain amount of time together, it is important to keep to that. Leaving early or going over time can indicate that you aren't reliable or trust-worthy. Giving someone a time check can ease into the ending, making it less abrupt.

> We've got a couple of minutes until we have to stop. Is there anything you'd like to say before we finish?

Using the skill of summarising near the end can bring the session to a gentle close by acknowledging what has been said and showing your attention and understanding.

> Gary, we are coming up to the end of our time together. We touched on a lot of things in relation to your new job, the enjoyable things and the not enjoyable things, and how difficult new beginnings can be, but despite the difficult feelings you are moving forward.

The final part of the helping session can attend to future meetings, stay-ing safe and well between meetings, if appropriate, and checking the person is safe to end.

> How are you feeling right now Gary?

The lead up to the ending needs to slow the session down and bring the conversation to a close. Once the details of further meetings have been addressed, the actually ending needs to be clear and prompt.

> We've run out of time Gary. Thank you. I look forward to seeing you next week. Goodbye.

EIGHT

Ethics, boundaries and confidentiality

Ethics

Counselling skills need to be used safely and appropriately. They form part of many roles and professions in many different settings. Ethical practice is essential for all roles and settings to ensure that the work is of benefit and is not harmful to anyone.

The term 'ethics' comes from the Greek *ethos*, meaning custom, habit or character. Ethics help us to decide what to do and how to do it and are fuelled by a desire to do the right thing based on sound moral principles. Ethics cover the following areas:

- Rights and responsibilities
- Moral decisions – what is good and bad?
- Issues of right and wrong
- How to best support someone to live a good life.

Richard William Paul and Linda Elder (2006, p. 2), define ethics as 'a set of concepts and principles that guide us in determining what behavior helps or harms sentient creatures'. The *Cambridge Dictionary of Philosophy* (R. Audi, 2015) states that the word 'ethics' is commonly used interchangeably with 'morality', and sometimes it is used more narrowly to mean the 'moral principles of a particular tradition, group or individual'.

So what does all that mean?

'Ethics' is a word I find difficult to describe and explain. It is the sort of word that dances around in my head until I can't make sense of it at all. In a nutshell, working ethically means to do the right thing. An ethical framework can help us to make decisions around what the right thing is. People are individuals and each person has a unique life, with its own joys, difficulties and problems. Each person brings a different set of strengths and weaknesses, abilities and challenges. An ethical framework can help us to offer support in a way that is not prescriptive but tailored to the needs of each person we work with.

The British Association for Counselling and Psychotherapy (BACP) provides an ethical framework for the counselling professions (BACP, 2018; see Appendix III for the complete BACP ethical framework for the counselling professions). The framework uses the terms 'client' and 'practitioner' but the commitments, ethics, principles, values and personal moral qualities of the BACP ethical framework are equally relevant to helping work using counselling skills. The framework puts clients first and works to professional standards by:

- Making the client the primary concern while we are working with them
- Providing an appropriate standard of service
- Working within our competence
- Keeping our skills and knowledge up to date
- Collaborating with colleagues to improve the quality of what is being offered to clients
- Ensuring that our wellbeing is sufficient to sustain the quality of the work
- Keeping accurate and appropriate records.

The framework promotes respect and builds an appropriate relationship by:

- Valuing each client as a unique person
- Protecting client confidentiality and privacy
- Agreeing with clients on how we will work together
- Working in partnership with clients
- Communicating clearly what clients have a right to expect
- Communicating any benefits, costs and commitments that clients may reasonably expect
- Respecting the boundaries between our work with clients and what lies outside that work
- Not exploiting or abusing clients
- Listening out for how clients' experiences our working together.

It asks that we maintain integrity and keep accurate and appropriate records by:

- Being honest about the work
- Communicating our qualifications, experience and working methods accurately
- Working ethically and with careful consideration of how we fulfil our legal obligations
- Being willing to discuss with clients openly and honestly any known risks involved in the work and how best to work towards our clients' desired outcomes by communicating any benefits, costs and commitments that clients may reasonably expect
- Ensuring that clients are promptly informed about anything that has occurred which places the client at risk of harm or causes harm in our work together, whether or not clients are aware of it, and quickly taking action to limit or repair any harm as far as possible
- Reviewing our work with clients in supervision
- Monitoring how clients experience our work together and the effects of our work with them.

The framework also offers values which are a useful way of expressing the general ethical commitments that underpin the purpose and goals of our actions. The values include a commitment to:

- Respecting human rights and dignity
- Alleviating symptoms of personal distress and suffering
- Enhancing people's wellbeing and capabilities
- Improving the quality of relationships between people
- Increasing personal resilience and effectiveness
- Facilitating a sense of self that is meaningful to the person(s) concerned within their personal and cultural context
- Appreciating the variety of human experience and culture
- Protecting the safety of clients
- Ensuring the integrity of practitioner–client relationships
- Enhancing the quality of professional knowledge and its application
- Striving for the fair and adequate provision of services.

Values inform principles. They become more precisely defined and action-oriented when expressed as a principle. Principles direct attention to important ethical responsibilities. Our core principles are:

- **Being trustworthy**: honouring the trust placed in the practitioner
- **Autonomy**: respect for the client's right to be self-governing

- **Beneficence**: a commitment to promoting the client's wellbeing
- **Non-maleficence**: a commitment to avoiding harm to the client
- **Justice**: the fair and impartial treatment of all clients and the provision of adequate services
- **Self-respect**: fostering the practitioner's self-knowledge, integrity and care for self.

Personal moral qualities are internalised values that shape how we relate to others and our environment. The practitioner's personal and relational moral qualities are of the utmost importance. Their perceived presence or absence will have a strong influence on how relationships with clients and colleagues develop and whether they are of sufficient quality and resilience to support the work.

Key personal qualities which are strongly encouraged include:

- **Candour**: openness with clients about anything that places them at risk of harm or causes actual harm
- **Care**: benevolent, responsible and competent attentiveness to someone's needs, wellbeing and personal agency
- **Courage**: the capacity to act in spite of known fears, risks and uncertainty
- **Diligence**: the conscientious deployment of the skills and knowledge needed to achieve a beneficial outcome
- **Empathy**: the ability to communicate understanding of another person's experience from that person's perspective
- **Fairness**: impartial and principled in decisions and actions concerning others in ways that promote equality of opportunity and maximise the capability of the people concerned
- **Humility**: the ability to assess accurately and acknowledge one's own strengths and weaknesses
- **Identity**: sense of self in relationship to others that forms the basis of responsibility, resilience and motivation
- **Integrity**: commitment to being moral in dealings with others, including personal straightforwardness, honesty and coherence
- **Resilience**: the capacity to work with the client's concerns without being personally diminished
- **Respect**: showing appropriate esteem for people and their understanding of themselves
- **Sincerity**: a personal commitment to consistency between what is professed and what is done
- **Wisdom**: possession of sound judgement that informs practice.

Activity – Inventory of personal moral qualities

Take each of the moral qualities identified by the BACP and reflect on your relationship with each of them. Identify the areas that need some work alongside the qualities you feel able and confident with.

Choose those you need to work on, identifying what the challenges are and what you need to grow. For example, it might be that you feel you lack knowledge and experience to make the sound judgements that wisdom call for.

Candour:

Care:

Courage:

Diligence:

Empathy:

Fairness:

Humility:

Identity:

Integrity:

Resilience:

Respect:

Sincerity:

Wisdom:

Boundaries

'Boundaries' is a term used to explain how a helping relationship works. They can be thought of as healing rules that manage expectations and let someone know what will happen and how they will be supported in a helping session or interaction. All relationships have boundaries and it is generally when these boundaries are broken that the relationship runs into trouble. Some boundaries are unspoken but accepted as part of a healthy relationship. Violence is not acceptable and when the boundary of personal safety is violated in a relationship, it can cause great harm and be very difficult to address and heal. A boundary in a romantic relationship can be around fidelity. Both people agree to be faithful to each other for the duration of the relationship. If that boundary is broken and someone is unfaithful, it generally causes pain and distress and can end the relationship. Loyalty is an important boundary in friendships. Friends talk to each other about sensitive and painful things with the expectation that their friend won't gossip about them. When friends do gossip outside the friendship, it breaks the trust and can cause someone to not feel safe in other relationships and make opening up and sharing about what is going on for them very difficult.

Some friendships need to negotiate the boundaries as the relationship develops. It is when boundaries cannot be agreed or maintained that the relationship is threatened. It may be that in a friendship, one person talks about their problems and the other person listens. After some time, this can feel unbalanced, with the risk of resentment and anger creeping in. It can be difficult to address these sorts of dynamics, and easier to carry on listening for hours until you feel as if your head will explode. Friendships can end rather than address the boundary issues. Money can be lent and not returned, which can fester in the friendship, but some people find it virtually impossible to ask their friend for the money back, even though it's eating them away inside. So many hurts in friendships go unsaid. If we struggle to manage our personal boundaries with family, friends, colleagues, etc., we will almost definitely have the same struggles in helping work. If we let a friend take up our time, talking for hours about their difficulties, and if we overlook our own feelings and needs because we are scared to end a conversation, we are likely to struggle to end a helping session or interaction in a timely manner for the same reasons. If someone asks us to do something for them that we really don't want to do and which will cause us problems in taking responsibility for our own life, and yet we simply feel unable to say no, we may find ourselves struggling with the same issues in our helping work.

Saying 'no' can be incredibly difficult for many, many reasons. We may fear rejection, hurting someone, conflict, discomfort, their anger or distress, losing the friendship, not losing the friendship, being judged, being talked about… the list is endless. Because of the problem of saying 'no', we can resort to a range of unhelpful behaviours to try to manage the situation – making excuses, manipulating, avoiding, agreeing over and over again and hating ourselves for being weak, lying, blaming, placating, rescuing. The behaviours and responses we have in our personal relationships will almost definitely follow us into our helping work. We need to find a way through our fears to find our 'no'. This is not necessarily an outward 'no'; it can be a quiet, internal 'no'. It is when we decide what our boundaries are and make a commitment to not allow them to be breached. This is much easier said than done and is most certainly a work in progress. For those of us who have been wounded and injured in relationships, it can be a long road to saying 'no'. For me personally, I can still hide the telephone in another room to avoid a difficult situation, or agree to things I know in my gut are not good for me because I can't find the courage to stand up to someone and say 'no'.

The next activity is not a stick to beat you with. It is a way of raising awareness of areas where your boundaries may be weak or broken. We cannot become strong at the broken places until we know where the broken places are.

Activity – Personal boundaries

The table below offers different scenarios. You are invited to reflect on each scenario, thinking about how you usually respond and feel, and then going on to identify what you would really like to do and say in each scenario.

Scenario	What would you do and why?	How would you feel?	What would you like to be able to do or say?
Your friend asks you to babysit and you had planned a quiet day to yourself.	Say yes because I hadn't got concrete plans and it didn't feel very nice as she was so stressed.	Guilty for not wanting to, resentful, upset because it was my first day off work for weeks.	I'm really sorry but I'm not available today.
Your son asks to borrow the car to go to a job interview but he bumped it last time you lent it.	Sorry, the clutch is broken and I'm waiting for the garage to come and get it.	Guilty for not helping and think it'll be your fault if he doesn't get the job. Scared he'll find out that you've lied.	No, sorry.
Your boss gives you additional work that you simply can't do without working in your own time.			

Scenario	What would you do and why?	How would you feel?	What would you like to be able to do or say?
Your friend is very needy and calls every day and talks for ages about how awful her life is for weeks and months on end.			
Your cousin asks for some money towards her wedding after hearing you got a bonus from work.			
You agreed to help at a village fete some months ago but now feel exhausted and overwhelmed by your life.			
A friend tells you that he and his new wife and two children want to come and meet you and would like to stay with you for a few days. You would prefer to eat your own head.			
Your mother asks you to drive her to a funeral 300 miles away and wait to bring her home. You had a day out planned.			
A colleague stands too close and you feel uncomfortable.			
An acquaintance comments on your appearance and makes suggestions on how you should do your hair or lose weight.			

(Continued)

(Continued)

Scenario	What would you do and why?	How would you feel?	What would you like to be able to do or say?
Someone talks about someone else in quite a horrible way and makes what you see as racist comments.			
Someone you hardly know wants to be friends and buys you a very expensive gift.			

Managing relationships can be like trying to negotiate a minefield and sometimes pain is unavoidable. It is too easy to put someone else's feelings in front of our own and only be able to say 'no' in extreme situations, for example, 'I'm sorry I can't look after your cat. My house exploded and both my kidneys have failed or else I would have loved to.' When maintaining personal boundaries, a very important question to ask is: 'Why do I value you more than me?' This applies to both personal and professional relationships. Helping someone does not mean abandoning yourself. Self-respect and self-esteem are important qualities to wear when working with others.

Boundaries can also be practical and physical

A baby is not safe in a bed and may roll out and hurt themselves. The sides of the cot are the boundaries that keep them safe and contained and unable to hurt themselves. Houses generally have boundaries, so that people know what land is theirs and what land belongs to someone else. Once this boundary is known, it helps prevent trespass and conflict around ownership. Countries have boundaries. Wars have been started when boundary lines have been crossed. Even a cup of tea needs the boundaries of the cup! When we consider the physical and practical boundaries in relation to helping work, we think about the setting. The setting may depend on the primary role, such as a nurse working in a hospital, or a teacher working in a school. Some helping interactions may be very brief and can happen in a wide range of settings, such as corridors, car parks, waiting rooms, churches, etc. However, ideally, the setting or environment needs to have boundaries in place in terms of:

Privacy – A closed door and lack of others interrupting.

Phones – Need to be turned off. Even when they are switched to silent, the buzz of a text or message can be intrusive.

Accessibility – If someone has a disability or difficulty, they need to be able to access the space. Even the most beautiful of spaces is useless if someone can't get into it.

Somewhere to sit – It sounds obvious but is not always available. It is important to be able to relax and broken or mis-matched chairs may not be conducive to helping work.

Clutter – If the space is cluttered, it can be a distraction, making it tempting to look at everything in the room rather than looking at all the feelings in the person.

Physical boundaries include touch and space

Touch is a very complex issue and the best approach is not to touch. If you are supporting someone who becomes distressed, your initial response may be to try to hug or comfort them physically. Some people might find this helpful, but others might not like being touched. They may have difficult experiences around touch, including violence and abuse. A caring hug could be received as something threatening and could cause the person to shut down. Sometimes we might offer a hug with the intention of stopping the pain and ending the distress, but helping work is not about shutting down the distress. It is about listening to the pain and distress, helping someone to understand and be able to manage their feelings. If we communicate to someone that their feelings need to be stopped, the message is that the feelings are too much. If we cannot hear and bear someone else's distress, how can we expect them to be able to bear it?

Confidentiality

Confidentiality means establishing a relationship of trust, so that all personal details are kept private and not passed on to a third party without the express consent of the person being helped or supported. Confidentiality ensures that someone's privacy is protected, especially when handling sensitive, often highly personal information. It involves having secure systems that limit access to someone's personal information. Confidentiality is important because it instils confidence in the working relationship and the support and service being provided. It allows someone to feel safe and at ease in disclosing personal, sometimes distressing, details with the understanding that such information will not be passed on without the client's expressed consent. Confidentiality contributes to the provision of a professional and accessible service.

Limits to confidentiality

Confidentiality cannot be absolute and will have to be broken in certain circumstances. There are some legal limits to confidentiality that have to be upheld. Different organisations and agencies may have additional limits, depending on their remit. For example, some agencies require confidentiality to be broken if any law is broken, whereas other agencies will not have this stipulation. Whatever the limits of confidentiality are for each particular setting, the person being supported needs to know exactly what they are before they start speaking. Only then can they decide what they can and can't talk about if they want complete confidentiality. It is not fair or ethical to let someone to talk without restraint and only then tell them you are going to tell someone else what they have said and/or inform the authorities. In some organisations, nothing is confidential between only the helper and helpee. All information is available to the whole team. Again, the person being supported needs to know that all people involved in their care will know what is spoken about.

Those using counselling skills do so under the umbrella of a primary profession and it is that profession that will dictate the policies and procedures, including confidentiality and its limits, under which someone will need to work. These are in place for both the helper and helpee and to further the aims and objectives of the profession. It is important to note that legislation changes rapidly and it is essential that all helpers keep up to date with relevant laws.

> My understanding of professionalism is having the discipline to be aware of and work to a set of values made up of legal statutes, of professional body frameworks and guidelines and of employer policies, frameworks and guidelines, which together detail expected conduct. Those statutes, policies, frameworks and guidelines should be used to identify roles and responsibilities which in turn define boundaries. (UK Essays, 2018)

Learning journal

Confidentiality

I was really surprised to learn that not everything is confidential when supporting someone with counselling skills. Even counselling itself is not completely confidential. I thought it would be like talking to a priest, where you can say anything without consequence. I had no idea it was so complicated, with all sorts of laws and things. I found it annoying and overly factual and detailed for me. I understand safety is vital, but all the rules and regulations can get in the way and become a barrier to building a trusting relationship. I agree that if a child is being harmed, something needs to be done, but how can anyone find out that a child is being harmed if someone is not offered confidentiality about what they say. For example, what if I was strug-gling to cope with my children and had taken to drinking too much alcohol and was becoming angry and frustrated and was hitting my children if they got on my nerves. I would know that what I was doing was wrong, but I could be caught in a spiral and could not stop on my own. I would know that I needed help, but I certainly wouldn't go for help if I thought the helper would tell the authorities what I was doing. I would need the helper to help me to stop what I was doing, but I wouldn't be able to say what I was doing. It feels like a vicious cycle to me.

Since starting this course, I have begun to do volunteering work in a drug rehabilitation centre. It has a drop-in centre and a needle exchange too. I volunteer in the needle exchange, which supports safer drug use. In some places, confidentiality has to be broken if someone breaks the law in any way. In drug services, this would mean there would be no confidentiality at all. One of the legal requirements for breaking confidentiality is 'drug trafficking'. What does this mean? Is it just drug dealing? Does it apply to all drugs? Does it mean bringing drugs into the country? Does it matter how much is brought into the country? Does it matter what drug is brought into the country? I just don't think it's adequate to say to people 'I will break confidentiality for drug trafficking' when I don't really know what it means myself. The same goes for 'money laundering'. How much are we talking about? What currencies apply, or does it mean all currencies? Is it only money obtained illegally? It seems strange to me that I have to report something to do with money but domestic violence isn't even mentioned. That says to me that money is valued more than life.

Some years ago I listened to a counsellor talking about working with sexual, physical and emotional abuse. She recalled a time when a young girl had disclosed to her that she was being abused by her father. The counsellor broke confidentiality and involved social services. When social services spoke to the girl, she denied what she had said and said that she was happy and well cared for at home. I don't know the answer, but I think that if the counsellor had not broken confidentiality so quickly, she might have been able to work with the girl for longer and hopefully get to a place where the girl would be able to get help for the abuse herself.

Tutor feedback

There is a lot of passion and emotion in your words as you write about confidentiality. It seems to raise the questions: 'Where am I safe to talk without fear of reprisal?' 'Who will keep my secrets with me?' I was left wondering whether your secrets have not been kept safe by the people you trusted them to. I do agree that the setting and role dictates some of the limits to confidentiality. Those working with children or the vulnerable are more likely to have more limits to confidentiality than those working in drug and alcohol services.

Going outside confidentiality or a circle of confidentiality is not about punishment or telling tales. It is about getting appropriate help and support for someone that is not currently being provided. It is also about getting help and support for someone else who is being harmed or at risk of harm. I take your point about the child who disclosed abuse and then retracted the disclosure, but there are no easy answers or responses to some situations and there is no way of looking into the future to see the right course of action. This dilemma does highlight the need to have professional support and guidance. No one person should have to carry things like this alone.

You touched on some of the legal limits to confidentiality and, to be honest, you raised questions I hadn't thought of in relation to drug trafficking and money laundering. The Drug Trafficking Act 1994 makes it a criminal offence not to report to the police suspicion or knowledge of drug money laundering. Money laundering does refer to money from crime. The Proceeds of Crime Act 2002 and the Money Laundering Regulations 2007 relate to this limit to confidentiality. I do not know if there are specific drugs and amounts of money involved but would be interested in knowing if you are able to research it.

Activity – Ethics inventory

Rate the following scenarios from 1 to 10:

1 = very unethical

10 = safe and ethical

Reflect on the possible consequences (the good, the bad and the ugly) of each scenario.

Helper has given the helpee his/her personal email, home address or phone number.

Helper borrows a book from the helpee.

Helper lends a book to the helpee.

Helper and helpee communicate with each other via texting on their personal phones.

Helper offers physical contact to the helpee, such as hugging or embracing, kissing on the cheek, rubbing hands or their face to provide comfort and support.

Helper spends lengthy phone hours with the helpee during the work day and in personal time.

Helper dresses provocatively during work time.

Helper freely shares and discusses his/her own personal experiences.

Helpee and helper meet in restaurants, pubs and parks.

Helper spends his/her personal funds to support the helpee's needs and wants.

Helper engages in a romantic/sexual relationship with the helpee once the helping work has ended.

Helper buys gifts for the helpee.

Helper uses drugs and/or alcohol with the helpee.

Some of the examples in the activity above may seem farfetched, but they do happen when professional boundaries are weak or non-existent, when the helper is having personal and/or professional challenges, and/or when training and professional support is lacking. Ethics are not just words on a page. They need to be alive and dynamic in the work. It is only by understanding and applying ethical standards that they ensure helping work is safe and effective.

NINE

Models, tools and techniques

This chapter offers a range of different tools and techniques that can support and/or enhance the use of counselling skills. The role and setting will dictate which tools, interventions etc. are the most helpful. Some of the models illustrate how a helping session can be structured and facilitated, whereas some of the techniques and interventions can be introduced as needed. There is a huge number of models, tools and techniques appropriate for counselling and what is contained within this chapter is far from exhaustive. Hopefully your appetite will be whetted to further explore the many things available to help you enhance your use of counselling skills. Therefore, this is very much a pick-and-mix array. Use the tools and techniques that make sense for your role and setting and theoretical approach/philosophy. Take what is helpful and leave the rest.

Carl Rogers and the person-centred model

Carl Rogers' person-centred model has had value and relevance in many areas of helping, counselling, education, health and workplace. Carl Rogers identified six necessary and sufficient conditions necessary to facilitate change. He first used the term in a paper published in 1957 by the *Journal of Consulting Psychology*, where he listed the six conditions as follows:

1. Two persons are in psychological contact.
2. The first, whom we shall term the client, is in a state of incongruence, being vulnerable or anxious.
3. The second person, whom we shall term the therapist, is congruent or integrated in the relationship.
4. The therapist experiences unconditional positive regard for the client.

5. The therapist experiences an empathic understanding of the client's internal frame of reference and endeavors to communicate this experience to the client.

6. The communication to the client of the therapist's empathic understanding and unconditional positive regard is to a minimal degree achieved.

Rogers continued:

No other conditions are necessary. If these six conditions exist and continue over a period of time, this is sufficient. The process of constructive personality change will follow. (Rogers, 1957, pp. 95–6)

For the purpose of using counselling skills in a range of roles and settings, the focus is generally on three of the *necessary and sufficient conditions,* which are known as the core conditions of empathy, unconditional positive regard and congruence. Most counselling skills models use these core conditions as a basis for their structure. The core conditions are arguably the bedrock of all work that involves one person supporting and helping another.

Congruence, empathy and unconditional regard, simply means to be aware of your own humanness in order to understand and accept another person. Although this sounds very simple, it is incredibly difficult to do and often requires a lot of personal development and self-awareness to be able to practise the core conditions honestly and with integrity. In *On Becoming a Person* (1961), Carl Rogers states:

The more that the client perceives the therapist as real or genuine, as empathic and having unconditional positive regard for him, the more the client will move away from a static, fixed, unfeeling, impersonal type of functioning, and the more he will move toward a way of functioning marked by a fluid, changing, acceptant experiencing of different personal feelings. The consequence of this movement is an alteration in personality and behavior in the direction of psychic health and maturity and more realistic relationships to self, others and the environment. (Rogers, 1961, p. 68)

The core condition of Empathy

Empathy is such a vital ingredient of all helping relationships and interactions that the whole of Chapter 5 is about empathy. Empathy basically means to understand someone else by seeing the world through their eyes, walking in their shoes, feeling with their heart.

The core condition of Unconditional Positive Regard

This condition is about valuing and respecting the client without exception. The person's value has no conditions placed upon it. The person is valued for who they are, not for how they should or could be. As children we are often on the receiving end of conditional regards. We are told we are lovable and acceptable if we are, for example, good, quiet, clever, dutiful. We are deemed unacceptable and worthless if we are, for example, naughty, dirty, rude, lazy, etc. Even as adults, value and respect can be conditional and dependent on how we behave. A helper may be the only person to show someone unconditional respect and value. Unconditional positive regard is a belief that the client, regardless of all their problems, feelings and behaviours, is simply a human being who has a right to acceptance. Acceptance paves the way for someone to speak honestly and openly about their issues without fear of judgement, rejection or punishment. Our role is to work hard to see past someone's behaviour to the real person at the core. We do not have to agree with what someone has done or said, but we can still value them as members of the human race, who are fallible and far from perfect.

We do not need to judge someone because their sins are different from our own.

The core condition of Congruence

This refers to our ability to be a real or genuine person with the client, without pretence or bluff, without making out we are something we are not. It is all too easy to hide behind a professional role and portray ourselves as better, more powerful and more perfect than we actually are. When congruent, a person has no need to act as an expert, to feel superior or to pretend in any way. They appear just as they are. Other people see this and somehow it gives them permission to be real and to be just as they are, warts and all. Rogers uses the word 'transparent' to describe the truly congruent or genuine person. Transparency means to see through, to be able to see past any defences, to see who someone really is in very imperfect, confusing, broken but beautiful humanness. Congruence demands the person being congruent to have the courage to be honest, to not manipulate to try to control and cajole in order to get their needs met or direct situations or people in the direction they want. When using counselling skills, honesty and openness are valuable qualities. If someone is able to say 'no', it becomes possible to trust their 'yes'.

People-pleasing and approval-seeking are not traits employed by congruent people. They are simply not needed by someone who has the courage and ability to be direct and open about what they want and need, their thoughts and feelings, opinions and values. In my opinion, congruence is very difficult to master. For me, it has been a very long and at times painful journey through a labyrinth of self-defeating behaviours, historic wounds and fears. Today, sometimes I am able to be congruent and sometimes I can't. I can forgive myself for not being perfect today. Congruence can be tricky to grasp and understand. Carl Rogers explained it beautifully:

> I realize that if I were stable and steady and static, I would be living death. So I accept confusion and uncertainty and fear and emotional highs and lows because they are the price I willingly pay for a flowing, perplexing, exciting life. (Rogers, 1980, p. 89)

Activity – The core conditions

For each of the vignettes in Table 9.1, think about whether you could offer all of the core conditions. Try to be honest about what you feel able to offer.

Identify areas you would struggle with and reflect on why that is for you. Think about how this could impact on the person and how the person might think and feel. How could it affect the helping work?

In the table below, we have completed one example to get you started.

Scenario	Congruence	Unconditional positive regard	Empathy
J talks to you about his recent holiday where his luggage went missing. He blames his sister and talks about wanting to slap her for being a stupid idiot.	I do think I was real and in touch with my own thoughts, feelings, etc.	I did judge him and disliked him for what he said about his sister and I think my tone changed and I felt secretly glad his luggage disappeared. He changed the subject after that.	Yes, I was able to understand his feelings of irritation and frustration.

Scenario	Congruence	Unconditional positive regard	Empathy
	I was aware of feeling triggered as my brother called me names and was a bully and we still have a difficult relationship.	There could have been things about the relationship with his sister he wanted to explore but I might have blocked that. If we work together again, I might mention that I noticed the subject changed after he expressed his anger towards his sister.	
You are a Reiki Healer and someone you are supporting is very much against alternative therapies and calls such therapists frauds and robbers.			
You are supporting someone who is married and having an affair with their son's girlfriend.			
Someone tells you something very painful and becomes distressed and sobs uncontrollably.			
Someone tells you that they find you sexually attractive and asks if you feel the same towards them.			
Someone talks to you about their weight and hating their body and appearance because of being fat. You are more overweight than they are.			

From this activity it can be seen that the core conditions are inextricably linked and when one is missing, it impacts strongly on being able to offer the others.

Activity – Reflecting on the core conditions

Can you recall a time in your life when someone offered you the core conditions? Can you describe this experience?

Can you recall a time when you needed acceptance and understanding which was not provided? Can you describe this experience?

Carkhuff's helping model

Carkhuff was a student of Carl Rogers. He took the core conditions identified by Rogers and created scales to rate, measure and give levels to empathy, unconditional regard and congruence. Carkhuff differed from Rogers in that he believed that the core conditions were skills that could be learnt and developed, whereas Rogers believed that they were attitudes that could not be taught (Hill & Lent, 1996). His model is Carkhuff's Human Resource Development model (1969). He believed strongly that the helping relationship itself was a vital ingredient when supporting someone through problems and challenges. Within it, he identified three distinct phases to helping work and their corresponding counselling skills. He believed that helping work is about facilitating each of the stages with specific skills in order to support the helpee's intrapersonal processing. He explored the relationship between each counselling skill and the helpee's response, examining how particular skills helped to enhance the helpee's intrapersonal processing skills.

Prior to the first phase of the work, he highlighted a period he called pre-processing. This is where the helper offers attention, observation and listening skills to engage the helpee in a supportive relationship. The aim is to build a relationship that enables someone to feel held and heard and safe enough to feel involved and to begin sharing their thoughts, feelings, problems and situation.

Phase 1: He called this phase helper responding – helpee exploring. This stage of his model sees the helper using responding skills, to both content and feeling. This supports the helpee to explore how they are experiencing their life and where they are in relation to their experience.

Phase 2: He identified this phase as helper personalising – helpee understanding. This does not mean the helper reflecting and using their own personal experience. It means the helper communicates understanding of the helpee's problems and experience. It gives meaning which allows the helpee to begin to reflect inwardly on where they want to be. This stage is about understanding, which gives the helpee the freedom to make sense of their internal world in a safe and non-judgemental environment.

Phase 3: Carkhuff identified this phase as helper initialising and helpee acting. The helper emphasises change by defining steps and goals that have been arrived at through understanding the helpee's situation and process. The helpee is supported to begin making the journey from where they are to where they want to be.

These phases are followed by a period of feedback, where reflection on the change process is explored and feedback is offered on the effectiveness of the actions taken.

This exchange of feedback and exploration is a tool in itself and someone can use this cycle of exploration, understanding and action throughout their life, for a myriad of problems and situations, in order to move forward and grow towards the person they want to be in order to live the life they want to live.

Egan's Skilled Helper Model

The Skiller Helper Model (Egan, 1998) is used in a wide range of roles and settings. In line with other models, its aim is to empower people to manage life more effectively and make lasting changes to engage with opportunities and to meet their full potential. The model has three stages:

1. **Exploration** – The first task is to find out what is going on for someone, where they are in life, where they would like to be and what they need to achieve this.

Skills needed: Active listening and warm attention, paraphrasing content and feeling, open questions, use of silence, focusing, summarising, receptive and open body language, appropriate eye contact, empathy and unconditional positive regard. The keys to this stage are to be fully in the person's world, to work hard to understand rather than to be understood, to not worry and to focus on the responses you want to make, to get out of your own way in order to be present to another, to challenge any personal prejudice in order to offer empathy and unconditional positive regard.

2. **Challenging** – This stage involves challenging someone's existing views that are no longer useful or helpful.

Skills needed: Timing and pacing, immediacy, careful self-disclosure, challenging, empathy, to take one issue at a time and not to focus on the whole picture. It is important not to direct someone to do something but rather to hold the range of possible actions and choices, recognising patterns and themes so that they can make an informed choice for themselves. It is OK to offer different viewpoints and options, but not to place value on any particular one. Your role is to facilitate choice, not to actually make the choice. Open questions are valuable to encourage exploration of different views and options. Goals can be set but need to be realistic and achievable and identified by the helpee rather than the helper. Once a goal is set, skills can be applied to move towards the destination of achievement in stage three.

3. **Action Planning** – This stage involves actually moving to achieve the goal identified. It is helpful to work with baby steps rather than giant leaps. The task can be broken into specific bite-sized pieces in order to turn good intentions into actual results.

Skills needed: Knowledge of the change process in order to work with someone to set and achieve realistic goals, using enquiry and challenge to ensure the goal is achievable, to reflect on where the person is in relation to the goal and to offer gentle challenge in times of detour or stuckness. It is important to acknowledge the different steps along the way.

The three stages are cyclical and each cycle is followed by evaluation, a little like the quickstep:

1 – 2 – 3 – evaluate   1 – 2 – 3 – evaluate   1 – 2 – 3 – evaluate

In his book *The Skilled Helper* (1998) Gerard Egan also offered the acronym SOLER, which identified and demonstrated how non-verbal communication can make an individual feel comfortable, secure and understood and able to open up and talk about their difficulties and challenges. It offers a useful checklist when supporting and helping others and can invite us to reflect on what prevents and/or blocks us from offering SOLER.

S   Sit at a comfortable distance to the helpee
O   Open posture with arms and legs uncrossed
L   Lean forward slightly to communicate interest and engagement
E   Eye contact must be appropriate and culturally sensitive
R   Relax and be present.

Activity – Reflecting on using SOLER

Use SOLER to take a short personal inventory.

When supporting/helping someone, what constitutes a comfortable distance for you?

Do you think that distance would be the same for everyone? Please qualify your answer.

How would you know if the person you were talking with feels comfortable with the space between you?

Do you normally sit with an open posture? Do you tend to fold your arms and/or cross your legs? If so, how does it feel to sit with open posture?

What do you think an open posture communicates?

What do you think leaning towards someone communicates?

How do you feel about initiating eye contact?

What does the term 'appropriate eye contact' mean to you?

Are there any cultural issues to consider around making effective eye contact?

Do you feel relaxed in a helping role?

What gets in the way of you feeling relaxed in a helping role?

After practising SOLER in a range of personal and professional interactions, reflect on its effectiveness. Did you find it helped or hindered the communication process?

Motivational interviewing

Motivational interviewing (MI) (Miller and Rollnick, 1991) is an approach that uses person-centred skills to direct someone towards positive behaviour change. It is important to note that it is conducive rather than coercive to change. The main focus of the approach is on ambivalence. It helps someone to recognise and explore their ambivalence in a non-threatening way in order for the person to increase their motivation in order to resolve their ambivalence and make a decision to change. Motivational interviewing has been used extensively in substance misuse and addiction settings and has been found to be effective for people who may be unwilling or unable to change.

When using motivational interviewing, it is important to honour the person's autonomy and freedom to choose.

Part of the process is to engage in 'change talk'. Change talk is communication linked to the desire to change and the ability to do so. Change talk includes a list of reasons for making the change and maintaining the commitment to change. Studies show that change talk, particularly in clinical settings, has been linked with successful behaviour change (Sobell & Sobell, 2008). It is worth emphasising that it is not helpful to try to push someone to change, no matter how much you believe they would benefit from making that change. If someone is self-harming or injecting heroin, it might seem obvious that it would be beneficial for them to change that behaviour but that decision is not yours to make. Motivational interviewing holds up the ambivalence – the reasons for and against change – and invites someone to choose. If someone responds with resistance and defensiveness, it is important not to push or try to convince someone to change; the term used in motivational interviewing is 'to roll with the resistance'. The helpee must be in the driving seat and be able to own the journey towards changing… or not changing!

Prince Hamlet described ambivalence perfectly when he said:

To be or not to be, that is the question. (*Hamlet*, Act 3, Scene 1; Shakespeare, 2005)

Counselling skills are used to evoke change talk. The acronym OARS captures the skills conducive to change and change talk:

- Open-ended questions
- Affirming
- Reflective listening
- Summarising.

Open-ended questions are used to clarify the person's situation and to identify the person's reasons for wanting to change.

Affirming recognises and acknowledges someone's strengths and abilities. This builds rapport and strengthens the working alliance or relationship between helper and helpee. Affirming uses empathic understanding to identify and validate someone's emotions.

Reflective listening puts the helper's agenda to one side and focuses solely on the helpee, using paraphrasing and restating to reflect content, emotion and meaning in order to encourage someone to continue talking. Reflective listening offers clarity and helps someone to hear what they have been saying in order to consider change. This is another skill that fosters the working alliance and strengthens the relationship between helper and helpee.

Summarising focuses on the core issues for consideration. It lays bare what is important to the helpee and gently offers a road towards change and evokes someone's own motivation for change.

The overall goal remains: to identify and resolve ambivalence and move forward. Self-efficacy is hugely important in motivational interviewing. Self-efficacy is about someone's belief in themselves. Self-belief is vital in the change process. If someone believes they are unable to achieve something, they are very likely to make that a reality. If someone believes they cannot change something, their motivation will be low and their effort will be minimal – what's the point in even trying if you believe you are going to fail?

Bandura (1986, p. 228) suggests:

Unless people believe that they can produce desired effects and forestall undesired ones by their actions, they have little incentive to act. Whatever other factors may operate as motivators, they are rooted in the core belief that one has the power to produce the desired results.

It is therefore important to work with someone to build their self-efficacy. Open questions can be useful alongside a safe and trusting relationship and working alliance. The types of question that can be useful are:

- When you have made changes in the past, how did you do it?
- What do you need to make a change?
- What personal strengths did you use then that could help you now?
- What in life is important to you, what do you value?
- What encourages and inspires you?
- Who could offer you support and help you to make this change?

These questions are designed to show that change is possible and the person has the strengths and skills needed to make the change. They are not manipulative or coercive but work to raise someone's ability in themselves and belief that they can make the desired change.

In summary, then, the five main principles of motivational interviewing are:

- Express empathy through reflective listening and the use of counselling skills
- Develop discrepancy between someone's goals or values and their current behaviour
- Avoid argument and direct confrontation
- Adjust to client resistance rather than opposing it directly
- Support self-efficacy and optimism by using change talk.

Motivational interviewing does not ask *if* someone is motivated. It invites and explores *what* motivates someone.

Activity – Making changes

It can be helpful to understand our own relationship and responses to the change process. Once we are aware of how difficult the change process can be, we are more likely to offer empathy and patience with someone who is stuck in ambivalence and struggling to make a change.

> Imagine that someone knocks on your door in the evening. You have finished work, just eaten tea and are enjoying a film on TV. You are told you have 12 hours to leave the house for good. Due to a legal loophole, you are not the owner of the home you believed to be yours.
>
> How would you feel?
>
> What would you do?
>
> Explore these questions fully: What would you take and leave? Where would you go? Would you ask for help? Who would you ask? What would you need?
>
> Think about the feelings you would experience. How would you manage these feelings?
>
> Ask other people how they would respond to being ordered to leave their home.
>
> What similarities and differences did you observe?
>
> What have you learnt from this activity in relation to change?

Change takes many forms and we can be certain that change will happen. Some changes happen against our will or without our active participation. Some turn out well and some don't. To make change happen, we must take action and sometimes taking that action seems almost impossible. The weight loss industry is huge and yet losing weight is challenging and impossible for some. It seems so easy. Eat less and lose weight, but something called hunger gets in the way and of course hunger can be emotional and psychological as well as physical. For many of us, we want our cake and we want to eat it too. Motivational interviewing will help us to explore the part of us that wants to eat and the part that wants to lose weight. Resolving that ambivalence is a huge step towards change.

Learning journal

This week focused mainly on the topic of change. I thought about change in relation to myself and also in relation to other people. If I was working with someone on changing a self-defeating behaviour and they didn't change, I think I would blame myself and feel guilty and inadequate. I used to sell meal replacement products for weight loss. People would come to me, get weighed and buy milkshakes, soups and meal bars to help them to lose weight. As long as they stuck to the weight loss plan, they would lose weight and get to their goal weight. If people came and hadn't lost weight, I would feel really bad about it. It was a bit mad actually, as they were the ones who had eaten extra food, but I was the one who felt bad about it. This is an issue that I need to work on in both my personal and professional life – what is my responsibility and what is not. A friend told me a little saying that I try to remember when I start feeling responsible for other people's feelings and thinking that I have to sort everything out: 'I didn't cause it and I can't cure it.'

I am learning that counselling skills facilitate change by offering a safe and non-judgemental relationship that supports someone to work things out for themselves. I think part of the problem is that I like to feel in control and if someone isn't changing the way I want them to, I feel out of control and I don't like that feeling. I can still often try to change people even though I have learnt that is impossible. I am learning that the only person I can change is me and often I can't even do that.

I have quite a short fuse and a hot temper. I can't even remember how many times I have lost my temper and said nasty things and afterwards felt absolutely wretched. I have sworn numerous times that I would never do it again and would see the warning signs and keep my mouth shut, but I have never managed to do it. Although this is very painful, it does help me to see how difficult change can be and to not be impatient and frustrated when other people don't change as quickly as I think they should.

I think it is best not to have any expectations at all when using counselling skills, but to try to be in the moment, listening to what someone is saying with interest and acceptance.

Tutor feedback

Isn't it interesting that we can expect others to achieve what we ourselves cannot? It is an easy trap to fall into – feeling adequate if someone we are working with does well or feeling inadequate if they do not. You are congruent about your own change process and how difficult it is at times to contain your anger and how that helps you to appreciate how difficult the process of change is for others. If you are willing, I would be interested in reading more about your personal relationship with anger. Often if we sit with our anger for long enough, it will tell us that its real name is grief or sadness or pain. If you sat with your anger for long enough, what would it tell you?

You wrote about feeling responsible for other people's feelings and perhaps getting confused between what belongs to them and what belongs to you. Is this with all people or only certain types of people? If you followed this behaviour into your past and to its root and beginning, where would it take you and to whom?

Your self-awareness is growing and you are able to apply this awareness to both your personal and professional relationships. Your understanding is blossoming and evolving. Well done!

The cycle of change

The cycle of change or transtheoretical model (Prochaska, DiClemente, & Norcross, 1992) identifies different stages in the process of change (Figure 9.1). Although a straightforward illustration of the process of change, it is based on principles developed from over 35 years of scientific research, intervention development and many research studies. It is used in countless setting and professions across the world, especially in the fields of addiction. The cycle has six stages: precontemplation,

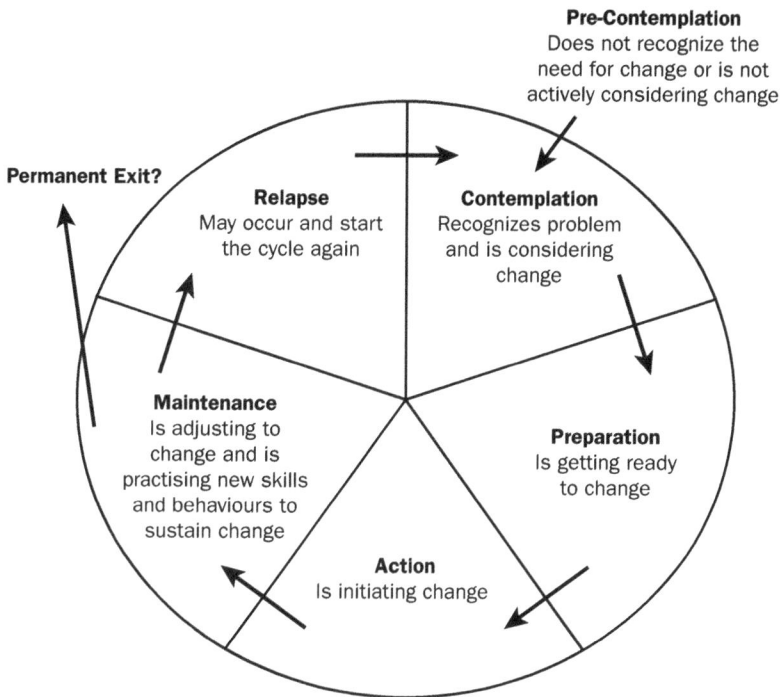

Figure 9.1   The cycle of change

Source: Prochaska and DiClemente's (1983) Stages of Change model. Reproduced by kind permission of the American Psychological Association.

contemplation, preparation, action, maintenance and relapse. It is very helpful in identifying where someone is in relation to change and what they need to move forward. Each stage of the cycle requires different skills and qualities, both from the helper and the helpee. It is impossible to force change onto someone. We may think we know what is best for someone, and if someone is engaging in self-harming behaviours it is obvious they need to stop, but we cannot compel someone to make a change that they are not ready and willing and able to make. This can be frustrating and at times very upsetting for those of us working with people who seem hell bent on destroying themselves, or even those of us who have family members or friends destroying themselves. We might think that if we love and care enough and can just find the right words, the right suggestion, the right advice, they will make the necessary change. This is simply not true; the decision to change must come from them. We can offer someone skills and qualities conducive to change, but we cannot make the change happen.

Stage 1 – Precontemplation

Here, the person has not even considered change, does not want to change or cannot see why change might be helpful. This is a stage of denial – 'I don't even know I am lying'. The person denies there is a problem despite evidence to the contrary. In this stage, trying to get the person to see what they are doing is harmful and can push them deeper into denial. There is a lack of self-awareness and a lot of resistance.

Stage 2 – Contemplation

The person becomes aware of problems associated with their behaviour but has a lot of ambivalence. It is difficult to resolve the part that wants to continue the behaviour and the part that wants to stop. There is often a willingness to find a way through the ambivalence, but it is very difficult to do alone. There can be little confidence in the ability to change and someone can be stuck in this stage for a long time. At some point the person is able to see how the negatives of the behaviour outweigh the positives and makes a decision to change.

Stage 3 – Preparation

The person plans towards making the change. There is a lot of willingness and anticipation in this stage and it is important that it does not dwindle and die. An achievable plan is designed on how the change will be made and what is needed to see it through. The steps to making the change must be realistic and specific within a timeframe. The longer things are left to drift, the more likely it is that willingness dissipates. It is also important not to push or rush.

Stage 4 – Action

The person makes the change and consciously chooses new behaviour. It can be easy to get stuck in the preparation stage and not actually to change.

Q There are five frogs on a lily pad who make the decision to jump into a pond. How many frogs are left on the lily pad?
A Five. The frogs only made the decision they didn't actually jump.

The decision means very little if it is not followed by action. It is important that the willingness is used to keep the momentum going to ensure that the frogs actually jump!

Stage 5 – Maintenance

This can be the forgotten stage. The fact that the decision has been made and a self-defeating behaviour changes can be so celebratory it can cause blindness around the fact that the new behaviour needs to be maintained and valued. Care is needed not to slip back into the old behaviour. Just wanting the new behaviour may not be enough to maintain it. Work is needed to maintain self-awareness and willingness and to engage with help and support that strengthens the new behaviour patterns and self-control. This is the long game, where the new behaviour needs to become part of the person's identity if they are not to risk relapse. Relapse is a reality and is something to be learnt from rather than punished. The cycle of change is often not a single event. The cycle can turn many times until someone feels free from certain behaviours. Even after many years relapse is possible. Personal distress, painful life events, underlying trauma and social pressures can all interrupt the healing process. Some relapses are temporary and brief, while some people may never be able to make the change again. The maintenance stage is risky, but also the doorway for lasting change.

Stage 6 – Termination

In this stage, the change is integrated into identity and the new behaviour becomes part of a lifestyle. Temptation does not lead to a relapse into old behaviour patterns. The person feels strong and able to manage the change in any situation and is appreciative and confident.

By realising where someone is on the cycle of change, counselling skills can be used to support the person where they are, rather than where we think they should be. It can be helpful to think about our own change process in relation to this model.

TEN

Professional roles

As already stated, counselling skills enhance a myriad of professional roles. Counselling skills enhance any role that requires communication and/or people skills, which makes the list virtually endless. Figure 10.1 identifies some of the roles but the list is far from exhaustive.

Adding counselling skills to a role does not change the role, but it does enhance it. A nurse using counselling skills is still a nurse; a police officer using counselling skills is still a police officer; a social worker using counselling skills is still a social worker. It is very important to remember this and it is equally important to remember that using counselling skills does not make someone a counsellor. Counselling is simply another role that uses counselling skills.

A nurse who uses counselling skills needs to be aware of what the patient needs and when using counselling skills would be helpful to them. If during the interaction, it becomes apparent that the patient needs further emotional or psychological help, a nurse can offer a sensitive referral to the appropriate support. If the nurse tried to address and work with these issues, they would have to step outside the nursing role to do so, and therefore step outside safe and professional boundaries. This could set up an unhealthy and potentially unsafe dynamic which could be harmful to both nurse and patient. Timing is important when using counselling skills to enhance a primary professional role.

If a police officer is chasing someone who has stolen something, bellowing at them about how they feel is not high on the list of appropriate actions. However, if the person is arrested and taken into custody, counselling skills would still respect and value the person, despite their behaviour, and would help the officer to find out what was going on for the person, what had led to the offending behaviour and what support could be useful in responding to the behaviour.

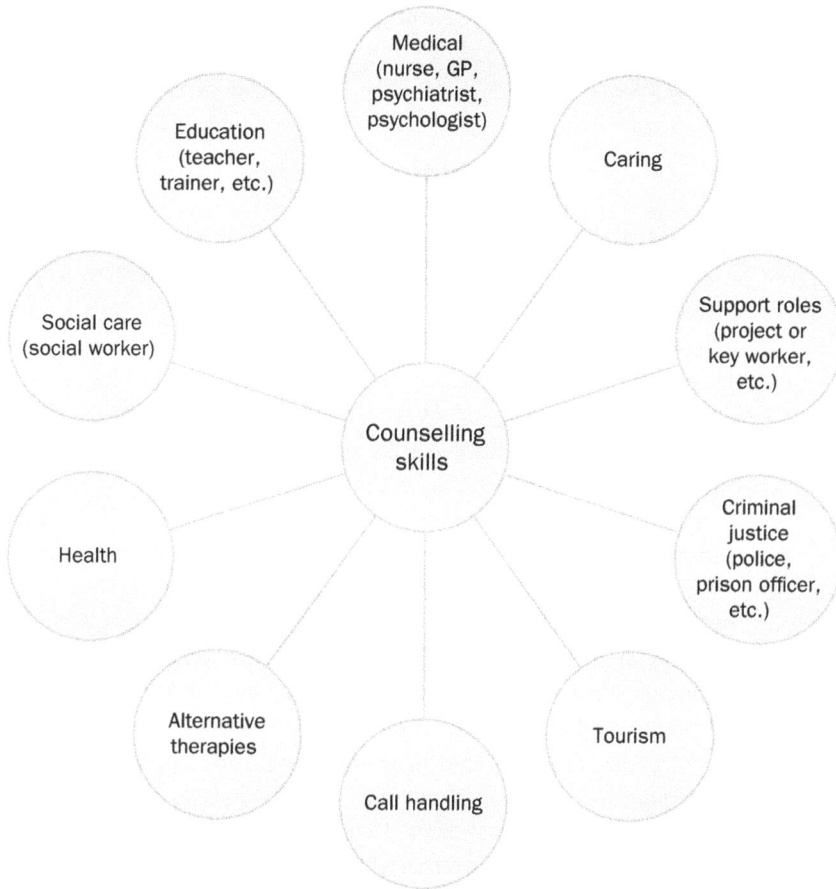

Figure 10.1   Professional roles that can use counselling skills

A housing officer has a responsibility to address someone's housing situation. If someone is homeless, the priority for them is to get a roof over their head. It may be that there are underlying problems that could be discussed with the housing officer. While the most pressing issue is the homelessness and this needs to be addressed first, perhaps long-term support from other professionals could be needed and the housing officer could help in accessing this support for their client.

A teacher notices a student acting out of character. Someone who is usually attentive and engaged has their head on the desk and has not completed any course work for a couple of weeks. It would not be appropriate to stop the lesson and try to get to the bottom of what is happening for the student, but it would probably be helpful if the teacher tries to engage the student after the lesson and create a listening space to explore how things are going and if the student needs help and/or support.

Learning journal

We have been looking at the range of different professional relationships that can be enhanced by incorporating counselling skills: nursing, teaching, health and social care roles, hospitality, police... an endless list. Personally, I think counselling skills could enhance more than just professional roles. In my opinion, all relationships would benefit from the skills, values and qualities that counselling skills offer. I like to think counselling skills are the fairy dust of relationships. A little sprinkle brings out the best in people.

I remembered when I was a volunteer at a family centre many years ago. My role was to set up activities for the children, circle time and games and singing groups. One of the mums arrived one day and looked really tearful and upset. During the day I found out her youngest child, a little girl called Khadija, had been diagnosed with leukaemia. She was only three years old. I can still remember the shock and horror I felt and also total discomfort. I didn't know how to be. I'm not giving myself a hard time because I didn't know any better, but I made the situation about me... my discomfort, my feelings of inadequacy, my fears, my shock. I couldn't cope with my feelings in relation to this desperate woman whose daughter could well be dying. On the whole I avoided her, and I noticed that the other mums and volunteers did too. When we did speak, I was overly cheerful and jolly and didn't mention her daughter because I didn't want to upset her. How ridiculous − as if I could upset her any more than she already was! I did want to support her, but I didn't know what to do. I didn't know at that time that I didn't have to DO anything. I just had to be with her (if that's what she wanted). I just had to listen. I like to think that I would respond differently today. I would hope to be able to acknowledge my feelings but then set them aside in order to offer a caring listening space.

There are other times in my life when I needed a listening space and kindness and didn't receive them. I have had relationships with professionals that have shown me how not to be with others. A kind of anti-role model. I remember a lesson at school... cookery... I was joking and messing about a bit and the teacher, Mrs Mayell, took me outside and rebuked me and said I was just a trouble-maker and she was sick of my stupid attention-seeking behaviour and so was everyone else. I can still recall how I felt that day in the corridor with her standing over me angry and critical. My home life was very difficult, very painful and it was all trapped inside me. No one ever asked me how I was or what was happening for me. I was just labelled as a trouble-maker, a nuisance. I'm reminded of the saying: 'When I behave at my very worst is when I need loving the most.' My behaviour was disruptive but no one cared enough to wonder why.

I have also had some experiences that stay with me because they were the opposite of harmful. They were healing and helpful and often came from unexpected sources. In my teens I was caught shoplifting. I'm not proud of this, but it was indicative of where I was in life at that time. I was arrested and taken to the police station. I was terrified, so scared. I was interviewed and was shocked that the police officer who interviewed me was gentle and seemed interested in more than just punishing me. She asked me if I was OK and checked that I was safe to go home. I was still charged with the offence and had to go to court, but I was treated with respect and kindness. I remember her saying that it sounded as if things were difficult at home and she asked if I would like some information on places that could help. At that time, I wasn't ready to open up and I said everything was fine at home. I was too frightened to tell the truth. However, seeds were planted on that day and those seeds rooted and grew in the time that followed. I have lots of memories of what helped and hindered, alongside experiences that were harmful and hurt. I think drawing on all those experiences help me to better understand how to respond to someone who is struggling and in pain.

I do believe that now I can be with someone in pain and I don't need to avoid them or placate or dismiss their feelings. Saying that, the place and time is important. I need to be clear when and when not to use my skills. It is not appropriate to leap in like the 'caped crusader' if I spot someone looking sad or hurt. Bellowing 'Make way everyone, I've got counselling skills and I'm not afraid to use them' is not helpful to anyone!

Tutor feedback

You are able to draw on your personal experiences to influence how you relate to others and how counselling skills and values can have a positive influence on both personal and professional relationships. You gave an excellent example of how counselling skills enhance a primary professional role but do not change it. When you were arrested, the police officer carried out her job and you were charged for the offence, but the process was facilitated with empathy and kindness, focusing on your safety and offering further support. It sounds like a horrendous experience which could have been made worse if you had been treated harshly, judged and shamed.

I smiled at your thoughts of counselling skills being like a sprinkle of fairy dust on relationships. Yes, counselling skills certainly add something to relationships. Perhaps they colour them in, highlighting the professional role to optimise its strengths and purpose. I like to think counselling skills help us to be the best person we can be in professional roles, personal relationships and also how we treat ourselves.

Your 'caped crusader' comment was amusing but made an important point. Timing is crucial and support must be wanted and not forced on someone, no matter how much we think they need it. Part of using counselling skills is carrying the hope for people when they have lost their own, but it is not about ramming it down their throats.

The three Rs are a reminder to know what to do and when to do it within a primary professional role:

- Recognise
- Respond
- Refer.

As already stated, the professional roles that can be enhanced by counselling skills are many and varied. In addition to this, the helping relationship or working alliance also varies from profession to profession. Some helping relationships are directive, although counselling skills are not. Some helping relationships involve personal care but counselling skills do not. Some helping relationships involve giving advice but counselling skills do not. The professional roles vary widely and wildly but counselling skills are a constant that weaves gently through each role, always enhancing, never changing.

Table 10.1 illustrates how the helping relationship varies across roles.

Table 10.1   Professional relationships

	Informing (teaching)	Nurturing (physical)	Guiding / directive	Encouraging	Challenging	Soothing	Collaborative	Reparative / developmental
Carer								
Nurse								
Doctor								
HR manager								
Drugs worker								
Social worker								
Teacher								
Police								
Hair dresser								
Priest								
Physio								
Mentor								

A patient with cancer arriving for their first radiotherapy appointment can exhibit an array of behaviours, such as anxiety or aggression, which are generated by intense emotions. Each patient will have their own individual concerns and their needs should be addressed, to make their first experience in the Radiotherapy Department as smooth and stress-free as possible. The radiographer's role at this point is undoubtedly to provide patients with information, while demonstrating a compassionate and genuine nature. This can make all the difference to the way a patient reacts and copes with the entire course of radiotherapy. The skills that will allow a radiographer to handle these situations are, in the first instance, good communication skills, but in addition to this the development of some basic counselling skills could further enhance patient care.
    Source: Martin & Hodgson, 2006

ELEVEN

Using counselling skills remotely

Historically, counselling skills have enhanced interactions that take place in person. However, counselling skills can be used online and via the phone in a wide range of contexts, including health and social care, homelessness, addiction education, mental health, social care and development and learning. Support and guidance offered remotely can actually be more effective and appropriate for some groups of people than meeting in person. There has been a dramatic increase in using counselling skills to support others via the phone and online. Using modern technology to support people using counselling skills can be cost-effective and tailored to meet the individual needs of service users across many professions. It provides an immediacy and flexibility that in-person provision cannot equal. In truth, online and telephone support is not better or worse than in-person support – it is different! In some quarters, there can be considerable resistance to offering counselling skills remotely. Change can be challenging and there are understandable fears and challenges inherent to this new way of working. Younger generations are generally better versed in the different online platforms and phone technology whereas older generations may struggle and lack confidence in their skills online, but will usually be more confident using the phone.

Counselling skills offered remotely are essential for people who are unable or unwilling to meet in person. There are numerous blocks to meeting in person, some of which prevent a high number of people accessing services: physical, financial, emotional and psychological barriers, distance and isolation are but a few. Online and telephone provision can offer support to those people who would otherwise be prevented from accessing help and support. Online or telephone support can reach people at a convenient time in the privacy of their own homes, which may be more appropriate for many different groups.

Table 11.1   Some reasons for offering support remotely

I'm a public figure and prefer the anonymity.	I live in the Outer Hebrides. There are no practitioners here.	I am a victim of domestic abuse and am frightened of bumping into my abuser.
I don't want anyone to know that I am seeing a mental health worker and online is more anonymous.	I have four young children and have no one to babysit.	I feel less intimidated and more able to be honest online.
My mental health difficulties prevent me travelling alone. I am agoraphobic.	I wanted an expert in my issue and I had to spread my net far to find someone. Language/accent/speech doesn't have to be a barrier.	I just don't feel able to talk in person. It's too much for me. I have been sexually attacked and don't want to be alone with anyone I don't know well. I know there is less chance of sexual misconduct working remotely.
I have a disability that prevents me leaving my bed.	I much prefer more time to reflect on and think about the session and using email gives me that space.	In my experience, times are more flexible and I save time by not having to travel.

Online support can also be a first step for the nervous and vulnerable who don't feel ready for in-person contact. Table 11.1 lists some of the reasons why remote support works better for some groups.

Offering counselling skills remotely may also be a way of continuing an effective and helpful support relationship, for example when someone moves out of an area and is unable to travel back for appointments. While it is clear that there are many advantages to offering counselling skills remotely, there are also possible disadvantages to consider (Table 11.2).

Different ways of working remotely

Technology is incredibly fast-moving and new methods come forward all the time. Because the technology of today could well be redundant by the end of the week it is quite pointless to focus on individual technologies. Rather, it feels more useful to provide an overview of working remotely and offering counselling skills safely, ethically and effectively

Table 11.2   Benefits and limitations of online and telephone support

Benefits	Limitations
Accessibility and location	Lacks human interaction and contact
Convenience – flexible hours	Lack of contact can make it harder to form a working alliance
Finances – fewer overhead costs for rooming, travel, etc.	Absence of visual and vocal cues can cause miscommunication
Issues and disabilities that make leaving home difficult	Can increase isolation and withdrawal from society
Flexibility	Typed words can appear cold and unfeeling
Social phobias and anxiety that impact on meeting in person	Technical failures and poor technical skills
Can engage more than one person who are in different locations	Using email can push the time boundaries and make it difficult to know where the support starts and ends
Reduces stigmas of going for help	Unable to afford computer, phone, etc.
May feel safer for some groups of people	Some risk issues might be difficult to respond to appropriately
Time delay can offer space for reflection and consideration	Time delay might leave someone feeling unsupported
Can provide a record of what has taken place	If both parties are working from home, boundaries could be harder to maintain
Writing itself can be therapeutic	Greater risk of interruption
Anonymity can help someone to open up	Anonymity may increase disinhibition and cause someone to disclose more than they wanted to or what is appropriate in a support session
Addresses the power imbalance – someone can write freely in an email or text without interruption or opinion from the person supporting them	If someone needs further support, it might be difficult to access further online resources

online or via the telephone. There are two distinctions to working remotely:

- Synchronously, which means in real time, e.g. by phone, video conferencing and via online platforms
- Asynchronously, which means communication without requiring an immediate response, e.g. via email, text or instant message.

Just as there are advantages and disadvantages to working in person and working remotely, there are advantages and disadvantages to working synchronously or asynchronously. At the end of the day, it may simply come down to personal preference and the competence of the person offering counselling skills.

Learning journal

Due to unforeseen circumstances, the course has had to take place online for a few weeks. We meet via video conferencing. Personally, I found this very challenging and felt resentful at having my studies interrupted; plus, I'm not good with technology and felt that this was an added pressure that I didn't want. I also learnt a lot about myself which will be helpful in the future. We were still able to practise our skills in triads on separate platforms. It took me a while to focus and listen as I was too busy looking at what I looked like, which was a massive distraction. This applied to all roles: as observer, helper and helpee. I hadn't realised I found myself so fascinating. I noticed every gesture and movement I made and have had to really fight with myself to not be critical.

Until now, I hadn't really thought about how people could be supported 'virtually' or 'remotely'. I just assumed 'in person' was best and that people needed real contact for the support and care to be helpful. Although I prefer attending this course in person, I am getting used to meeting on a 'platform'. Maybe I didn't like it initially because it was something new, different and unknown to me. To be honest, the more I get used to it, the more I like it. I have noticed that some of the things I think of as an advantage also have the potential to be a disadvantage. This week, I didn't bother getting dressed or leaving the house. I attended the course with a hoody on, no make-up, I had bare feet and I hadn't showered. I felt very comfortable and liked that I had so much more time and much less to do, but I can see how easy it would be for me to get a little too comfortable and start to let myself go. I didn't need to be motivated and I am not sure this is good for me.

I thought about how help and support could be delivered online or on the phone and I started to feel scared in case meeting in person started to fade away. It would be a lot cheaper to provide support online... there would be no room costs, no travel costs and also the time someone spent travelling could be better used to support someone. Although these are all really good things, they don't feel good to me and I still think there are huge benefits to seeing someone in person. I feel very stirred up about this. Am I just resistant to change? I guess when something is gained, something is lost, but it would be a great shame if person-to-person contact was a casualty.

I've just read the above paragraph and realise I sound quite negative and I need time to think about and reflect on that. I do believe that for some people online and phone support is a life-saver. My nan recently broke her hip and has been housebound ever since. The doctor and practice nurse speak to her via video conferencing and it works really well. There is no way she could get to the practice and the practice does not have the resources to send the doctor out a couple of times a week. It was funny because my nan didn't have a clue about the internet, but I lent her my laptop and showed her how to connect with her GP and nurse meetings and she was off. Her Facebook comments are a bit embarrassing, though!

I also think there is a risk for some people of becoming more isolated and withdrawn. I know that some people find leaving the house difficult and prefer to stay indoors. This could be due to a number of reasons – trauma, mental illness, fear, shyness, anxiety. I wanted to write laziness too but was worried that I was being judgemental. I think that having support online or on the phone could keep some people stuck indoors and even make things worse. I also think age makes a difference. I was able to support my nan to get online, but I'm not very confident myself. Younger people are much better with technology on the whole. They have grown up with it. When I was young not everyone had a home telephone and mobile phones were from sci-fi films. How quickly things have changed.

The jury is out about online and phone support. I hope it never completely replaces in-person relationships. Maybe it's about providing a service that someone needs rather than going for something that is cheaper and more convenient.

Tutor feedback

This is a very emotive subject and I could hear your ambivalence. It was a shock when we had to meet online as a group, rather than face to face, and how difficult that was, but I also read how quickly you began to adapt to the new circumstances. I agree with you about the appropriateness of providing support online and in person. The most important consideration is what someone needs and also what is in that person's best interest. As you wrote, someone might be very resist-ant to leaving their house but getting out into the world could be the best thing for them or it could retraumatise them or be too challenging.

These are difficult decisions and decisions that should ideally be made with the person concerned. You wrote about the economics of technology. Yes, overhead costs are lower, and less time is consumed by travel and preparation. In an ideal world, this wouldn't matter, but budgets and time constraints are real and do impinge on service provision.

There is a cloud that lurks over online and phone support that says that it is not as good as in-person support, but the cloud is not specific about why exactly it isn't as good. So, what exactly is different about meeting in person in the same room? How is this better than meeting virtually? Why is an in-person relationship felt to be superior to a virtual one? What exactly are the special ingredients that make meeting in person better? Can you reflect on how working remotely might impact on forming and maintaining the helping relationship?

Ethics and safety when working remotely

Before even thinking about what work can be conducted remotely, the person using counselling skills needs to be confident using the technology and be able to support the person they are working with to use the technology effectively. Technology is great until it stops working! If you are working with someone on a digital platform and the internet stops working, the work also stops. Therefore, there is a need for a back-up plan, such as by phone, to ensure that the person isn't left high and dry. Similarly, if working on the phone and the signal drops, a back-up plan might be to use email or another text-based internet medium.

One difference is that using counselling skills via the telephone means visual cues are lacking and undertaking counselling skills through written text (e.g. email) means visual and auditory cues are missing. It is therefore important to consider how this impacts the working alliance and building a safe and valuable relationship. There can be a tendency to make assumptions and it is important to check out observations and understandings for accuracy.

Using counselling skills on the phone and online has many similarities to using counselling skills in person, but there are some important differences to consider. It would be unwise to assume that working remotely is the same as working in person. Additional training is required, covering technology, the professional role in relation to remote work (a nurse using counselling skills online uses different skills and qualities from those needed by a social worker or a tutor), online and phone ethics and boundaries, adapted communication skills for virtual environments, spacing and pacing techniques, commonly used symbols and emoti-cons, managing risk and making appropriate referrals. It is crucial to remember that although the environment is virtual, the person being supported most definitely is not!!

Confidentiality

Confidentiality is an interesting consideration when offering counselling skills remotely, as taking responsibility for confidentiality falls on both parties, not just the person offering counselling skills.

Confidentiality using the phone

Helpers and helpees need to consider the following:

> Can anyone overhear?
> Where are phone numbers stored?
> How is identity protected?
> Where is the phone kept?
> Is the phone password protected?

Confidentiality using online platforms

Helpers and helpees need to consider the following:

> Is the connection or platform safe?
> Can it be accessed by others?
> Has an email trail the potential to be sent to others?
> Do others have access to emails and text-based correspondence?
> Can the computer or tablet be locked?
> How long are online recordings and records kept?

It can be more difficult to evaluate risk remotely, both the risk to self and to others. Identity authentication can be challenging if working without visual clues. It could be that you are talking to a family member rather than the person you are meant to be supporting. It is important to ensure that you are communicating with the right person and there may need to be an agreed password. Working remotely carries a differ-ent shopping basket of challenges and problems for the unprepared and unaware. Let us look at an array of situations using the following extended activity as a guide.

Activity – Ethical dilemmas

Reflect on the situations outlined below and consider:

How could the problems have been avoided?

What needs to be done next?

The telephone

1. Jan is a social worker and is in the kitchen occupied with washing up. Her phone rings in another room and as Jan stops washing up and walks into the other room, she sees her visiting niece has already answered her phone and is in conversation with one of her clients.
2. Frank works in the field of addiction. He feels his mobile phone vibrating in his jacket pocket. When he picks the phone up, he realises that the phone has somehow dialled one of the residents he supports in the rehabilitation centre where he works. He sees a long voicemail message has been left on the service user's answerphone. He has no idea what he was doing or saying when the message was left.
3. Bill supports women who are considering a termination and saves their details on his personal phone by first name only and with a number to protect their identity and ensure confidentiality. His mum asks to use his phone and notices an unusual name. She asks if it is Willow North, a colleague of hers. It is Willow North. She wants to know how Bill knows her.
4. Julie is on a counselling skills course and is also a volunteer in a drop-in centre for people suffering from depression and anxiety. She obtained someone's permission to record their counselling skills session together to support her learning. Her phone has been lost or stolen.
5. Graham is a tutor and has been having an extra marital affair. His wife finds out. She takes his school phone, which he never takes out of house because it has all his students' information on it. She rings them all to tell them what sort of man he really is.

Video platforms

The phone isn't the only place where things can go wrong. Video platforms also present problems.

Reflect on the following scenario and consider:

How could the problem have been avoided?

What needs to be done next?

Scene 1 – Preparing for a holiday

Linda is a physiotherapist and looks up from packing a suitcase and shouts:

> David, can you grab my laptop please, I am speaking to my client on Zoom tomorrow as I can't be there to see her in person. I want to make sure I can get on the internet in the chalet. It's only the second session with this client and I want it to go smoothly. I need to be able to see her to check she's doing the exercises correctly. And don't forget the dongle too, just in case there's no Wi-Fi.

David walks downstairs and hands Linda a laptop bag. He picks up a suitcase and they leave the house.

Scene 2 – At the holiday cottage

The laptop is set out on a table with a chair next to it. Linda tells David to go outside or wait in the bedroom as she has a session with her client in 15 minutes and needs to get ready online. Linda opens her laptop and realises that there is no accessible internet connection and tries to connect to 4G. The signal is not stable and Linda feels irritated and concerned about the upcoming session.

Linda connects with the client on a video-conferencing platform via her phone's hotspot and starts the session. The sound is quite poor and there is little Linda can do as she left her headset and speakers at home.

The session begins and the client opens up about her health fears. After several minutes, the screen suddenly goes dark and Linda is unable to get the laptop to respond at all. In frustration, she shouts 'I'm going to throw this bl***y thing through the window in a minute. David, please come and help me.' Linda then hears her client's voice calling, 'Linda are you OK? You don't sound like yourself at all.'

At that minute, the connection does end and cannot be restored. Linda has no other way of contacting her client as her personal details are stored safely at home.

Social media

This is an area where a myriad of challenges and difficulties can arise.

> Consider the following scenarios and:
>
> Offer an opinion on the situation
>
> Reflect on whether there are any ethical or safety issues.

1. You are a personal assistant and carer. Your business page is linked to a page on your personal Facebook account. You are happy to let clients and prospective clients see your personal Facebook page as you don't post very much and do not post anything personal.

2. You are a teacher and you go on a night out and drink far too much alcohol. You post a picture of yourself in a very provocative pose, looking very much the worse for wear. In the morning you look at your emails, messages and social media and see that one of your students has 'liked' the picture.
3. You are a business coach and sometimes look up clients on Facebook to help you gain a better understanding of their lives and relationships.
4. You are a community psychiatric nurse and are having a big clear out at home. You advertise a table top/garage sale on Gumtree, Friday Ads and Marketplace. On the day of the sale, a patient turns up and introduces her two children to you.

All of the instances in the above activity illustrate the necessity for careful thought and reflection about an online presence – both personally and professionally. There are no clear-cut answers that cover all bases but professionalism and safety have to underpin any and all interactions both remotely and in person.

Blended working

Blended support is a mix of remote and in-person work. Perhaps blended work can be seen as the best of both worlds if it is offered safely and skilfully, and focused on what someone wants and needs. For blended work to be helpful and effective it must do just that... blend. The virtual and in-person elements must work together and not be two completely separate things. Both elements need to support someone's health and wellbeing, and they must both be instrumental in the support. The blended support needs to be tailored to meet someone's individual and unique needs. This might not be a 50/50 split. Some people might need more in-person support, or vice versa. The online support may need to be more creative and dynamic to compliment the in-person work. It is not enough simply to do the same things online as is done in person. They are different settings and need different considerations. The approach needs to fit with the person's abilities and technical capability.

An example of blended working

Joan is a carer whose role is to support people in the community who have additional needs. She works with Malcolm, who has learning difficulties and mental health problems. Her role is to offer both emotional and physical support. She visits Malcolm at his home to help him manage his living space and to prompt him to take care of his personal hygiene and self-care. She supports him via video conferencing at the beginning of each week to help him plan and prepare for the week ahead. During times when Malcolm struggles, she offers additional phone calls to check in with him and assess whether he needs further support.

Activity – Blended working

Can you think of other examples where blended working would be helpful?

Technology and remote working have come a long way since 'Ask Uncle Ezra', which was the first online advice column provided for students at Cornell University in 1986. Today there is a wide range of tools, systems and gadgets that help us to communicate wherever we may be. Alongside using counselling skills in person, remote working weaves a rich tapestry of skills, qualities and abilities that can reach into the furthest corners and the most isolated of people.

There is also an ACE up the sleeve of helpers who work remotely which highlights the advantages:

- Accessibility
- Convenience
- Economics.

American business professional Martha Crawford summed things up perfectly, when she tweeted:

And we are still all just human beings in authentic relationship, trying to hear and understand and accept and respond to each other with open hearts in a less than ideal world. That is always the case.

Activity – Working remotely

What are your thoughts, feelings and opinions about remote working?

TWELVE

Self-awareness, personal qualities and feelings

When using counselling skills to support someone, self-awareness and personal qualities and skills are just as important as the actual counselling skills themselves. Self-awareness is needed to respond appropriately to each unique person and situation. Without the insight that self-awareness offers, there is a risk of making assumptions and judgements. There needs to be an objective view in order to have an unbiased insight into the situation, so the person being supported can be offered understanding and support. It is important that the helper's own personal feelings and opinions do not cloud their understanding.

Self-efficacy, in relation to counselling skills simply means, knowing what to do and being able to do it (well). Knowing what to do and when to do it requires the ability to put to one side any rigid, formulaic ways of working in order to respond to someone's changing situation and needs. Simply having a set of skills that is delivered in the same way to everyone is not sufficient. Being able to use counselling skills requires a high degree of emotional literacy in order to work with someone in a congruent and responsive way. Personal development enhances self-awareness, which enables awareness of when a helper's own agenda, feelings and opinions impinge on working with others. Personal development also offers opportunities for change and personal growth. Self-awareness will support someone to identify and draw on helpful personal attributes, while addressing and working through self-defeating behaviour and patterns of relating. Understanding how personal feelings can impinge on working with others, both positively and negatively, will allow a clearer focus on the needs and agenda of the other person. As human beings we are all wounded. Some of us are more wounded than others. The wounds may have happened in childhood, through painful relationships, events and circumstances. Some of us may have wounded ourselves as a response to pain, trauma and the complexities of shame, self-hatred and damaged self-esteem. Being wounded does not prevent us being able to help and support another; the wounds do not make us less than, inadequate or incapable. In some cases, our woundedness is what drives us to be the best we can be. Our woundedness can sharpen understanding and compassion. However, we need to know where our wounds are, how they were caused and how they can be healed. Without this self-awareness, there is a risk our wounds will bleed on other people without us even being aware that it is happening. We can unconsciously harm others through our woundedness, but self-awareness can address this and allow us to protect ourselves and others from our hidden pain and distress. Earlier in the book, we looked at blocks to listening. If someone talks about something painful that we have also experienced, there is a danger that without self-awareness we will defend ourselves as best we can. We might change the subject, offer advice, criticise the person, or try to placate and dismiss their feelings. We don't do this because we are bad people; we do this because of old ways of coping which we can address and challenge with self-awareness. The rest of this chapter is dedicated to raising self-awareness through a range of activities, questions, reflections and considerations aimed at introducing yourself to yourself.

Self-awareness theory, developed by Duval and Wicklund in their 1972 landmark book – A Theory of Objective Self-awareness *– states that when we focus our attention on ourselves, we evaluate and compare our current behaviour to our internal standards and values.*

It is important for a helper to be aware of their strengths and weaknesses. To be mindful of personal behaviours that are self-healing and those that are self-harming or self-defeating. The activities in this chapter meander through feelings, relationships, helping work and life in general.

Personal inventory

The term 'inventory' means a complete list. The word 'complete' is key here. An inventory attempts to include everything – the good, the bad and the ugly. An inventory includes things forgotten, ignored and denied. An inventory includes things we are proud of and things we are ashamed of, things that caused deep joy and things that caused heartbreaking sorrow; it includes when we hurt others and when others hurt us. It includes parts of our character we prefer to keep hidden as well as the parts we like to share with others. An inventory reflects back on the past and can therefore touch on very painful memories. An inventory can be seen as a bad neighbourhood – not somewhere to go alone!!

It can be helpful, even necessary, to have additional support during this process of preparing an inventory, especially if there is a history of trauma. Personal therapy is not a prerequisite to using counselling skills, but it is something I would recommend. To engage in person therapy is an act of self-care. We tend to care about the things we value and therefore we value ourselves by engaging in personal therapy. By learning how to value ourselves, we learn how to value others. The aim of creating an inventory is to build self-awareness in order to enhance the use of counselling skills. It is not intended as a therapeutic tool, but can be a useful companion on a healing journey.

Activity – Undertaking a personal inventory

How do you feel about undertaking a personal inventory?

How do you feel it could help you?

Feelings

Feelings are an integral part of using counselling skills. Below is a list of feelings and it can be useful to refer to this when it is difficult to identify or give language to certain feelings and experiences. The point here is not to assign value judgements to individual feelings. There are not good and bad feelings, and some are more pleasurable and comfortable than others, but all feelings are messengers to let us know what is going on and how we are reacting to ourselves, others and the world.

Some feelings are tricky to negotiate and need further attention to understand their role in our lives.

Fear

Fear is a huge and pervasive emotion. It can colour all areas of life and can be the foundations of many people's lives. The threat of harm triggers fear and the threat can be physical, psychological, emotional

---

Feelings... nothing more than feelings

Angry	Excited	Loving	Envy
Sad	Bored	Jealous	Scared
Overwhelmed	Happy	Content	Discontented
Anxious	Ashamed	Comfortable	Desperate
Inadequate	Joyful	Lonely	Resentful
Embarrassed	Guilty	Hopeful	Hurt
Grieving	Hateful	Miserable	Insecure
Worthless			

Activity – Feelings

For each of the feelings above, consider how you feel about it:

- In yourself
- In others.

For each of these feelings, reflect on:

- What you do with each feeling, how you respond to it, what others see you do when you experience the feeling
- What your experience is of other people responding to the feeling. What did they do? What did they do to you? What was it like for you?

For each feeling, consider how you would respond to it in a helping session:

- In yourself
- In the person you are supporting.

How do you identify individual feelings? Where in your body do you experience each feeling? Use the template below to locate individual feelings. Allocate a colour to symbolise how each feeling is experienced.

What feelings do you have the most trouble allowing yourself to feel?

What feelings in others do you struggle to be with?

Do you try to shut off or deny certain feelings? Why?

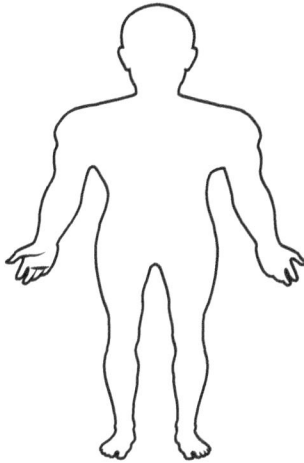

Example – Anger

I hate my own anger and am ashamed of it. I don't want other people to know I get angry.

I am frightened of other people's anger in case they hurt me.

I often don't show anger at what I'm really angry with, but tend to take it out on those close to me, which makes me feel guilty.

---

or spiritual. The threat does not have to be real or actual; fear is just as real and powerful if the threat is imagined. Although fear is generally an unpleasant feeling, it serves a very important role, which is to alert us to danger, threat or harm. Sometimes fear becomes wrong-sized and we can react with terror and horror over a very small threat. An unexpected knock at the door can send someone into a spasm of fear and panic; a loud noise can trigger a panic attack in some. Our past experiences can impact on how we experience and respond to fear in the here and now. For our example, if our childhood was frightening because our parents and/or caregivers were unpredictable and volatile, we could become hypervigilant, braced for and ready to react to danger at all times. We would never know when the danger would present itself, so we would have to be in a state of hypervigilance and fear all the time. Hypervigilance is when we are in a 'red alert' state. Our senses are heightened and we are constantly on the lookout for threat and danger. There may not be any danger but our senses are operating on a 'just in case' basis. Hypervigilance is exhausting as it entails a constant scanning of the environment and it is therefore impossible to relax. If we think of a soldier on sentry duty. They have to be ready at all times for an enemy attack. The enemy could appear at any second and the soldier needs to be ready to deal with the threat. The enemy could be as small as an ant or be an entire battalion; it matters not, because the soldier has to be ready for all eventualities. Someone who is hypervigilant is like a soldier who is never able to step down from being on guard.

Fear can attach to any number of things:

Fear of being hurt
Fear of living
Fear of death, our own and others'
Fear of the future
Fear of not having or being enough
Fear of spiders, storms, outside, flying, sex, giving birth, not giving birth, dogs, people, men, women, and children… the list is endless
Fear of ourselves, of relationships, of not being able to look after ourselves in relationships, of being alone.

Fear is composed of two primary reactions to some type of perceived threat: biochemical and emotional. As already mentioned, our emotional response to fear is very personal but, physically, we tend to respond in similar ways. When faced with a threat, whether real or imagined, our bodies prepare to manage the threat. A very common response to fear is the 'flight/fight' response, whereby we automatically prepare to fight or we try to run away. This is a primitive response and is not altogether helpful in today's modern world. When a horrendous telephone bill pops through the letterbox, we can neither fight it nor run away, but our bodies may still enter that heightened state. In flight/fight mode, our body releases adrenaline in order to manage the situation, the heart rate increases, along with sweating. Our muscles tense and we are extremely alert. These reactions are perfect when facing a sabre-toothed tiger, but are not helpful in the face of the horrendous telephone bill!

Fear can consist of both physical and emotional symptoms and some of the common signs and symptoms include:

• Chest pain
• Chills

- Dry mouth
- Nausea
- Rapid heartbeat
- Shortness of breath
- Sweating
- Trembling
- Upset stomach.

In addition to the physical symptoms of fear, people may experience the psychological symptoms of being overwhelmed, upset, feeling out of control or having a sense of impending death. It can be easy to see how fear can cast a shadow over life, preventing us from being all we can be. Fear can be said to be on a continuum. Nervousness is akin to fear but so is terror and panic. What makes one person nervous will make another person panic. We each have a personal relationship with fear that is unique to us.

Fear has many names

There are numerous terms and words used to describe fear. Some suggest less fear than others, itself revealing fear as being on a continuum. Below are just some of the synonyms associated with fear:

- Nervousness
- Terror
- Trepidation
- Panic
- Alarm
- Scared
- Dread
- Jittery
- Worried
- Anxious
- Foreboding
- Trepidation
- Apprehension.

You can use the synonyms above to help you engage with a personal inventory on fear.

Activity – Me and fear

What does fear mean to you?

Who or what do you fear? Why?

How have you responded negatively or destructively to your fear?

Has fear controlled your life? How?

What is your earliest memory of fear? How do you feel now remembering that memory?

What would you like your relationship with fear to be going forward?

Anger

Anger is a primary, natural emotion that aims to help us to survive and protect ourselves against attack or real or perceived wrongdoings from others, including society as a whole. Anger often gets a poor press and can be judged as a 'bad' thing. Angry people can be judged as being difficult and/or unpleasant. As children, we are often told off or punished for expressing anger. It is important that feeling anger is very different from acting out on our anger, and also that anger is different from rage and aggression. Anger exists to protect us. We can imagine it as a protector that appears to ensure we are not violated, invaded or impinged upon.

If we are stressed and/or overwhelmed by life, we may react angrily to people, places and things that generally would not be a bother to us. Our anger can be a barometer to measure how we are feeling in other areas, such as estimating where our stress levels are and monitoring our self-care. Other possible anger triggers include:

- Threats to security – personal, environmental, financial, relational
- Grief and loss
- Other people's behaviour, e.g. rudeness, rejection, criticism
- Hunger
- Tiredness
- Frustration
- Stress, both personally and professionally
- Disappointment with self and others
- Physical or mental ill health.

Table 12.1   Possible symptoms of anger

Physical symptoms	Emotional symptoms
Shallow breathing or breathlessness	Irritation, frustration, feeling overwhelmed
Rapid heartbeat	A desire to run away from the situation
Shaking / trembling	A desire to lash out verbally and/or physically
Pacing	Feeling resentful and/or hateful
Clenching fists or jaw	
Being rude and losing sense of humour	Self-hatred
Shouting and/or swearing	Inability to cope
Sweating	Feeling depressed
Increased use of tobacco, alcohol, comfort food, drugs, etc.	Fear

We are using our anger effectively when we address our unmet needs, grievances, frustrations and hurts in a rational but assertive and boundaried way. When we lose control of our anger it can become destructive and we become more likely to say or do unreasonable and/or irrational things that we might come to regret when the anger passes. There are physical and emotional signs of anger that can help us to recognise our own anger and also to begin to recognise when others, including those we work with, might be feeling angry. Some of the physical and emotional symptoms of anger are listed in Table 12.1.

Anger has many names

Anger can be difficult to manage in ourselves and difficult to respond to in others. Anger can be hidden deeply and rarely shown, or it can lie just below the surface, leaping out at the slightest provocation. Similarly to fear, it can be experienced and shown in a number of ways and goes by many different names:

- Irritation
- Frustration
- Rage
- Vexation
- Umbrage

- Acrimony
- Exasperation
- Annoyance
- Fury
- Impatience
- Ire
- Resentment.

You can use the synonyms above to help you engage with a personal inventory on fear.

Activity – Me and anger

What is your current relationship with anger? Has it changed over the years?

How have you and do you experience anger?

Who or what do you feel angry about currently?

When was the last time you acted out on anger? What happened?

Name a positive and a negative experience of anger – yours or another's.

Would you like to change your experience with anger – yours or another's? In what ways?

If someone you were supporting got angry with you, how would you feel? What would you do or say?

Anger is sometimes thought of as a secondary emotion, a defence against feeling other, more painful emotions, for example getting angry rather than feeling hurt, abandoned or rejected. What is your opinion on this statement?

Guilt and shame

Guilt and shame are two very powerful feelings that can be extremely difficult to experience, process and manage. The two emotions can be seen as similar, even interchangeable, but there is a clear and profound difference. Guilt is generally a feeling we get when we do something wrong, whereas shame tends to be a feeling we get when we think there is something wrong with us. Guilt is in relation to something we may have said or done that goes against our own values and/or causes hurt or pain to someone else. With guilt there is a 'wrong' and when there is a 'wrong', there is a way of putting things right, making amends, apologising and saying sorry. Shame, on the other hand, is something that affects our entire being; we feel bad about who we are, we feel we are the mistake, the 'wrong'. We cannot change who we are, our entire sense of self, and therefore shame becomes a toxic, pervasive emotion that impacts on self-esteem, personal value and our ability to feel loved and cared for and also to love and care for ourselves.

Our sense and experience of guilt can become unbalanced. We can feel incredibly guilty for the smallest of mistakes, which suggests the guilt is tipping over into shame and our own judgement of ourselves as not good enough. Shame is a feeling of being exposed. A word that is strongly associated with shame is 'embarrassed'. Breaking the work down, it becomes 'in bare ar**d' – we are exposed and naked in all our imperfections. Shame can be linked to failure and fears of being judged and found unworthy. For some, it is a fear of being seen as they see themselves – weak and horrible, defective and broken, weird and different. Shame makes us cover up, hide who we are and adopt a mask or a variety of masks to show to the world. We present people with what we think is a better version of ourselves, one that will be seen as more lovable and attractive than we really think ourselves to be. Shame is linked to having our failings exposed and being judged in the eyes of others. Shame can create an inner voice telling us that we'll never be good enough. Shame can make us feel humiliated and worthless. Shame flourishes in the darkness and can keep us hidden away from others, isolated and alone. It can be difficult to right-size guilt and shame. We can magnify small misdemeanours and feel awful; we can even feel guilty when someone else does something wrong. We need to create a healthy conscience, one that will tell us when we have let ourselves and others down but not one that feels guilty about everything. We need to own what is truly ours and let go of what is not. Offering support using counselling skills is a powerful antidote to shame. Exposing it and talking things through in an empathic and accepting relationship can ease the burden and hurt that shame causes.

Activity – Guilt and shame

What is your relationship with guilt and shame?

How have you and do you experience these two feelings?

Who or what do you feel guilty or ashamed about currently?

Is your shame and guilt justified or are you taking responsibility for things that don't belong to you?

How might you feel if someone you were supporting said you weren't helping them? What might you do in this situation?

Relationships

In relationships, what values and principles are important to you? Throughout this book, the value of the helping relationship is highlighted as being the crucial element of using counselling skills to support and encourage someone's wellbeing and process of change. A relationship needs to be built on strong foundations of care, trust, understanding and listening.

Learning Journal

I've got myself in a real mess on this course and feel all over the place. I'm in a place I know well and yet I find myself here again and I just want to run and hide.

My heart is beating really fast just writing this because I feel so many feelings. I feel silly, embarrassed and guilty. I feel scared and trapped. I feel angry with other people and with myself. I want to try to manipulate my way out of this but that is something I've done all my life. I want to change and I want to stop situations like this happening. They have happened all my life and I'm sick and tired of them. I feel full of resentment and that makes me feel poisoned inside. Someone on the course said that resentments are like mushrooms. If we keep them in the dark and cover them with the manure of our feelings, they grow and grow, but if we expose them to the light, they shrivel and die. As a first step, I'm writing here. The second step is to take it to the group and expose the situation and hopefully find some closure. I am so frightened I feel sick just thinking about it. I'm sure I will be hated and rejected by the group and wonder if I'm setting myself up for that. Whatever, I need to change this pattern and, if nothing else, speaking out will stop people talking to me... a blessing and a curse.

I've just read back what I've written and realise it sounds very dramatic and actually it is not. It's quite a small thing but it's a big deal to me. In a nutshell, I have a tendency to agree with whoever I am with, regardless of how I really feel. Someone in the group expressed a negative opinion about another member of the group and not only did I agree, I even added some comments of my own. A few weeks later another group member expressed feeling fed up with the negativity of the group member who had talked with me about them and I agreed with them too, and again said a few things myself about the other person and their negativity. Now both members of the group talk to me about the other and I agree with both and I actually gossip about them both.

I want to write I'm sorry. I feel awful, but no matter how awful I feel I keep doing it. It's got to the point where I want to leave the course. Honesty and integrity are vital for counselling skills and I'm showing neither. I like to think I'm an honest person and I say I hate gossips, but I'm being really two-faced. It's not even as if this is a new thing. I do it everywhere and with just about everyone. I wrote in an earlier journal entry about feeling guilty when someone expressed really racist opinions to me. I wrote that I felt bad because I hadn't challenged them, but actually I felt bad because I'd nodded and agreed with them. I didn't really agree with them but I acted as if I did. I just get really scared to disagree with anyone. I think I might know where some of it comes from. My mum was only 17 when she had me and was a single mum. She was quite impatient and bad-tempered and would throw things and shout really loudly. I was very wary of her temper from a young age. I also really wanted her to love me. I would have done anything for her. From age three, I lived with my Nan and she brought me up. She was lovely and spoilt me a bit and was just always there for me. My mum was nasty about my Nan and sort of sneered at her and criticised her and made jokes about her. I hated myself but I agreed with her and laughed at my Nan with her. I can't even explain how I felt.

I have a tendency to lose myself in relationships and then I wonder how I can ever be a counsellor. This has been so hard to write. I'm going to stop now before I change my mind.

Tutor feedback

What an awful position for a young child, a little girl, to be in. So eager to please and be loved and also afraid to be on the receiving end of what sounds like a volatile mother with a ferocious temper. That old situation has followed you throughout your life and even into this course, and once again you find yourself between two people agreeing, placating and pleasing even when you don't want to and don't agree with them. It took a lot of courage to write this journal entry and it will take even more courage to speak out in the group. What do you need to do this? How can I support you?

The echoes from the past are very loud, but you are willing to stop the pattern repeating any more. This is a huge step. Have you considered personal therapy? In an earlier journal entry you wrote that you had found it useful in the past.

Five words, five simple words, but they are five of the hardest words you will ever say in situations like this:

'I don't agree with that.'

Five simple words.

What you are doing is learning to protect that younger part of you who didn't have the power to say those five words and who has suffered ever since. You simply wanted to please your mum and that need to please has transferred onto other people. I think the person who has been the most hurt by this pattern is you. You have taken the first and most important step. I would urge you to think about personal therapy. Not because you are doing something wrong, but because you are doing something right. Well done.

Another relationship that is vitally important is the relationship we have with ourselves. When considering what makes a good helping relationship, it is necessary to ask the same questions about the relationship with self.

Activity – Relating to self

Reflect on your relationship with yourself by completing the table below.

Relating to self

Care is needed to form an effective working alliance or helping relationship.
How do you care for yourself? Please explain.
Understanding is needed to form an effective working alliance or helping relationship.
Do you judge or criticise yourself? Please explain.
The ability to listen is needed to form an effective working alliance or helping relationship.
Do you listen to yourself, your fears, hopes, dreams and worries? Please explain.
Reliability and consistency are needed to form an effective working alliance or helping relationship.
Do you stand by yourself or do you abandon yourself? Please explain.
Rapport is needed for an effective working alliance or helping relationship.
Do you get on with yourself? Do you enjoy your own company? Please explain.
Unconditional positive regard is needed to form an effective working alliance or helping relationship.
Do you like and value yourself? Please explain.
Kindness is needed to form an effective working alliance or helping relationship.
Are you kind to yourself? Please explain.
Humility is needed to form an effective working alliance or helping relationship.
Are you honest with yourself about who you really are? Please explain.

The list in the above activity could go on and on. Often our patterns of relating in personal relationships creep into our professional relationships. We take ourselves wherever we go. The more we become aware of who we are in relationships, the better we are able to make changes. It can be helpful to look back to past relationships as well as current ones to raise self-awareness. By making a list of past and current relationships we can become aware of whether each was/is helpful or not, if each was/is harmful or healing. We can look at relationships with relatives, partners, friends, colleagues, neighbours, school peers and authority figures, such as the police, teachers, managers and acquaintances.

Activity – Relating to others

Reflect on your role in these relationships and on what maintained or ended the relationship?

Are you different in romantic or sexual relationships compared to platonic relationships?

How do you feel about being alone?

Can you identify any patterns in your relationships?

Are you a different person with different people?

How do you consider the feelings of others in your relationships? Are they equal to your own? Or do they have more or less value?

Have you done things in your relationships that you did not want to do? Have you behaved in ways you didn't want to? Why?

Have any relationships left you feeling ashamed and guilty? What were they? Why did you feel that way?

How have you got on with acquaintances, neighbours, colleagues and people from school, etc.? Are there any patterns that emerge?

What role does trust play in your relationships, past and present?

What personal behaviours in relationships would you like to change?

What does a healthy relationship mean to you?

If any of your relationships have been abusive and you haven't been able to talk this through in a safe and loving environment, you could give yourself the gift of healing. Many of us are called to the helping professions and tend to give others the love and healing we struggle to give ourselves. This poem, 'The Cosmic Dancer', by Brigit Anna McNeil (2020), eloquently sets out the work we may need to do:

Before I could ease the weight of grief and sorrow.

I had to first meet those parts of me.

The parts I had pushed out onto the wastelands.

The parts I had treated with neglect and fear.

These parts of me,

Born from moments of pain and trauma, had become monstrous to my mind.

I was scared of greeting them,

Seeing what I had done from shutting them away and tearing out their tongues.

Fearful of the guilt and shame these monstrous parts of me might make me feel.

Guilt for my actions, words and deeds.

Scared of being filled with shame, as the smears of dirt still held in my fibre are revealed in all their shitty glory.

Yet, when I entered the wastelands, to call these ugly parts of me back, waiting to be filled with disgust at the mere sight of them.

I saw instead, broken parts of me, in need of love and care. Each needing to be seen, heard and felt; no longer neglected.

To be, instead, acknowledged in love.

I no longer felt to push these parts of me away.

But only to hold these pieces of myself; the broken child, the lost woman, the distorted teen; holding them into my heart.

Hugging them with tenderness and strength, until they started to melt back into me, filling my heart and making me whole again.

No longer fragmented.

No longer fearing the monster, instead feeling me.

Source: Reproduced by kind permission of Brigit Anna McNeil.

Values and qualities

It is important to acknowledge our value and qualities. It is all too easy to concentrate on all that is wrong and ignore the many attributes present. When using counselling skills, our attributes and qualities will help form the relationship which is key to help, healing and change. These will include:

- Kindness and care
- Compassion and consideration
- Integrity
- Patience and tolerance
- Emotional maturity.

Activity – Values and qualities

Can you relate to the values and qualities above and bring them to bear in your work with others?

What do you need in order to be able to use these qualities effectively when using counselling skills?

Self-awareness

Philippe Rochat has undertaken extensive research in self-awareness. He has identified five distinct levels of self-awareness (Rochat, 2003). The first stage (Level 0) begins in the early years, when we have no self-awareness. Self-awareness increases at each level until it reaches 'Level 5' (explicit self-awareness). The mirror that is mentioned here relates to another person or, in the case of an infant, the mother.

- **Level 0:** Confusion. At this level the individual has a degree of zero self-awareness. They are unaware of any mirror reflection or of the mirror itself. They perceive the mirror as an extension of their environment. Level 0 can also be displayed when an adult frightens themselves in a mirror, mistaking their own reflection as another person just for a second.
- **Level 1:** Differentiation. The individual realises the mirror is able to reflect things. They see that what is in the mirror is different from what is surrounding them. At this level they can differentiate between their own movement in the mirror and the movement of the surrounding environment.
- **Level 2:** Situation. At this point an individual can link the movements on the mirror to what is perceived within their own body. This is the first hint of self-exploration on a projected surface where what is visualised on the mirror is special to the self.
- **Level 3:** Identification. This stage is characterised by the new ability to identify self: an individual can now see that what's in the mirror is not another person but actually them. It is seen when a child, instead of referring to the mirror while referring to themselves, refers to themselves while looking in the mirror.
- **Level 4:** Permanence. Once an individual reaches this level, they can identify the self beyond the present mirror imagery. They are able to identify the self in previous pictures looking different or younger. A 'permanent self' is now experienced.

- **Level 5:** Self-consciousness or 'meta' self-awareness. At this level not only is the self seen from a first-person view, but it is realised that it is also seen from a third person's view. They begin to understand they can be in the mind of others. For instance, how they are seen from a public standpoint. (Rochat, 2003, pp. 719–22)

Self-awareness can be enhanced and increased by feedback from others. Other people may be able to see things about us that we are unaware of. It can be very painful to be criticised and given feedback harshly. However, feedback from caring people that is delivered mindfully and sensitively can help us to see our hidden areas and blind spots and increase our self-awareness and insight.

The Johari window model

The Johari window is a technique that helps people to better understand their relationship with themselves and others and to develop greater self-awareness. It was created by psychologists Joseph Luft (1916–2014) and Harrington Ingham (1916–95) (Luft & Ingham, 1955). It uses a simple technique that allows people to identify their strengths, weaknesses and blind spots. It is best carried out in groups or pairs as it relies on giving and receiving feedback. The exercise works like this:

1. **Each person selects a set number of adjectives from the list below that they feel best describe themselves.**

able	accepting	adaptable	bold
brave	calm	caring	cheerful
clever	complex	confident	dependable
dignified	empathetic	energetic	extroverted
friendly	giving	happy	helpful
idealistic	independent	ingenious	intelligent
introverted	kind	knowledgeable	logical
loving	mature	modest	nervous
observant	organised	patient	powerful
proud	quiet	reflective	relaxed
religious	responsive	searching	self-assertive
self-conscious	sensible	shy	silly
		sentimental	spontaneous

Figure 12.1   The Johari window

	Known to self	Not known to self
Known to others	Known self Things we and others know about ourselves	Blind self Things others know about us that we do not know
Not known to others	Hidden self Things we know about our self that others do not know about us	Unknown self Things neither we nor others know about us

2. **Each person then selects, from the same set of adjectives, the characteristics that best describe another person.**

Once the adjectives are selected, they are then placed into the four cells or quadrants of the Johari window (Figure 12.1).

Known self

Adjectives that both the subject and peers select go in this cell (or quadrant) of the grid. These are traits that subject and peers perceive.

Blind self

Adjectives not selected by the person but only by their peers go here. These represent what others perceive but the person does not.

Hidden self

Adjectives selected by the person but not by any of their peers go here. These are things the peers are either unaware of and are only known by the person, who may keep them hidden on purpose.

Unknown self

Adjectives that neither the person nor peers select go here. They represent the subject's behaviours or motives that no one participating recognises, either because they do not apply or because of collective ignorance of these traits.

A completed Johari window can be a real eye-opener. The insight you have about yourself and the awareness you have about how you are seen by others helps you to raise your self-awareness. When we learn about our 'Blind Spot' behaviours and understand more about the contents of our hidden selves, our 'Façade', these two windows/quadrants become smaller and we are more open with others and ourselves.

This chapter has offered some challenging questions to reflect on. The questions may bring up painful memories and events. It is important to be kind to yourself, and gentle.

> Self-awareness, which encapsulates self-knowledge and self-insight, has long been recognised as being a critical component of a successful therapeutic process. (Brown & Lent, 2009, p. 306)

THIRTEEN

Professional support, guidance and self-care

Using counselling skills can be emotional and draining. It can raise many different ethical dilemmas, including issues around risk, safeguarding, competence and confidentiality, to name but a few. Counselling skills are used in a wide range of roles and settings, and the type of professional guidance and support will vary too. Some professions will have their own professional body. For example, the biggest professional body in the United Kingdom is the Royal College of Nursing (RCN); and not far behind is the British Medical Association (BMA). The General Teaching Council (GTC) is the professional body for teaching in England. The overall purpose of all professional organisations is to work in the public interest to help improve standards. Many health and social care professionals have regulators to ensure that the professional is competent and works safely and professionally, offering an effective service. For example, social workers must be registered with one of four UK regulators: Social Work England (SWE), Social Care Wales (SCW), the Northern Ireland Social Care Council (NISCC) and the Scottish Social Services Council (SSSC).

The Health and Care Professions Council (HCPC) is an interesting organisation. It protects the public by regulating health and care professions. To do this it:

- Sets standards for professionals' education and training and practice
- Keeps a register of professionals, known as 'registrants', who meet their standards
- Takes action if professionals on the Register do not meet the standards.

For each profession the HCPC outlines:

- Standards of conduct, performance and ethics
- Standards of proficiency

- Standards of continued professional development (CPD)
- Standards relevant to education and training.

Some of the professions covered by the HCPC are:

Chiropodist
Art therapist
Paramedic
Physiotherapist
Practitioner Psychologist
Occupational Therapist
Dietician.

The professional landscape can be confusing, with multiple professional bodies, registers, associations, regulators. What does it all mean? In a nutshell, they all have one thing in common – standards. Many professions are regulated, and many are not. Counselling, for example, is not a regulated profession but some of counselling's professional bodies hold voluntary registers which acknowledge that registrants meet the standards of the professional body. The BACP is such a register holder.

Skills for Care is another important organisation and is the strategic body for workforce development in adult social care in England. Skills for Care is an independent registered charity working with thousands of adult social care employers in England to set the standards and qualifications for social care workers. Carers and support workers can join various organisations that offer support and guidance but do not hold members to an ethical framework or set of standards. The National Association of Care & Support Workers (NACAS) is such an organisation. It is impossible to detail all the different organisations, regulators and professional bodies that relate to the roles and settings that benefit from the use of counselling skills. What they highlight, however, is the need for professionals to have an umbrella of support and guidance. Roles and settings vary and as such might require different forms of professional support and guidance. Some of those forms include:

- Consultative support
- Supervisory support and guidance
- Line management
- Mentoring
- Coaching.

The different forms of professional support and guidance offer a relationship that can:

- Monitor own personal and professional wellbeing
- Reflect on the effectiveness of the work and the relationship.

Professional support and guidance do not necessarily focus solely on the job. They can also help with personal and family needs, mental health assistance, educational goals and career decision making. What happens in our personal lives definitely impacts on our professional lives. The two do not operate in a vacuum. Professional support and guidance should be available to you regularly to help you manage your professional role, reflect on your work with others and how the role impacts on you and how you impact on the role. Unfortunately, not all employers and organisations provide adequate professional support and guidance. You might need to consider accessing this support outside the organisation you work for. There may be a financial consideration which will have to be weighed up against other commitments and, more importantly, against your own health. What price for your personal wellbeing?

All professionals have a line manager and some also have a supervisor. It can be helpful to reflect on how these relationships can be supportive. For example, prior to meeting with a line manager, supervisor, etc., it is helpful to identify what you want and need to talk about. This will provide a focus to the meeting, rather than risk the meeting becoming a general chit-chat about the job. Some areas you might want to talk about could include:

- How you are feeling in the role
- How capable and competent you are feeling in the role
- Workload – too much, too little?
- Areas you are struggling with
- The individuals you are helping/supporting (ensuring the confidentiality boundaries are in place, etc.)
- How the relationship/work is going with each person
- How you feel towards each person you support
- What is challenging and difficult about your role
- How things are at home
- Whether there are any new or ongoing challenges
- Learning and development requirements and requests
- What personal and professional support is in place.

It can be hard to be honest with employers, especially when we are struggling or feeling incompetent or have made mistakes. It could be that we have done or said something that could jeopardise our role and employment. We might have irrational fears that make us pretend that everything is going well when it isn't.

Activity – Honesty at work

It can be hard to be honest at work due to a number of factors. Below are some scenarios that some people might find challenging to talk about in line management or supervision meetings.

How would you feel talking about these issues?

How would you feel and respond if you were the line manager/supervisor?

1. You are sexually attracted to someone you are caring for.
2. You are a nurse and think a consultant has made a poor judgement about a client.
3. You feel useless in the job, as if you just can't get anything right.
4. You work with someone with severe learning disabilities and have become frustrated and shouted at him.
5. You are a victim of domestic abuse and are regularly beaten by your partner.
6. You really don't like someone you are caring for.
7. You work in a rehab centre and are also in recovery. A new resident is someone you used drugs with in the past.
8. You offer floating support to a care scheme that supports elderly people to stay in their own homes. You left early one day and the person fell while trying to wash up.
9. You feel stressed all the time and feel overwhelmed and unable to cope.
10. You saw a colleague, who is also a friend, be very rough with a patient.
11. You are bored of the job and of the people you are supporting.
12. You lied to someone about something you had done and are now constantly scared that you will be found out.
13. You are a teacher and have been drinking far too much alcohol. A student said they could smell alcohol in the classroom. You are scared of losing your job.
14. Your GP has referred you to counselling in order to work on your own childhood trauma.
15. You really struggle to use your counselling skills and keep giving advice, asking too many questions and trying to cheer people up.
16. You have a criminal record and have been asked for an enhanced DBS check.

Developing a professional development plan

A 'professional development plan' is a roadmap containing the skills, strategies and education you need to further yourself to achieve your professional goals. There are various steps involved in a professional development plan, which could include the following.

1. Reflecting on where you are now

What have you done over the past year, three years or five years to help your professional development?

Are you doing what you want to do in your professional life?

If not, why not?

What things have you done recently to help or hinder your professional life?

2. Identify a specific career goal

What ambitions to you have? Where would you like to be? What exactly do you want to be doing?

Make sure you set goals that are SMART:

- Specific
- Measurable
- Achievable
- Realistic
- Timely.

To help you identify your goals, reflect on the following questions:

- What does success mean to you? Do you feel successful in your current job?
- What does/would success look and feel like?
- What activities and things do you love doing the most? Are these a part of your current job? If not, can you change this?
- Are you feeling successful in your current job?
- Where would you like to be in one year, three years, five years and ten years? Begin to identify both long- and short-term goals. It is OK to think big or small!

3. Gather any information you might need

What professional skills, qualities and attitudes are needed for the professional life you want?

Take time to look at job descriptions and person specifications to identify gaps in your skill set. Practise interview techniques to get where you want to go.

Break down your long-term goals into more manageable steps, identifying the baby steps needed for your dream job. On a practical level, what skills, training, etc. does your dream job require? All jobs require different skills and it is impossible to bake a cake without knowing what ingredients it contains. Once we know what the ingredients are, we can check which ones we have and which ones we need to acquire. Gather as much information as possible on the role, company and job. There may be opportunities within your current organisation or job and a meeting with a line manager or supervisor can help you to identify available training opportunities or promotion.

4. Identify what professional skills and personal qualities you already have and those skills and qualities you need to learn or work on

List the training, experience, skills, qualities and attitudes you already have… and don't underplay yourself! Don't forget to include your transferable skills, that is those skills you use in other roles. For example, a parent uses a multitude of skills that are invaluable in the workplace.

5. Draw up a timeline for accomplishing your ambitions and goals

Open-ended plans are more likely to fail than those that have a time boundary attached. The timeline needs to be realistic and achievable, but equally there does need to be one. Attach rewards along the way. If you reach a goal (e.g. attending a workshop on interview skills), reward yourself in some way. You could take yourself to lunch and order your favourite food, or have a head massage to acknowledge the great thinking you've been doing. Be creative but don't forget to acknowledge the achievements, no matter how small.

Change is incredibly hard, and each tiny baby step takes courage and perseverance. Be generous with your timeline. Change rarely happens as quickly as we would like it to. Do not create a timeline that will give you permission to beat yourself up if you don't achieve it. Plot the small steps along your timeline that will take you in the direction you want to go until you are doing what you want to be doing. Measure your progress regularly to ensure that you don't lose heart and lose your way.

Remind yourself why you want to change.

Get support to encourage and empower.

Activity – A virtual manager/supervisor

Use this virtual tool to reflect on where you are in your professional role.

Hello, my name is Work Bot and I am here to help you.

- How is everything going today? Tell me about this last week.
- What's on your mind this week?
- Last time we spoke you said X was a challenge for you. How is that going?
- What are your plans and priorities this week?
- How confident do you feel with where your job is going?
- What has energised you in your role [over a period of time]?
- What has challenged you [over a period of time]?
- What has gone well/not so well for you [over a period of time]?
- What's one thing (or a few) you learned this week?
- Do you feel confident in how you/your team are progressing?

- How are you/your team progressing towards established goals?
- How is everything going with people you work with/on your team?
- Are there any interactions you'd like to discuss?
- What feedback do you have for me?
- When you think about yourself in two years' time, what comes to mind?
- What are two or three new skills you'd like to learn on the job?
- How are you progressing towards your bigger career and life goals?
- Is there someone at the company (or outside) that you'd like to learn from?
- What progress have you made on your career goals this week?
- What are you committing to between now and the next time we meet?
- What can I help you with between now and the next time we meet?
- Is there anything we didn't cover that you'd like to discuss next time?

Goodbye and happy work life, from... Work Bot

Self-care

Self-care is integral both personally and professionally. Working with others can be challenging in many ways, and it is important that caring for others does not come before caring for self. Self-care fosters personal resilience and an ability to manage and cope. Lack of self-care can exacerbate other difficulties. Although stress and being overwhelmed can be seen as personal issues, they do influence working with others. Self-care needs to include professional support and guidance and an awareness of the need for a work–life balance. Self-care is not intended to be a one-time task, but rather an ongoing practice of caring and esteeming the self in order to be able to offer care and esteem to others.

Self-care is needed in the following areas (Figure 13.1):

- Physical
- Emotional
- Social
- Spiritual
- Personal
- Psychological
- Financial
- Professional.

The template in Table 13.1 can help you to arrive at a self-care plan and also to identify the areas that need further attention. Some examples are

TYPES OF SELF-CARE

Physical	Emotional	Social	Spiritual	Personal	Psychological	Financial	Professional
Sleep Stretching Walking Physical release Healthy food Yoga Rest	Stress management Emotional maturity Forgiveness Compassion Kindness	Boundaries Support system Positive social media Communication Time together ask for help	Time done Meditation yoga Connection Nature Journaling Sacred space	Hobbies Knowing yourself Personal identity Honouring your true self	Safety Healthy living environment Security and stability Organised space	Saving Budgeting Money management Sparging Paying bills	Time management Work boundaries Positive work-place More learning Break time

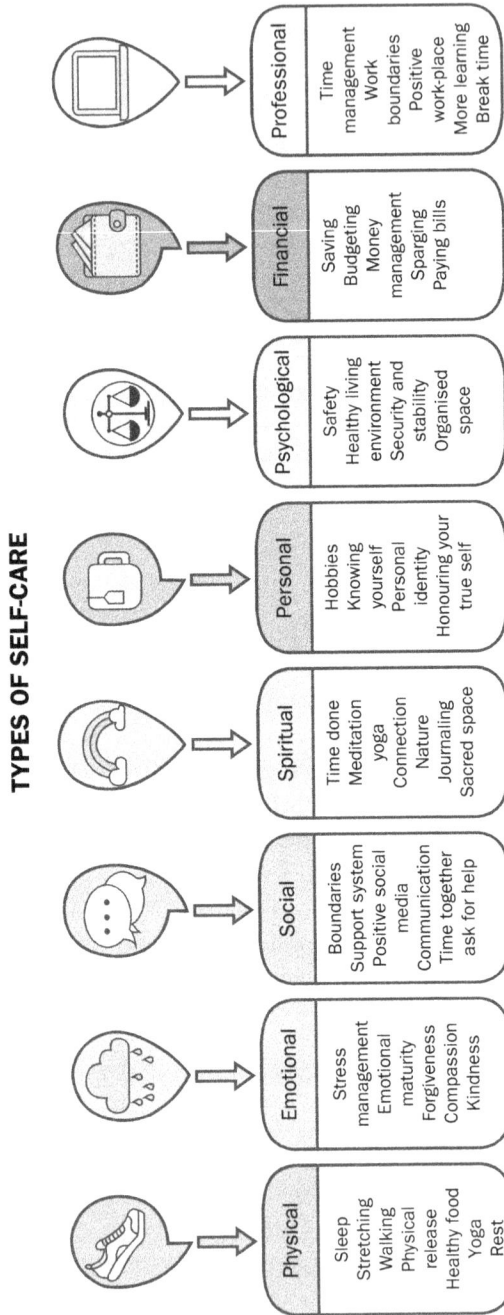

Figure 13.1   Types of self-care

Table 13.1   Caring for myself

Caring for myself – What is needed?	
Professional	Physical
Supervision, peer support	*Healthy diet*
Relationships	Psychological
Friendships	*Journal*
Emotional	Spiritual
Talking honestly	*Yoga, meditation*
Which areas need further input?	
What stops you practising self-care in some or all of the areas?	
What stops you loving yourself?	
What do you need to put this self-care plan into practice?	

given to set you on your way, but each can be personalised with further details.

Completing Table 13.1 has hopefully identified areas for personal and professional development and acknowledged the importance of practising self-care to protect oneself from the emotional impact of working with others and to foster personal resilience. Working with others who have experienced traumatic events can have a profound impact on the people helping and supporting them. The term 'secondary traumatic stress' (STS) refers to the presence of symptoms caused by empathic engagement with other people's traumatic experiences. Other terms used to describe STS are 'compassion fatigue' or 'vicarious trauma'. Anyone who engages empathetically with survivors of traumatic incidents and material relating to their trauma is potentially affected, including doctors and other health professionals. In order to do our best work with the people we help and support, we need to be aware of how our work affects us. It is important to recognise the warning signs when we are being affected by trauma – whether it is our own or others' trauma.

Symptoms of STS may include:

- Increased anxiety and concern about safety
- Intrusive, negative thoughts and images related to the traumatic stories you may have heard
- Fatigue and physical complaints
- Feeling numb or detached from others
- Feeling powerless or hopeless about the people you are helping/supporting
- Diminished concentration and difficulty with decision making
- Physically or emotionally withdrawing from people

- Experiencing lingering feelings of anger, rage and sadness about someone's victimisation
- Becoming overly involved emotionally with the person you are supporting and thinking about them outside working hours
- Experiencing bystander guilt, shame or feelings of self-doubt
- Loss of hope, pessimism, cynicism
- Difficulty in maintaining professional boundaries, e.g. over-extending self (trying to do more than is in the role to help).

It is important to notice and attend to symptoms of secondary trauma stress. Professional support and guidance are invaluable and other strategies include:

- Taking care of yourself emotionally
- Looking after your physical and mental wellbeing
- Maintaining a healthy work–life balance (i.e. having outside interests)
- Being realistic about what you can accomplish
- Taking regular breaks and taking time off when you need to
- Seeking support from colleagues, family members (always remembering confidentiality)
- Taking up training opportunities
- If you need it, engaging in individual therapy
- Detaching from work and not letting it follow you home.

APPENDIX I

Counselling skills competence framework

Counselling skills competence framework

Areas of competence				
Professional context	**Empathy**	**Skills and techniques**	**Working alliance**	**Personal qualities**
Ability to use counselling skills within legal, ethical and professional guidelines	Ability to use counselling skills to communicate empathic understanding	Ability to use a range of listening and responding skills appropriately	Ability to use counselling skills to establish, maintain and end the work	Ability to use counselling skills with self-awareness
Ability to work within professional boundaries appropriate to role and setting	Ability to use counselling skills empathically, to understand and respond appropriately to those experiencing painful and distressing emotions		Ability to use counselling skills collaboratively	Ability to draw on helpful personal attributes

(Continued)

(Continued)

Areas of competence

Professional context	Empathy	Skills and techniques	Working alliance	Personal qualities
Ability to use counselling skills to enhance but not change the primary role	Ability to use counselling skills to work empathically with a diversity of persons, settings and situations		Ability to use counselling skills in interactions with other professionals, carers, friends and family of the person you are working with	
Ability to offer appropriate care and support Ability to identify, assess and respond to risk and emergency Ability to make use of professional support and guidance				

Professional context

1. Ability to use counselling skills within legal, ethical and professional guidelines

Commit to working ethically and safely.
Follow policies and procedures relevant to role and setting.

2. Ability to work within professional boundaries appropriate to role and setting

Maintain a professional role appropriate to the setting.
Communicate and work within personal and professional limits of ability, maintaining ongoing personal awareness of own capacity and limitations.
Ability to establish and maintain agreed time boundaries.
Ability to explain to the person you are supporting why boundaries are important.
Ability to explain and maintain confidentiality and its limits including:

- Legal limits to confidentiality, for example, safeguarding, terrorism.
- Ethical limits of confidentiality, for example, risk of harm.
- Agency or organisational confidentiality policies (where relevant).

Ability to breach confidentiality safely and appropriately where necessary, acknowledging that sharing relevant information with relevant people at the right time may be necessary.

Work sensitively to try to gain someone's consent if confidentiality needs to be breached, to share confidential information where needed and work together to access appropriate services.

Comply with data protection law and protect privacy according to role and context.

3. Ability to use counselling skills to enhance but not change the primary role

Ability to:

- Integrate counselling skills into a primary role.
- Remain focused on the purpose of the primary role.
- Use terminology specific to role and setting.
- Identify and manage any potential tensions when embedding counselling skills in a primary role.

4. Ability to offer appropriate care and support

Assessment

Ability to:

- Support someone to identify what they need and want; understanding how care and support could help them achieve those outcomes.

- Assess the needs and wants of the person you are working with, identifying what support the person needs and wants.
- Reflect on own limits of ability to ensure the provision of appropriate and adequate care and support.
- Regularly review the work, to ensure that the support you offer is responsive to someone's needs and circumstances.

Referral and signposting

Make appropriate referrals to relevant services by:

- Using knowledge of own role, capacity and limitations when making referral decisions.
- Drawing on knowledge of a range of professions and professional roles and how they work together to provide the care and support someone needs.
- Communicating with other relevant agencies and organisations.
- Identifying external resources and supporting an individual to access and make the best use of these resources.
- Involving the person in the process, being sensitive to their need for privacy and confidentiality; unless the level of risk precludes this.

5. Ability to identify, assess and respond to risk and emergency

Ability to identify areas of risk, and work with someone to monitor and manage the risky and (or) harmful behaviour(s) by:

- Ensuring appropriate support is in place and making referrals where necessary
- Supporting someone to make a safety plan, identifying steps and resources needed to stay safe.

Ability to assess and respond to thoughts of suicide.
   Ability to respond appropriately to emergency and crisis situations by:

- Following risk and emergency procedures
- Calming the situation where possible and looking for ways of reducing or removing risk
- Informing relevant services or organisation(s) where appropriate.

6. Ability to make use of professional support and guidance

Engage with professional support and guidance:

- Consultative support
- Supervisory support and guidance
- Line-management
- Mentoring
- Coaching.

Use professional support and guidance to:

- Monitor own personal and professional wellbeing
- Reflect on the effectiveness of the work and the relationship.

Use reflection and self-appraisal to review own use of skills.

Develop a professional development plan.

Be open to receiving constructive feedback to improve and develop own use of skills.

Empathy

1. Ability to use counselling skills to communicate empathic understanding

Communicate empathic understanding and acceptance.

Demonstrate the qualities of empathy, unconditional positive regard and genuineness.

Ability to apply empathic understanding to communicate kindness, compassion and consideration.

Use empathy, self-awareness and counselling skills to respond appropriately and in a timely manner to meet the needs of the person you are working with.

Ability to respond appropriately by being aware of own evoked feelings when working with others.

2. Ability to use counselling skills empathically, to understand and respond appropriately to those experiencing painful and distressing emotions

Listen to difficult and challenging emotions and let the person know you have heard and understood.

Listen to someone talk about difficult and challenging emotions without trying to change the subject or avoid painful feelings.

3. Ability to use counselling skills to work empathically with a diversity of persons, settings and situations

Facilitate choice; supporting people to make their own decisions wherever possible to promote and maintain autonomy, dignity, choice and independence.

Focus on the person's priorities and wishes, by identifying and being sensitive to difference, and responding to their unique cultural, emotional, psychological and spiritual needs and offering understanding, respect and acceptance.

Understand and work within the spirit of the Equality Act 2010, by:

- Recognising own values, beliefs and principles and acknowledging that they may differ from other peoples.
- Recognising and addressing own prejudice, bias, stereotypes and assumptions.
- Recognising and addressing the impact of judgement, discrimination, bullying and harassment.
- Challenging discrimination in self and others.
- Appreciating and being curious about different cultures, values and beliefs.
- Listening with an open mind without judgement or opinion.

Skills and techniques

1. Ability to use a range of listening and responding skills appropriately

Use a range of listening and responding skills appropriate to the role and setting, including both verbal and non-verbal communication.

Provide clear and straightforward information and communication, avoiding jargon and overly complicated terminology.

Use a range of counselling skills effectively, for example:

- Listening – to verbal and non-verbal communication.
- Paraphrasing – to communicate attention and understanding of content.

- Reflecting – to acknowledge feelings and emotions.
- Restating – repeating back to the person to acknowledge what has been said and to encourage the person to continue.
- Summarising – giving an overview of what has been said.
- Focusing – supporting someone to prioritise what to talk about or work on.
- Minimal encouragers – using small gestures or verbal comments to acknowledge listening and offer encouragement for someone to continue talking, for example, nods, saying mm..., facial expressions, hand gestures.
- Non-verbal communication, for example, open posture and appropriate eye contact.
- Reframing – to offer a different view.
- Questions – use a range of different types of questions: open questions to support someone to explore their situation; closed questions to gather facts, details and information.
- Self-disclosure – a rarely used counselling skill and only appropriate when the self-disclosure is for the other person's benefit and not used to coerce, induce or direct.
- Immediacy – the ability to use what is happening in the moment for someone's benefit.
- Silence – to allow someone the time and space to think things through in a safe and supportive environment.
- Challenge – to gently bring someone's awareness to something they may have avoided or overlooked.
- Attend to verbal and non-verbal cues with understanding and insight.
- Ability to facilitate appropriately paced communication, offering both space and structure.
- Ability to provide a safe and private space for someone to talk about their concerns and (or) worries.
- Ability to work collaboratively and be actively and flexibly engaged in motivating, encouraging and supporting the wellbeing of others.

Ability to recognise and understand how unhelpful responses can impact on others, for example:

- Giving unsolicited advice
- Interrupting and talking over
- Asking too many questions
- Placating
- Controlling
- Rescuing.

Ability to recognise and address own blocks to listening, for example:

- Own emotions, thoughts, problems and issues
- Physical discomfort
- Thinking of what to say
- Judgement and prejudice.

Use counselling skills and their related values and principles in other areas of communication, including:

- Writing
- Telephone and text
- Internet and social media.

Working alliance

1. Ability to use counselling skills to establish, maintain and end the work

Ability to establish and foster a facilitative relationship.

Establish a relationship appropriate to role, setting and desired outcomes.

Form an effective relationship informed by the other person's needs and wants.

Let the person know exactly what they can expect from you.

Proceed at the other person's pace, giving them space to talk.

Maintain the focus of the conversation on the other person's agenda and follow their lead.

Build rapport and trust, acknowledging that a strong relationship is key to supporting wellbeing.

End the relationship and work safely and appropriately by:

- Giving someone notice that your time together is coming to an end
- Exploring how they feel about ending
- Understanding that endings can be painful and challenging
- Identifying coping strategies.

Ability to:

- Reflect on the effectiveness of the relationship and the work
- Use counselling skills to learn about someone's life and situation

- Work with people with a range of different support needs
- Draw on knowledge of a wide range of life issues
- Respond to difficult and challenging behaviour and situations.

2. Ability to use counselling skills collaboratively

Ability to:

- Actively engage someone to work together
- Negotiate a meaningful focus for your time together
- Understand the role empathy, acceptance and empowerment have on working collaboratively.

3. Ability to use counselling skills in interactions with other professionals, carers, friends and family of the person you are working with

Ability to:

- Collaborate and communicate with colleagues and other services and organisations in ways that respect and value the person at the heart of the work
- Communicate appropriately with carers, friends and family of the person you are working with:
  - within the boundaries of confidentiality
  - with the person's consent.

Personal qualities

1. Ability to use counselling skills with self-awareness

Ability to:

- Acknowledge how personal feelings can both help and hinder the use of counselling skills
- See past own feelings and experiences to clearly and accurately focus on the other person

- Identify areas for personal development and access appropriate resources, for example: counselling, training, coaching, colleague support.

2. Ability to draw on helpful personal attributes

Ability to support others with:

- Kindness and care
- Compassion and consideration
- Integrity
- Patience and tolerance
- Emotional maturity.

Ability to acknowledge the importance and practice of self-care to protect oneself from the emotional impact of working with others and to foster personal resilience.

APPENDIX II

A guide to the BACP counselling skills competence framework

A guide to the BACP counselling skills competence framework

The competences required to use counselling skills in a range of different roles and settings

Copyright information:

A guide to the BACP counselling skills competence framework is published by the British Association for Counselling and Psychotherapy, BACP House, 15 St John's Business Park, Lutterworth, Leicestershire, LE17 4HB.

T: 01455 883300
E: bacp@bacp.co.uk
W: www.bacp.co.uk

BACP is the largest professional organisation for counselling and psychotherapy in the UK, is a company limited by guarantee 2175320 in England and Wales, and a registered charity, 298361.

A guide to the BACP counselling skills competence framework is available online at www.bacp.co.uk

Contents

Executive summary

This guide identifies the competences required to use counselling skills safely and effectively in a wide range of professional roles and settings. It describes the advantages offered by the competence framework for professionals, trainers and commissioners, and its applications.

The role of counselling skills is often not clearly defined. It is a term used broadly with no clear remit about the role or responsibilities of those using counselling skills in their primary professional role.

Developing competences for the use of counselling skills to enhance a wide range of primary professional roles is a challenge; but it's a much needed one to improve quality of care, and the safety and wellbeing of both service users and professionals; the cared for and the carers.

The overall message of the framework is to use counselling skills safely and ethically in line with the limits of the associated professional role. Competent use of counselling skills provides the ability to:

- **Recognise** when someone needs to talk

- **Respond** using appropriate skills to facilitate a safe listening space

- **Refer** by sensitively signposting or referring when someone needs further help or assistance

The framework identifies five key 'areas of competence' that are required to use counselling skills safely and effectively in a primary professional role:

1. Professional context
2. Listening and responding skills
3. Empathy
4. Working alliance
5. Personal qualities

In summary, this guide will explain the principles and processes that informed the development of the competence framework and offer detailed information for each area of competence.

Finally, the guide will discuss how the framework can be implemented, whilst promoting and upholding strong professional standards.

Background

The process of our competence development has historically aligned with Roth and Pilling (2008) methodology, whereby the competence framework is developed through a Systematic Review (SR) of the available research literature, conducted by an information analyst.

In applying this methodology to the development of the counselling skills competence framework, it became evident that the SR carried definitional and logistical challenges and limitations. Therefore, the project team agreed to employ a further research method to supplement the findings of the SR with additional evidence.

A Constructivist Grounded Theory study (GT) was introduced to add authority and allow a more interpretive and critical review of relevant literature. The project team considered that this mixed methods' approach added quality and validity to the research findings.

The final analytic step was to incorporate the opinions of expert and peer reviewers to arrive at the final competence framework.

The counselling skills competence framework is designed to be inclusive; care was taken to balance detail with flexibility to avoid a prescriptive and non-inclusive framework that would not encompass the wide range of professional roles that are enhanced by incorporating counselling skills and values.

Rationale for development

Counselling skills rest loosely within our *Ethical Framework for the Counselling Professions* (EFfCP), with no clarity of role, remit or responsibility. The roles that could benefit from counselling skills span many diverse professions, settings and specialisms and cover a wide range of responsibility, knowledge, skills and ability. Currently there is no commonly agreed standard of performance for those using counselling skills and therefore quality assessment is either highly subjective or non-existent. Without a shared understanding, there can be no appropriate standards and no entry standards for many roles. An evidence-based, expert-informed framework for counselling skills provides a common language, which can be used across professions, specialisms, roles and settings.

A foundation of counselling skills is therefore appropriate for many professional roles, for example: social worker, doctor, police officer or healthcare professional.

As an analogy: most houses have foundations, but they are generally hidden from view. The house itself is what is noticed and there are many different types of house. If counselling skills are the foundations, and all the different houses are the professional roles that can be safely built on them, solid foundations form the basis for safe and reliable houses and professionals!

This framework aims to highlight and value a wide range of roles that offer support, care and assistance in many different places and in different ways. Counselling skills can find a home in all of these roles and by understanding the relationship between the primary professional role and counselling skills, the support and care offered will have an additional layer of quality, skill and safe, ethical understanding. Most professionals will already have the skills, knowledge and abilities related to their role; the framework offers counselling skills and values to enhance the relational aspects.

Definition

For the purpose of creating the framework, the project team was tasked with formulating and agreeing a definition for counselling skills. The definition went through several iterations until the team agreed and adopted the following:

"Counselling skills are a combination of values, ethics, knowledge and communication skills that are used to support another person's emotional health and wellbeing. They are not exclusive to counsellors since a wide range of people use them, often to enhance a primary role. Their use is therefore dependent on who is using them and the setting in which they're used."

Who is the competence framework for?

The primary audience for the framework, includes but is not exhaustive of:

- employers
- employees
- educators
- commissioners
- carers and those who are cared for

Counselling skills can be used to enhance many professional roles.

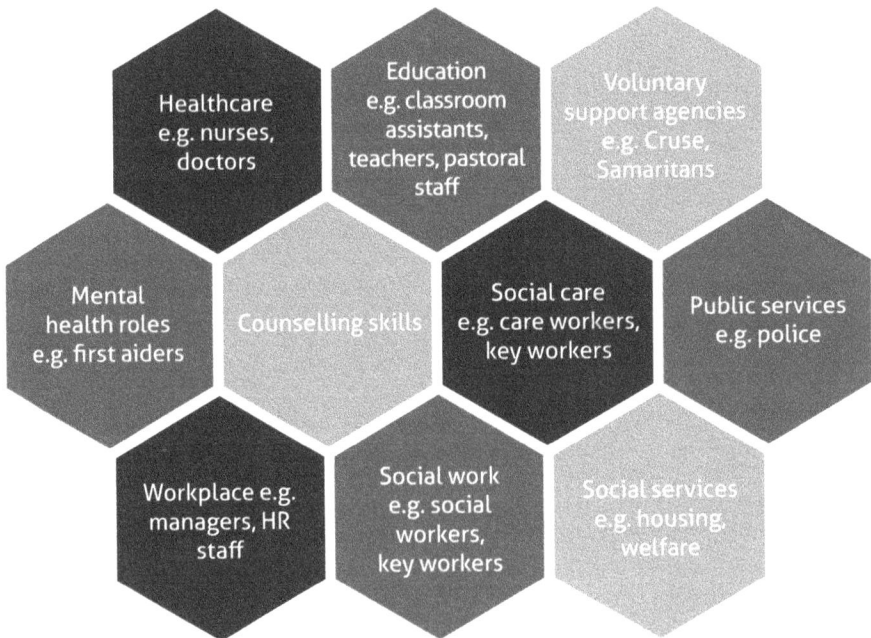

About the competence framework

The competence framework aims to broadly define the knowledge, skills, abilities, behaviours and attitudes needed to use counselling skills safely and effectively within relevant professional roles and settings.

The framework consists of five areas of competence, which can be generically applied to a broad number of contexts. Each of these competences is defined and broken down into manageable components; using language that is clear enough to ensure that everyone has a common understanding of what the effective use of counselling skills means. This common understanding becomes the benchmark against which the performance of an individual can be assessed in education and training and appraised in the workplace.

A competence framework is only helpful if it accurately reflects the professional role in terms of knowledge, skills, experience, qualities and behaviour. This framework is not a tool in isolation. The competences are an integral part of other standards and systems related to the primary professional role.

How to use the competence framework

The framework can be used:

- to set standards, and inform person specifications

- to identify and clarify aspects of job roles and responsibilities

- to design, develop and evaluate qualifications and training programmes

- for recruitment, staff development and appraisals

- to commission services

- as a reflective tool and for personal and professional development

Employment

The competences are generic, adaptable and directly transferable across roles and settings, making them relevant to anyone in a health, social care, support and advice/guidance role.

Interview questions can be taken from the competences. This approach helps to ensure a good match between the role (where counselling skills are part of the role) and the candidate's level of competence both at the point of recruitment and in subsequent performance appraisal. The objectivity offered by evidence-based competences allows fairer decisions around recruitment and promotion.

Many professionals will already have some of the competences in the counselling skills framework. They can cross-check their current skills base with the framework. Gaps in learning and development will be revealed and could form future professional development opportunities.

Not every competence will apply to all roles, and the competences do not replace the need for professionals to meet their own professional role requirements.

The framework responds to the question. "What do people need to be able to do, to be effective in their role?" There are many relational professions that offer help and support to others in a range of different ways. The counselling skills framework offers a common understanding of how to use counselling skills and values to enhance those roles.

Training

The competence framework provides a resource for building a qualification with learning outcomes and assessment criteria related to the counselling skills competences. The qualification and training can be tailored by the learning provider to meet the needs of different learning populations.

The framework can also help counselling skills users to think about where they are currently and where they want to be in the future and plan their learning accordingly. Customised training can address learning gaps.

As well as employment and training, the framework is relevant to commissioning. It will support commissioners to have a greater understanding of the nature and use of counselling skills in a number of professional roles and settings. It may also help commissioners to commission an appropriate range and level of services.

Applying the competence framework

The competence framework includes a wide range of skills and knowledge. Not all competences will be relevant in all contexts. The spirit and underlying elements of the framework are universal. Counselling skills enable professionals to **recognise** when someone needs support and a space to talk; and **respond** to the person's needs. If the person needs help that sits outside of the professional's limits of ability, an appropriate and sensitive **referral** can be made.

As mentioned previously, the areas of competence identified by the framework cover; safe and ethical use of counselling skills, understanding and acceptance of self and others and a strong working alliance meaning that professionals need also to focus on self-care, resilience and professional support and guidance.

The centrality and use of counselling skills as part of another primary role will differ according to the context. What is common is the ability to recognise emotional pain and distress, help an individual/person to talk through their concerns, and be able to respond appropriately within their role.

Overarching benefits of a competence framework for counselling skills

The framework acknowledges and offers a benchmark standard to a diverse workforce encompassing many settings and roles. This can, in turn, enable employers to recruit skilled and competent employees and support the development of their existing employees.

Counselling skills qualifications mapped to this competence framework will be a strong foundation of learning and achievement for those progressing onto higher level and practitioner level qualifications and training, as well as those taking the skills and knowledge learnt into the workplace.

It will enable the helping professions to recognise the needs of the person being supported in relation to the professional's own role and limits of ability. This will ensure they are able to work effectively, or signpost, or refer to another service such as, counselling and psychotherapy. This will provide a coherent care continuum, whereby people will be able to benefit from care and support tailored and appropriate for their individual needs. Improved engagement, clarity of role and communication will ensure people are able to access personalised and appropriate services and care.

The key benefit is the promotion of emotional and psychological health and wellbeing for those in need and for the general public and society as a whole.

Structure

The structure of the framework has been kept deliberately simple to show clearly and succinctly how the competences have relevance to and can enhance many professional roles across sectors and contexts. We will now consider the five areas of competence in more detail.

Competence one – Professional context

This area of competence is very closely allied to the primary professional role and it is important that the professional context for the primary role is not compromised by conflicting information and values from other standards (including this framework). The primary role is to be enhanced by embedding counselling skills, but not changed. In relation to this framework, there will always be an overarching role and set of professional boundaries already in place.

Legal frameworks apply to most professional work but can vary across sectors and settings.

The legal requirements will cover for example; equality and discrimination, mental health capacities and consent, data protection and confidentiality. People may be members of different professional bodies and follow different ethical frameworks or codes of practice. For example, practising nurses have an affiliation with NMC (Nursing and Midwifery Council) where there will also be an underlying requirement for safety and appropriateness. This framework will support those ethical frameworks and codes of practice, whilst ensuring the counselling skills' component is facilitated safely with skill and understanding.

Across roles and settings, there is likely to be some conflict or differences in how this competence area is understood and utilised, and it is important that the framework is seen as an addition to a role, rather than a replacement.

Professional boundaries are essential but again will be different across roles and settings. In many situations, someone using counselling skills will also be fulfilling different tasks related to their primary role, and this can be challenging in terms of establishing and maintaining professional boundaries. A nurse, for example, could listen to a patient's fears about a cancer diagnosis and an hour later be taking blood from that patient or serving them dinner. It takes considerable skill to manage the emotional aspects of the working alliance; to provide a warm and empathic space, whilst taking into consideration the situation and aims of the time spent together. At some points the more practical elements of the nurse's role will take a back seat to allow a space where the patient can voice their feelings and thoughts about their diagnosis. It takes skill and empathic sensitivity to know what to do and when.

Confidentiality (and limits) is an area that can also differ across settings and could cause conflict with a person's beliefs, looking through a therapeutic lens. For example, a counsellor in private practice has relative autonomy (within the law) of when to break confidentiality and may choose not to break confidentiality when certain crimes are disclosed. Conversely, other professional roles may require confidentiality to be broken whenever the law is broken or according to agency policies and procedures.

Other policies and procedures in relation to the primary professional role can include assessing and responding to risk and emergency situations. This competence framework supports the need to identify, assess, monitor and respond in these situations.

In relation to the counselling skills interactions, the care and support offered needs to be appropriate. The professional needs to recognise what someone needs and be able to assess whether they have the skills and knowledge required to help them. Part of this competence is the ability to recognise and work within limits of ability, being able to signpost or refer to someone further qualified or experienced, for example, a counsellor or psychotherapist.

Professional support and guidance vary widely across the health and social care professions and across roles and settings. There are many areas where adequate professional support and guidance are sadly lacking, and people are often left alone to work with people who can have complex and challenging needs. The lack of professional support and guidance can lead to a very high staff turnover, which impacts on building trust and working alliances. The lack of professional support can impact on someone's ability to offer care and support. This framework highlights the importance of professional support and guidance, making it a necessary component of working with others. Adequate and appropriate professional support and guidance fulfil a number of roles; they help someone to monitor their own wellbeing and ability to work effectively and safely with others; they also enable reflection on the effectiveness of the work, the working alliance and the use of counselling skills and values.

Competence two – Empathy

The nature, application and value of empathy and how this is communicated and developed is key to offering someone understanding and acceptance. Empathy and understanding are closely linked to difference and diversity and both are held within this competence area. Responsivity is also held here.

Responsiveness requires empathy to see and understand the world from another's perspective. Responsiveness is also the ability to identify and respond to empathic opportunity. This framework highlights the importance of knowing when to stay with the primary remit of the professional role and when to offer a listening space; and offers the skills and abilities needed to make those decisions.

It is important to work appropriately and sensitively with emotion, within the limits of personal and professional ability. When working with emotion, there is a risk that the conversation will go 'too deep', leaving the professional overwhelmed and under skilled to manage the situation. Appropriate responses ensure the person feels heard and understood, rather than shut down and abandoned.

Understanding and acceptance are not possible when prejudice and stereotyping taint situations. Assumptions can be made based on the professional's experiences and perceptions but assumptions risk discounting the person being supported from the conversation. Personal and professional development will help to identify and challenge personal prejudice and stereotypes and any worn out beliefs and values. This will enable a professional to listen to who the person is and what they are saying, rather than through the filters of their own opinions.

Using counselling skills with a diversity of persons, settings and situations requires understanding, both of self and others. To work with others requires the knowledge that other people's values, beliefs and principles may differ from our own; and with that knowledge, be able to understand the impact of prejudice and discrimination and also recognise and challenge personal areas of prejudice and misunderstanding.

It is important to retain humility, curiosity and an openness to new perspectives, cultures and ways of being. We shouldn't make assumptions that 'we know already' as it's the individual's experience of their own cultural beliefs that's important e.g. just because we know someone is from a certain religious denomination, or have read a book about it, doesn't mean we know what it's like for the individual before us. This approach to working with others enables an appreciation of their unique cultural, emotional, psychological and spiritual needs and an ability to offer understanding, respect and acceptance. By facilitating choice and supporting people to make their own decisions; autonomy, dignity, choice and independence are promoted.

Competence three – Skills and techniques

This competence area has a plethora of terms for similar things – counselling skills, active listening skills, helping skills, counselling micro-skills, communication skills.

This framework offers a list of listening and responding skills with definitions. The list is not exhaustive, and the priority is for the skills to have meaning to the person using them, alongside the ability to offer them in an appropriate and timely manner.

There is an emphasis on using accessible and straightforward language, avoiding jargon and overly complicated terminology.

Appropriate use of listening and responding skills, helps professionals to know what to do, when and how to do it.

There are several counselling skills-based models and approaches but in order to be appropriate and relevant to the wide range of professional roles that could benefit from embedded counselling skills, this competence framework does not include theories or particular techniques or models. It does however, include the core conditions from person-centred theory as outlined by Carl Rogers. Carl Rogers identified the core conditions as: empathy, unconditional positive regard and congruence (Rogers, 1957). These conditions of understanding, acceptance and genuineness are relevant and helpful in all human interactions and offer professionals the skills and qualities that enhance the work and enable a collaborative and respectful working alliance to be formed.

Although this framework remains generic to roles, settings and sectors, and is not restricted by any one approach or model, it is important to acknowledge that many roles could benefit from understanding and working within a particular counselling or helping skills' approach. e.g. Egan's Skilled Helper Model (Egan, 1998), Carkhuff's Human Relations training (Carkhuff, 1969), Hill's Three Stage Model (Hill, 2009).

It is important to identify and use the listening and responding skills that are facilitative and helpful, but it is also important to identify communication styles that are unhelpful and potentially harmful. Often, unhelpful communication styles require self-awareness in order to understand and challenge them. For example, there may be an urge to give someone advice and tell them what to do, when they show pain, fear or distress. Research shows that these responses aren't helpful but the urge to give advice remains. Through personal and professional support and development, personal patterns of relating can be identified and understood. It could be that someone gives advice because they don't know what else to do and can't cope with their own feelings of inadequacy. Perhaps past hurts are triggered by what someone is saying, and the impulse could then be to stop the person talking to avoid the subject and personal pain.

Unhelpful patterns of relating hinder many professionals from offering a safe and accepting listening space. Both personal and professional development will address and hopefully resolve unhelpful patterns of relating and enable professionals to offer a safe listening space free from their own agenda and needs. Personal blocks to listening can be identified and overcome in order to give someone full attention.

Appropriate use of listening and responding skills will offer both space and structure to an interaction that is neither rushed nor hindered but facilitated to allow appropriately paced communication. These skills are not isolated to face-to-face interactions but should also be applied to other areas of communication. Writing, telephone, text, internet and social media can all be enhanced by the skills and values inherent in this framework.

Competence four – Working alliance

Working alliance is also known by many other terms, including: helping relationship, therapeutic relationship, support dyad, support relationship. The overall meaning remains the same; one person assisting another. All these terms are allied to a professional role – nurse, teacher, support worker, manager, doctor etc. It is important that the 'working alliance' is in line with the requirements of the primary role and the values of the counselling skills framework.

The working alliance varies tremendously. It can be a relationship with a GP over many years or an interaction lasting minutes with a housing officer and many others. The goals and purpose of the working alliance also vary widely. Care and support can be defined and interpreted very differently across professions and cultures. A police officer and support worker can both use counselling skills to form a working alliance with others, but the alliance would be different due to their different roles. A carer's use of counselling skills to form a working alliance would depend on the people they are working with: their level of personal agency, autonomy and capacity.

The working alliance needs specific knowledge and skills for each stage of the interaction: establishing, maintaining and ending.

All these factors impinge on what sort of working alliance is formed but the underlying message of this competence framework is to keep the focus on the person's wants, needs and abilities, within a respectful, safe and ethical working alliance.

The main focus is on the person being supported but there are occasions where other professionals, carers, relatives and friends may be considered or consulted. The same skills, values and attitudes conveyed by this competence framework, also apply to these interactions.

This reinforces the value of collaboration, both with the person being supported and between professionals, within the circle of confidentiality, through referrals and with friends, family and carers. A collaborative interaction is one where, the action of working with someone, produces 'something'. It's about working with someone to agree the goals of working together and exploring ways of achieving those goals.

Competence five – Personal qualities

When using counselling skills to support someone, personal qualities and skills are just as important as the actual counselling skills themselves. Self-awareness and personal development are extremely valuable keys to many doors.

Self-awareness is needed to respond appropriately to each unique person and situation. It is required in order to have insight into the situation, the person and oneself and necessary so the person can be offered understanding and support.

Self-efficacy, in relation to counselling skills simply means, knowing what to do and being able to do it (well). This captures the overall spirit of the entire framework. Knowing what to do and when to do it also fall under responsiveness, which requires the ability to respond to someone's changing situation and needs, rather than simply having a set of skills that are delivered in the same way to everyone.

Personal development enhances self-awareness, which enables awareness of when a professional's own agenda, feelings and opinions impinge on their work with others. Personal development also offers opportunities for change and personal growth. Self-awareness will support someone to identify and draw on helpful personal attributes, whilst addressing and working through self-defeating behaviour and patterns of relating. Understanding how personal feelings can impinge on working with others, both positively and negatively, will allow a clearer focus on the needs and agenda of the other person.

Self-care is integral to this competence framework. Working with others can be challenging in many ways, and it is important that caring for others does not come before caring for self. Self-care fosters personal resilience and an ability to manage and cope. Lack of self-care can exacerbate other difficulties. Although stress and being overwhelmed can be seen as personal issues; they do influence working with others. Self-care needs to include professional support and guidance and an awareness of the need for a work-life balance. Self-care is not intended to be a one-time task but rather an ongoing practice of caring and esteeming the self in order to be able to offer care and esteem to others.

Conclusion

Our competence framework for counselling skills offers a benchmark standard for those whose primary professional role is, or could be, enhanced by using counselling skills.

We recognise the valuable contributions that different professionals make to the wider mental and emotional health of the general population, hence the commissioning of this project. By also clearly distinguishing between levels of competence and ability, it ensures that people receive an appropriate and helpful service.

The development and research phase of the framework was hindered by the differences in language and terminology across settings and roles: helping skills, counselling skills, supporting skills, mentoring skills, communication skills, active listening skills etc. The challenge was, how to provide a framework with a common language that had meaning for all these roles and settings? As a result, the final framework uses simple, inclusive language.

Overall, the priority is to ensure that people receive the support, care and treatment most fitting for their needs; which gives rise to the questions: what does someone need to address their problems and who is the best person to help them do that?

This competence framework responds to these questions by ensuring professionals have the knowledge, skills and understanding to:

- **recognise**

- **respond**

- **refer**

It ensures personalised support and a professional and coherent continuum of care.

The quality, integrity and authority of the competence framework can be enhanced by employers, professional bodies and awarding organisations creating partnerships to further promote and uphold competence.

References

Carkhuff, R.R. (1969). *Helping and human relations: A primer for lay and professional helpers: I. Selection and training.* New York: Holt, Rinehart & Winston.

Egan, G. (1998). *The Skilled Helper – a problem management approach to helping* 6th edition California: Brooks Cole,

Hill, C.E. (2009). *Helping skills: Facilitating, exploration, insight, and action* (3rd ed.). American Psychological Association.

Rogers, C. (1957). The necessary and sufficient conditions of therapeutic personality change. *Journal of Consulting Psychology*, Vol. 21(2), pp. 95–103.

Roth, A.D. and Pilling, S. (2008). Using an evidence-based methodology to identify the competences required to deliver effective cognitive and behavioural therapy for depression and anxiety disorders. *Behavioural and Cognitive Psychotherapy*, 36(2), 129–147. https://doi.org/10.1017/S1352465808004141

Acknowledgements

This project was commissioned by the British Association for Counselling and Psychotherapy (BACP). The development process began in 2018. The project team was headed by Fiona Ballantine Dykes (Chief Professional Standards Officer) and Traci Postings (Professional Standards Development Facilitator). Professor John McLeod was a 'critical friend' to the project.

Jessie Emilion was the Information Analyst for the Systematic Review. Professor John Nuttall and Doctor Maria Luca acted as external advisors to the project.

A group of experts in the field met regularly to support the development of the framework. This expert reference group, ERG, consisted of BACP staff and external experts.

Membership of the ERG

Fiona Ballantine Dykes
Chief Professional Standards Officer

Traci Postings
Professional Standards Development Facilitator

Professor John McLeod
'Critical friend' to the project

Professor John Nuttall and Doctor Maria Luca
Regent's University

Jessie Emilion
Information Analyst for the Systematic Review

Diana Balsom
Commissioner of Services Dorset County Council

Victoria Collier
Project Manager Skills for Care

Doctor Anthony Crouch
Chief Executive CPCAB Awarding Organisation

Andy Langford
Chief Operating Officer – CRUSE

Faisal Mahmood
Counsellor and Programme Lead Newman University

We are also grateful to colleagues who commented on the framework and to those who peer-reviewed it.

Glossary

Analysis
Detailed examination of the elements or structure of something.

Attending
Responding to verbal and non-verbal cues with understanding and insight.

Autonomy
The right or condition of self-government. The capacity to make an informed, uncoerced decision.

Benchmark
A standard or point of reference against which things may be compared.

Blocks to listening
Things that get in the way of really listening and hearing someone. There are external blocks to listening - noisy surroundings, accents or language barriers, distractions. There are also internal blocks to listening - personal thoughts, feelings, opinions, physical health and comfort etc.

Boundaries
Offer safe limits to each encounter with someone. Boundaries provide a framework to work from. They set the structure for the relationship and working alliance.

CGT
Constructivist grounded theory. A systematic methodology in the social sciences involving the construction of theories through methodical gathering and analysis of data. The theory is literally grounded in the actual data.

Challenge
Also known as confrontation, means to gently bring a discrepancy to someone to raise their awareness. It could be noticing someone smiling or laughing when they talk about something very sad.

Clinical skills
A discrete and observable act within the overall process of patient care.

Collaboratively
Working together.

Competence and competence framework
A cluster of knowledge, skills, abilities, behaviours and attitudes related to job success and failure. Therefore, a competence framework is something that broadly defines the knowledge and skills needed to be effective within a role or sector.

Confidentiality
Keeping something private or secret; not disclosing to others.

Confidentiality limits
When working with others, not everything can be kept private and confidential. There are legal limits where confidentiality must be broken including: terrorism, money laundering, drug trafficking. Confidentiality may be broken where there is a serious risk of harm too.

Counselling
A talking therapy that is delivered by a trained practitioner, who works with people either short or long term to help them bring about effective change and enhanced wellbeing.

Counselling skills
Can also sometimes be called helping skills, active listening skills.

Counselling skills are a combination of values, ethics, knowledge and communication skills that are used to support another person's emotional health and wellbeing. They are not exclusive to counsellors since a wide range of people use them, often to enhance a primary role. Their use is therefore dependent on who is using them and the setting in which they're used.

Diversity
Variety. A range of different things or people. Understanding that each individual is unique with a unique set of characteristics.

Empathy and empathic understanding
The ability to understand the feelings of another. To understand feelings, thoughts, and experiences from someone else's frame.

Equalities Act
A law which protects people from discrimination. It means that discrimination or unfair treatment based on certain personal characteristics is against the law.

ERG (expert reference group)
A group of experts in a particular field who form a time limited task and finish group. They generally refine the scope of the work and make recommendations to inform the research tasks.

Ethics
Principles that govern a person or group of people. A moral philosophy. BACP's *Ethical Framework for the Counselling Professions* could be seen as a moral philosophy.

Focusing
Helps someone to direct their conversational flow into what is most important for them. Enables them to get in touch with the emotions behind the story or narrative. It is a little like zooming into a photograph and seeing a close up of a particular place, thing or relationship.

Frame of reference
A set of ideas and beliefs upon which someone makes judgments about themselves and the world.

Helping skills
See counselling skills.

Information analyst
Responsible for creating reports, researching and analysing data.

Interpersonal skills
The ability to communicate or interact well with other people.

Kindness
A personal quality that enhances working with others. It is the quality of being considerate, generous, nice and caring towards self and others.

Limits of ability
Something that controls what someone is able to do. They are determined by levels of training and experience and competence in a given area, which dictate who and what someone is safely able to work with.

Listening and responding skills
Key counselling skills. Listening is a process of selecting, attending to, creating meaning from, remembering and responding to someone's verbal and non-verbal messages: responding skills are communication skills that show interest and understanding in what someone is communicating by careful focusing and listening techniques.

Motivation
Willingness and desire to do something. Creates action.

Peer counselling
A helping process that involves one-to-one support between members of a group, with a common purpose.

Peer reviewer
Someone with knowledge and experience in a particular field who offers feedback on a piece of work or research in that particular subject area.

Personal qualities
Personal attributes helpful to support others which include, kindness and care, compassion and consideration, integrity, patience and tolerance and emotional maturity.

Person-centred
A person-centred approach focuses on an individual's personal needs, wants, desires and goals so that they are central to the care and support they need.

Prejudice
An unfair and unreasonable opinion or feeling, usually formed without thought or knowledge. An unreasonable dislike of a particular group of people or things.

Primary role
The main role into which counselling skills are embedded: nursing, caring, psychology, paramedic, support work, social work.

Referral
The act of directing someone to a different person or place for further or more appropriate help, support, information.

Reflecting
Reflecting feelings is determining the feelings and emotions in a person's verbal and non-verbal communication and stating them back to the person. A reflective listener focuses on the feelings in someone's story, rather than the facts.

Resilience
The ability to mentally or emotionally cope with a crisis or to return to pre-crisis status quickly. The capacity to recover from difficulties. Toughness.

Responsiveness
Timely and helpful responses that acknowledge and meet someone's wants and needs. The quality of responding quickly and positively.

Self-awareness
Conscious knowledge of one's own character and feelings.

Self-care
The practice of taking action to preserve or improve one's own health. Protecting one's own wellbeing and happiness.

Stereotype
A widely held but fixed and oversimplified image or idea about a particular category of people. Generalisations that prejudge who someone is based on certain characteristics, for example, race, gender, sexuality.

Summarising
Bringing together all the threads of an interaction into a single statement that covers the content of what has been said; especially useful at the end of a period of time with someone. It condenses the main points of a conversation, giving someone the opportunity to listen and recap.

Supervision and supervisory support
Showing and giving support to someone to help them progress in their work and feel valued and comfortable. It develops good practice in the workplace, builds skills and knowledge and builds a collegiate relationship. The person offering supervision, generally has more knowledge and experience than the person they are supporting.

Systematic Review
A type of literature review that uses systematic methods to collect and critically appraise data, followed by synthesising findings quantitatively or qualitatively. They are designed to provide a whole picture of a given subject or question through existing evidence.

Unhelpful responses
Responses that hinder rather than support someone's wellbeing. Unhelpful responses include interrupting and talking over, giving advice and telling someone what to do, overuse of questions, rescuing etc.

Working alliance
The relationship formed when working with or supporting someone. It is important to develop an effective bond and to set out the boundaries and limits of the relationship as well as establishing the tasks and goals of the work.

APPENDIX III

Ethical framework for the counselling professions

Ethical
Framework
for the
Counselling
Professions

Copyright Information

Contents

Introduction

Our commitment to clients

Ethics

Values

Principles

Personal moral qualities

Conclusion

Good practice

Putting clients first

Working to professional standards

Respect

Building an appropriate relationship

Breaks and endings

Integrity

Accountability and candour

Confidentiality

Working with colleagues and in teams

Supervision

Training and education

Trainees

Research

Care of self as a practitioner

Responding to ethical dilemmas and issues

Introduction

The *Ethical Framework* sets out the expected ethical principles, values and good practice standards for BACP members.

As members and registrants of BACP, we have committed ourselves to the principles and values set out in this *Ethical Framework* and recognise that our membership or registration may be at risk if we fail to fulfil our commitments.

This *Ethical Framework for the Counselling Professions* is the main point of reference for decisions in professional conduct hearings.

Using the *Ethical Framework*

You should read and understand the *Ethical Framework* before working with clients. This framework is designed to help you provide your clients with a secure base for your work together. It is good practice to integrate the *Ethical Framework* into your work and to use it as a resource to help you face any challenges and issues as they arise. This works much better than just turning to it in an emergency or after something has gone wrong.

As a framework, it creates a shared structure within which we all work but with the flexibility to respond to the needs of different contexts and client groups. There are three main sections:

- *Our commitment to clients* provides a summary and overview. You may use this as a separate document to give to your clients or include it in the information you provide about your service.

- *Ethics* is designed to help you understand the thinking behind how we work with clients. It can be used in supervision to think through any issues or dilemmas.

- *Good practice* considers the practicalities of putting our ethics into action.

The *Good Practice in Action* resources, and other resources on the BACP website, provide additional non-binding practice guidance which you may find relevant or useful. The binding words are those used in the *Ethical Framework for the Counselling Professions*, which should be your ultimate point of reference to decide what is appropriate to your role and setting.

Key terms

A *practitioner* is a member or registrant of the British Association for Counselling and Psychotherapy who is providing therapeutically-informed services, particularly coaching, counselling, pastoral care, psychotherapy or using counselling skills. This includes being a supervisor, trainer, educator of practitioners, or researcher of any aspect of the counselling professions.

Therapeutically-informed services are developed from and informed by the theory and practices used in talking and listening therapies, typically coaching, counselling, pastoral care, psychotherapy or using counselling skills. Such theories and practices may be drawn from a wide academic and professional base, including neurology, psychoanalysis, psychology, social sciences and other disciplines.

A *client* is anyone in receipt of coaching, counselling, pastoral care, psychotherapy or counselling skills from a member or registrant of the British Association for Counselling and Psychotherapy. All clients are entitled to receive services that satisfy the commitments stated in this *Ethical Framework* in ways that are appropriate to the type of service being provided and its setting.

All the principles of the *Ethical Framework* will apply to working with trainees and supervisees, particularly to ensure that they are treated with respect, provided with services that meet the required standards, and are protected from exploitation or abuse by anyone with professional power or authority over them. Trainees and supervisees will receive the same commitments and ethical standards as any client receiving services from a member of the counselling professions.

Trainees will fulfil all the commitments to clients within the *Ethical Framework* when working as practitioners with members of the public as their clients. Good Practice point 81 sets out the commitments for working with other trainees to learn new knowledge and skills.

The principles of the *Ethical Framework* apply where appropriate to the participants in research – for further guidance see Good Practice points 84–90 and the BACP *Ethical Guidelines for Research in the Counselling Professions*.

Our *responsibilities* are set out as full or qualified commitments. We are fully and unconditionally committed to fulfilling a specific requirement where we state 'we will ...' or 'we must ...'. Where we consider that a requirement may need to be varied for good ethical reasons, we state that 'we will usually ...'.

We are committing ourselves to being openly accountable and willing to explain how we have implemented any of these obligations to people with a valid interest in our work.

Our commitment to clients

Clients need to be able to participate freely as they work with practitioners of the counselling professions towards their desired goals. This requires clients to be able to trust their practitioner with their wellbeing and sensitive personal information. Therefore, as members or registrants of BACP, we take being trustworthy as a serious ethical commitment. We have agreed that we will:

1.
Put clients first by:

a. making clients our primary concern while we are working with them

b. providing an appropriate standard of service to our clients.

2.
Work to professional standards by:

a. working within our competence

b. keeping our skills and knowledge up to date

c. collaborating with colleagues to improve the quality of what is being offered to clients

d. ensuring that our wellbeing is sufficient to sustain the quality of the work

e. keeping accurate and appropriate records.

3.
Show respect by:

a. valuing each client as a unique person

b. protecting client confidentiality and privacy

c. agreeing with clients on how we will work together

d. working in partnership with clients.

4.
Build an appropriate relationship with clients by:

a. communicating clearly what clients have a right to expect from us

b. communicating any benefits, costs and commitments that clients may reasonably expect

c. respecting the boundaries between our work with clients and what lies outside that work

d. not exploiting or abusing clients

e. listening out for how clients experience our working together.

5.
Maintain integrity by:

a. being honest about the work

b. communicating our qualifications, experience and working methods accurately

c. working ethically and with careful consideration of how we fulfil our legal obligations.

6.
Demonstrate accountability and candour by:

a. being willing to discuss with clients openly and honestly any known risks involved in the work and how best to work towards our clients' desired outcomes by communicating any benefits, costs and commitments that clients may reasonably expect

b. ensuring that clients are promptly informed about anything that has occurred which places the client at risk of harm or causes harm in our work together, whether or not clients are aware of it, and quickly taking action to limit or repair any harm as far as possible

c. reviewing our work with clients in supervision

d. monitoring how clients experience our work together and the effects of our work with them.

Ethics

1.

Our ethics are based on values, principles and personal moral qualities that underpin and inform the interpretation and application of *Our commitment to clients* and *Good practice*.

Values

2.

Values are a useful way of expressing general ethical commitments that underpin the purpose and goals of our actions.

3.

Our fundamental values include a commitment to:

- respecting human rights and dignity
- alleviating symptoms of personal distress and suffering
- enhancing people's wellbeing and capabilities
- improving the quality of relationships between people
- increasing personal resilience and effectiveness
- facilitating a sense of self that is meaningful to the person(s) concerned within their personal and cultural context
- appreciating the variety of human experience and culture
- protecting the safety of clients
- ensuring the integrity of practitioner-client relationships
- enhancing the quality of professional knowledge and its application
- striving for the fair and adequate provision of services.

4.

Values inform principles. They become more precisely defined and action-orientated when expressed as a principle.

Principles

5.

Principles direct attention to important ethical responsibilities. Our core principles are:

Being trustworthy:
honouring the trust placed in the practitioner.

Autonomy:
respect for the client's right to be self-governing.

Beneficence:
a commitment to promoting the client's wellbeing.

Non-maleficence:
a commitment to avoiding harm to the client.

Justice:
the fair and impartial treatment of all clients and the provision of adequate services.

Self-respect:
fostering the practitioner's self-knowledge, integrity and care for self.

6.

Ethical decisions that are strongly supported by one or more of these principles without any contradiction with the others may be regarded as well-founded.

7.

However, practitioners may encounter circumstances in which it is impossible to reconcile all the applicable principles. This may require choosing which principles to prioritise. A decision or course of action does not necessarily become unethical merely because it is controversial or because other practitioners would have reached different conclusions in similar circumstances. A practitioner's obligation is to consider all the relevant circumstances with as much care as possible and to be appropriately accountable for decisions made.

Personal moral qualities

8.

Personal moral qualities are internalised values that shape how we relate to others and our environment. They represent a moral energy or drive that may operate unconsciously and unexamined. This moral energy or drive is ethically more beneficial when consciously examined from time to time and used to motivate our ethical development or shape how we work towards a good society.

9.

'Personal moral qualities' are a contemporary application of 'virtues' from moral philosophy.

10.

The practitioner's personal and relational moral qualities are of the utmost importance. Their perceived presence or absence will have a strong influence on how relationships with clients and colleagues develop and whether they are of sufficient quality and resilience to support the work.

11.

High levels of compatibility between personal and professional moral qualities will usually enhance the integrity and resilience of any relationship.

12.

Key personal qualities to which members and registrants are strongly encouraged to aspire include:

Candour:
openness with clients about anything that places them at risk of harm or causes actual harm.

Care:
benevolent, responsible and competent attentiveness to someone's needs, wellbeing and personal agency.

Courage:
the capacity to act in spite of known fears, risks and uncertainty.

Diligence:
the conscientious deployment of the skills and knowledge needed to achieve a beneficial outcome.

Empathy:
the ability to communicate understanding of another person's experience from that person's perspective.

Fairness:
impartial and principled in decisions and actions concerning others in ways that promote equality of opportunity and maximise the capability of the people concerned.

Humility:
the ability to assess accurately and acknowledge one's own strengths and weaknesses.

Identity:
sense of self in relationship to others that forms the basis of responsibility, resilience and motivation.

Integrity:
commitment to being moral in dealings with others, including personal straightforwardness, honesty and coherence.

Resilience:
the capacity to work with the client's concerns without being personally diminished.

Respect:
showing appropriate esteem for people and their understanding of themselves.

Sincerity:
a personal commitment to consistency between what is professed and what is done.

Wisdom:
possession of sound judgement that informs practice.

Conclusion

13.

The challenge of working ethically means that practitioners will inevitably encounter situations that require responses to unexpected issues, resolution of dilemmas, and solutions to problems. A good understanding of the ethics that underpin our work is a valuable resource which is helpful in making significant decisions. The use of an ethical problem-solving model and discussion about ethics are essential to good practice. This *Ethical Framework* is intended to assist practitioners by directing attention to the variety of ethical factors that may need to be taken into consideration and to identify alternative ways of approaching ethics that may prove more useful.

14.

No statement of ethics can eliminate the difficulty of making professional judgements in circumstances that may be constantly changing and full of uncertainties. By accepting this statement of ethics, members and registrants of the British Association for Counselling and Psychotherapy are committing themselves to engaging with the challenge of striving to be ethical, even when doing so involves making difficult decisions or acting courageously.

Good practice

1.
As members of the British Association for Counselling and Psychotherapy (BACP) we are committed to sustaining and advancing good practice.

2.
This section of the *Ethical Framework* looks behind *Our commitment to clients* and *Ethics* to consider their implications for *Good practice* in more detail.

3.
It sets out what can be expected of all members and registrants of BACP as practitioners providing therapeutically-informed services, particularly coaching, counselling, pastoral care, psychotherapy and using counselling skills. This includes being a supervisor, trainer, educator of practitioners, or researcher of any aspect of the counselling professions. Trainees will fulfil all the commitments to clients within the *Ethical Framework* when working with members of the public as their clients. Good practice point 81 sets out the commitments for working with other trainees to learn new knowledge and skills.

4.
As members and registrants of BACP, we have committed ourselves to the principles and values set out in this *Ethical Framework* and recognise that our membership or registration may be at risk if we fail to fulfil our commitments.

5.
Our responsibilities are set out as full or qualified obligations. We are fully and unconditionally committed to fulfilling a specific requirement of Good practice where we state 'we will...' or 'we must...'. Where we consider a requirement may need to be varied for good ethical reasons, we state that 'we will usually...'.

6.
We are committing ourselves to being openly accountable and willing to explain how we have implemented any of these obligations to people with a valid interest in our work.

Putting clients first

7.

We will make each client the primary focus of our attention and our work during our sessions together.

8.

Any professional or personal interests that conflict with putting a client's interests first will be carefully considered in consultation with a supervisor, an independent experienced colleague or, when appropriate, discussed with the client affected before services are offered.

9.

We will give careful consideration to how we manage situations when protecting clients or others from serious harm or when compliance with the law may require overriding a client's explicit wishes or breaching their confidentiality – see also 10, 55 and 64.

10.

In exceptional circumstances, the need to safeguard our clients or others from serious harm may require us to override our commitment to making our client's wishes and confidentiality our primary concern. We may need to act in ways that will support any investigations or actions necessary to prevent serious harm to our clients or others. In such circumstances, we will do our best to respect the parts of our client's wishes or confidences that do not need to be overridden in order to prevent serious harm.

11.

We share a responsibility with all other members of our professions for the safety and wellbeing of all clients and their protection from exploitation or unsafe practice. We will take action to prevent harm caused by practitioners to any client – see also 24.

12.

We will do everything we can to develop and protect our clients' trust.

Working to professional standards

13.

We must be competent to deliver the services being offered to at least fundamental professional standards or better. When we consider satisfying professional standards requires consulting others with relevant expertise, seeking second opinions, or making referrals, we will do so in ways that meet our commitments and obligations for client confidentiality and data protection.

14.

We will keep skills and knowledge up to date by:

a. reading professional journals, books and/or reliable electronic resources

b. keeping ourselves informed of any relevant research and evidence-based guidance

c. discussions with colleagues working with similar issues

d. reviewing our knowledge and skills in supervision or discussion with experienced practitioners

e. regular continuing professional development to update knowledge and skills

f. keeping up to date with the law, regulations and any other requirements, including guidance from this Association, relevant to our work.

15.

We will keep accurate records that:

- are adequate, relevant and limited to what is necessary for the type of service being provided

- comply with the applicable data protection requirements – see www.ico.org.uk.

16.

We will collaborate with colleagues over our work with specific clients where this is consistent with client consent and will enhance services to the client.

17.

We will work collaboratively with colleagues to improve services and offer mutual support – see 56–59 Working with Colleagues and in Teams.

18.

We will maintain our own physical and psychological health at a level that enables us to work effectively with our clients – see 91 Care of self as a practitioner.

19.

We will be covered by adequate insurance when providing services directly or indirectly to the public.

20.

We will fulfil the ethical principles and values set out in this *Ethical Framework* regardless of whether working online, face-to-face or using any other methods of communication. The technical and practical knowledge may vary according to how services are delivered but all our services will be delivered to at least fundamental professional standards or better.

Respect

21.

We will respect our clients' privacy and dignity.

22.

We will respect our clients as people by providing services that:

a. endeavour to demonstrate equality, value diversity and ensure inclusion for all clients

b. avoid unfairly discriminating against clients or colleagues

c. accept we are all vulnerable to prejudice and recognise the importance of self-inquiry, personal feedback and professional development

d. work with issues of identity in open-minded ways that respect the client's autonomy and be sensitive to whether this is viewed as individual or relational autonomy

e. challenge assumptions that any sexual orientation or gender identity is inherently preferable to any other and will not attempt to bring about a change of sexual orientation or gender identity or seek to suppress an individual's expression of sexual orientation or gender identity

f. make adjustments to overcome barriers to accessibility, so far as is reasonably possible, for clients of any ability wishing to engage with a service

g. recognise when our knowledge of key aspects of our client's background, identity or lifestyle is inadequate and take steps to inform ourselves from other sources where available and appropriate, rather than expecting the client to teach us

h. are open-minded with clients who appear similar to ourselves or possess familiar characteristics so that we do not suppress or neglect what is distinctive in their lives.

23.

We will take the law concerning equality, diversity and inclusion into careful consideration and strive for a higher standard than the legal minimum.

24.

We will challenge colleagues or others involved in delivering related services whose views appear to be unfairly discriminatory and take action to protect clients, if necessary – see 11.

25.

We will do all that we reasonably can to ensure that our clients are participating on a voluntary basis. Hesitant clients or clients who feel under pressure from other people or agencies to work with us will have their reservations acknowledged and taken into account in how services are offered.

26.

We will work with our clients on the basis of their informed consent and agreement. We recognise that exceptional situations may arise where we may need to prioritise the safety of the client or others over our client's wishes and confidentiality – see 10.

27.

Careful consideration will be given to working with children and young people that:

a. takes account of their capacity to give informed consent, considering whether it is appropriate to seek the consent of others who have parental responsibility for the young person, and their best interests

b. demonstrates knowledge and skills about ways of working that are appropriate to the young person's development and how relationships are formed

c. demonstrates a sound knowledge of the law relevant to working with children and young people and their human rights

d. is informed about the current culture and customs that affect parenting/care giving and how children and young people interact with each other and other significant people in their lives.

28.

We will give careful consideration to obtaining and respecting the consent of vulnerable adult clients, wherever they have the capacity to give consent, or involving anyone who provides care for these clients when appropriate.

29.

Our work with clients will be based on professional partnerships with them that aim to increase their wellbeing, capability and/or performance.

Building an appropriate relationship

30.

We will usually provide clients with the information they ought to know in advance in order to make an informed decision about the services they want to receive, how these services will be delivered and how information or data about them will be protected. Where the urgency or seriousness of the situation requires us to intervene before providing such information, we will do so at the first appropriate opportunity.

31.

We will give careful consideration to how we reach agreement with clients and will contract with them about the terms on which our services will be provided. Attention will be given to:

a. reaching an agreement or contract that takes account of each client's expressed needs and choices so far as possible

b. communicating terms and conditions of the agreement or contract in ways easily understood by the client and appropriate to their context

c. stating clearly how a client's confidentiality and privacy will be protected and any circumstances in which confidential or private information will be communicated to others

d. providing the client with a record or easy access to a record of what has been agreed

e. keeping a record of what has been agreed and of any changes or clarifications when they occur

f. being watchful for any potential contractual incompatibilities between agreements with our clients and any other contractual agreements applicable to the work being undertaken and proactively strive to avoid these wherever possible or promptly alert the people with the power or responsibility to resolve these contradictions.

32.

We will periodically review each client's progress and, when practicable, seek our client's views on how we are working together.

33.

We will establish and maintain appropriate professional and personal boundaries in our relationships with clients by ensuring that:

a. these boundaries are consistent with the aims of working together and beneficial to the client

b. any dual or multiple relationships will be avoided where the risks of harm to the client outweigh any benefits to the client

c. reasonable care is taken to separate and maintain a distinction between our personal and professional presence on social media where this could result in harmful dual relationships with clients

d. the impact of any dual or multiple relationships will be periodically reviewed in supervision and discussed with clients when appropriate. They may also be discussed with any colleagues or managers in order to enhance the integrity of the work being undertaken.

34.
We will not have sexual relationships with or behave sexually towards our clients, supervisees or trainees.

35.
We will not exploit or abuse our clients in any way: financially, emotionally, physically, sexually or spiritually.

36.
We will avoid having sexual relationships with or behaving sexually towards people whom we know to be close to our clients in order to avoid undermining our clients' trust in us or damaging the therapeutic relationship.

37.
We will avoid continuing or resuming any relationships with former clients that could harm the client or damage any benefits from the therapeutic work undertaken. We recognise that conflicts of interest and issues of power or dependence may continue after our working relationship with a client, supervisee or trainee has formally ended. Therefore:

a. We will exercise caution before entering into personal or business relationships with former clients

b. We will avoid sexual or intimate relationships with former clients or people close to them. Exceptionally, such a relationship will only be permissible following careful consideration in supervision and, whenever possible, following discussion with experienced colleagues or others concerned about the integrity of the counselling professions, when:

- enough time has elapsed or the circumstances of the people concerned have sufficiently changed to establish a distinction between the former and proposed new relationship

- any therapeutic dynamics from the former relationship have been sufficiently resolved to enable beginning a different type of relationship. (This may not be possible with some clients or inappropriate to some therapeutic ways of working.)

- an equivalent service to the one provided by the practitioner is available to the former client, should this be wanted in future

- the practitioner has taken demonstrable care in ensuring that the new relationship has integrity and is not exploitative

c. We will be professionally accountable if the relationship becomes detrimental to the former client or damages the standing of the profession.

Breaks and endings

38.

We will inform clients about any fixed limits to the duration or number of sessions as part of the contracting process.

39.

We will endeavour to inform clients well in advance of approaching endings and be sensitive to our client's expectations and concerns when we are approaching the end of our work together.

40.

We will inform clients in advance of any planned breaks in working together, for example, holidays or medical treatments, and give as much notice as possible.

41.

Any unplanned breaks due to illness or other causes will be managed in ways to minimise inconveniencing clients and, for extended breaks, may include offering to put clients in touch with other practitioners.

42.

In the event of death or illness of sufficient severity to prevent the practitioner communicating directly with clients, we will have appointed someone to communicate with clients and support them in making alternative arrangements where this is desired. The person undertaking this work will be bound by the confidentiality agreed between the practitioner and client, and will usually be a trusted colleague, a specially appointed trustee or a supervisor.

Integrity

43.

We will maintain high standards of honesty and probity in all aspects of our work.

44.

We will be as open and as communicative with our clients, colleagues and others as is consistent with the purpose, methods and confidentiality of the service.

45.

Whenever we communicate our qualifications, professional experience and working methods, we will do so accurately and honestly. All reasonable requests for this information will be answered promptly.

46.

We will give conscientious consideration to the law and how we fulfil any legal requirements concerning our work – see also 14f, 23 and 70.

47.

We will promptly notify this Association about any criminal charges or disciplinary procedures brought against us. We will also notify this Association of civil claims arising from work in the counselling professions, or if we have been declared bankrupt.

48.

We will avoid any actions that will bring our profession into disrepute.

49.

We will encourage clients to raise any concerns about our work with them at the earliest possible opportunity, give any concerns careful consideration and, when appropriate, attempt to resolve them. Clients will be informed of any applicable complaints processes open to them including the Professional Conduct Procedures of this Association www.bacp.co.uk/about-us/protecting-the-public/professional-conduct.

Accountability and candour

50.

We will take responsibility for how we offer our clients opportunities to work towards their desired outcomes and the safety of the services we provide or have responsibility for overseeing.

51.

We will discuss with clients how best to work towards their desired outcomes and any known risks involved in the work.

52.

We will ensure candour by being open and honest about anything going wrong and promptly inform our clients of anything in our work that places clients at risk of harm, or has caused them harm, whether or not the client(s) affected are aware of what has occurred by:

a. taking immediate action to prevent or limit any harm

b. repairing any harm caused, so far as possible

c. offering an apology when this is appropriate

d. notifying and discussing with our supervisor and/or manager what has occurred

e. investigating and take action to avoid whatever has gone wrong being repeated.

53.

We will consider carefully in supervision how we work with clients – see 60–73.

54.

We will monitor how clients experience our work together and the effects of the work with them in ways appropriate to the type of service being offered.

Confidentiality

55.

We will protect the confidentiality and privacy of clients by:

a. actively protecting information about clients from unauthorised access or disclosure

b. informing clients about how the use of personal data and information that they share with us will be used and who is within the circle of confidentiality, particularly with access to personally identifiable information

c. requiring that all recipients of personally identifiable information have agreed to treat such information as confidential in accordance with any legal requirements and what has been agreed with the client at the time of disclosure

d. informing clients about any reasonably foreseeable limitations of privacy or confidentiality in advance of our work together, for example, communications to ensure or enhance the quality of work in supervision or training, to protect a client or others from serious harm including safeguarding commitments, and when legally required or authorised to disclose

e. taking care that all contractual requirements concerning the management and communication of client information are mutually compatible

f. ensuring that disclosure of personally identifiable information about clients is authorised by client consent or that there is a legally and ethically recognised justification

g. using thoroughly anonymised information about clients where this provides a practical alternative to sharing identifiable information.

Working with colleagues and in teams

56.

Professional relationships will be conducted in a spirit of mutual respect. We will endeavour to build good working relationships and systems of communication that enhance services to clients.

57.

Practitioners will treat colleagues fairly and foster their capability and equality of opportunity.

58.

Practitioners will not undermine any colleague's relationship with clients by making unjustifiable or ill-judged comments.

59.

All communications between colleagues about clients should be on a professional basis and thus purposeful, respectful and consistent with the management of confidences agreed with clients.

Supervision

60.

Supervision is essential to how practitioners sustain good practice throughout their working life. Supervision provides practitioners with regular and ongoing opportunities to reflect in depth about all aspects of their practice in order to work as effectively, safely and ethically as possible. Supervision also sustains the personal resourcefulness required to undertake the work.

61.

Good supervision is much more than case management. It includes working in depth on the relationship between practitioner and client in order to work towards desired outcomes and positive effects. This requires adequate levels of privacy, safety and containment for the supervisee to undertake this work. Therefore a substantial part or preferably all of supervision needs to be independent of line management.

62.

Supervision requires additional skills and knowledge to those used for providing services directly to clients. Therefore supervisors require adequate levels of expertise acquired through training and/or experience. Supervisors will also ensure that they work with appropriate professional support and their own supervision.

63.

All supervisors will model high levels of good practice for the work they supervise, particularly with regard to expected levels of competence and professionalism, relationship building, the management of personal boundaries, any dual relationships, conflicts of interest and avoiding exploitation.

64.

All communications concerning clients made in the context of supervision will be consistent with confidentiality agreements with the clients concerned and compatible with any applicable agency policy.

65.

Careful consideration will be given to the undertaking of key responsibilities for clients and how these responsibilities are allocated between the supervisor, supervisee and any line manager or others with responsibilities for the service provided. Consideration needs to be given to how any of these arrangements and responsibilities will be communicated to clients in ways that are supportive of and appropriate to the work being undertaken. These arrangements will usually be reviewed at least once a year, or more frequently if required.

66.

Trainee supervision will require the supervisor to collaborate with training and placement providers in order to ensure that the trainee's work with clients satisfies professional standards. The arrangements for collaboration will usually be agreed and discussed with the trainee in advance of working with clients.

67.

When supervising qualified and/or experienced practitioners, the weight of responsibility for ensuring that the supervisee's work meets professional standards will primarily rest with the supervisee.

68.

Supervisors and supervisees will periodically consider how responsibility for work with clients is implemented in practice and how any difficulties or concerns are being addressed.

69.

The application of this *Ethical Framework* to the work with clients will be discussed in supervision regularly and not less than once a year.

70.

Supervisors will conscientiously consider the application of the law concerning supervision to their role and responsibilities.

71.

Supervisors will keep accurate records of key points discussed in supervision.

72.

Supervisees have a responsibility to be open and honest in supervision and to draw attention to any significant difficulties or challenges that they may be facing in their work with clients. Supervisors are responsible for providing opportunities for their supervisees to discuss any of their practice-related difficulties without blame or unjustified criticism and, when appropriate, to support their supervisees in taking positive actions to resolve difficulties.

73.

Supervision is recommended to anyone working in roles that require regularly giving or receiving emotionally challenging communications, or engaging in relationally complex and challenging roles.

Training and education

74.

All trainers will have the skills, attitudes and knowledge required to be competent teachers and facilitators of learning for what is being provided.

75.

Any information about the teaching, education or learning opportunities being provided will be accurate and enable potential students to make an informed choice.

76.

Any selection of students will be fair, respectful and transparent to candidates and use procedures designed to select suitable students.

77.

Any assessments of students will be fair, respectful and provide reasoned explanations for the outcome to the students.

78.

Care will be taken when using examples of work with clients for teaching purposes that the client information is used with the consent of the person or sufficiently anonymised so that the person concerned cannot be identified by any means reasonably likely to be used.

79.

Trainers and educators will model high levels of good practice in their work, particularly with regard to expected levels of competence and professionalism, relationship building, the management of personal boundaries, any dual relationships, conflicts of interest and avoiding exploitation.

80.

Trainers and educators will encourage trainees to raise any concerns at the earliest opportunity and have processes and policies for addressing any trainee's concerns. Trainers and educators are responsible for providing opportunities for trainees to discuss any of their practice-related difficulties without blame or unjustified criticism and, when appropriate, to support trainees in taking positive actions to resolve difficulties.

Trainees

81.

Trainees working with each other will:

a. relate respectfully to others and endeavour to support each others' learning

b. follow good ethical practice when working with each other, for example when practising skills or in personal development.

82.

In the interests of openness and honesty with clients:

a. trainees on a practitioner-qualifying course working with clients will inform clients (or ensure that clients have been informed) that they are trainees

b. trainees who are undertaking post-qualification CPD or further training will be guided by any applicable training requirements when using their professional and ethical judgement about whether to inform clients that they are in training.

83.

All trainees will:

a. seek their clients' permission to use any information from work with them for training purposes, for example, in presentations, case studies or as assessed practice. Alternatively, any report of work undertaken will be so thoroughly anonymised that the identity of the person concerned cannot be identified by any means reasonably likely to be used. Consent is required if anonymity cannot be assured or when required by the training provider's instructions or regulations

b. ensure that they deliver services that satisfy the minimum professional standards when working as practitioners with members of the public. This standard may be achieved with the assistance of appropriate professional support

c. collaborate with their trainers, placement providers, supervisors and other professional advisers to provide services to their clients that satisfy professional standards by being undertaken with reasonable care and skill

d. be watchful for any incompatibilities between contractual requirements that have implications for work with clients, for example, between agreements with clients, training providers and placements, and seek appropriate support in order to ensure that all contractual requirements are compatible

e. be open and honest with trainers, placement providers and supervisors about all issues relevant to their selection, training, supervision and professional practice.

Research

84.
We value research and systematic inquiry by practitioners as enhancing our professional knowledge and providing an evidence-base for practice in ways that benefit our clients.

85.
We will usually support and provide opportunities for research if it is compatible with the services we provide.

86.
When undertaking research we will be rigorously attentive to the quality and integrity of the research process, the knowledge claims arising from the research and how the results are disseminated.

87.
All research that we undertake will be guided by the *BACP Ethical Guidelines for Research in the Counselling Professions.*

88.
All participants in research will do so on the basis of explicit informed consent.

89.
All research will be reviewed in advance to ensure that the rights and interests of participants have been considered independently of the researcher.

90.
The research methods used will comply with standards of good practice in any services being delivered and will not adversely affect clients.

Care of self as a practitioner

91.

We will take responsibility for our own wellbeing as essential to sustaining good practice with our clients by:

a. taking precautions to protect our own physical safety

b. monitoring and maintaining our own psychological and physical health, particularly that we are sufficiently resilient and resourceful to undertake our work in ways that satisfy professional standards

c. seeking professional support and services as the need arises

d. keeping a healthy balance between our work and other aspects of life.

Responding to ethical dilemmas and issues

92.

We recognise that professional and ethical issues, problems and dilemmas will arise from time to time and are an unavoidable part of our practice.

93.

We will use our supervision and any other available professional resources to support and challenge how we respond to such situations. We will give careful consideration to the best approaches to ethical problem-solving.

94.

We will take responsibility for considering how best to act in such situations and will be ready to explain why we decided to respond in the way we did.

References

Adler, A. (2002). *The Collected Clinical Works of Alfred Adler: Journal Articles: 1927–1931*. Chicago, IL: Alfred Adler Institute.

Aguert, M., Laval, V., Lacroix, A., Gil, S., & Le Bigot, L. (2013). Inferring emotions from speech prosody: Not so easy at age five. *PLoS One*, 8(12): e83657.

American Heritage Dictionaries (2016). *The American Heritage Dictionary of the English Language* (5th edition). Boston, MA: Houghton Mifflin Harcourt.

Armstrong, K. (2010). *Twelve Steps to a Compassionate Life*. Toronto: Knopf Canada.

Audi, R. (ed.) (2015). *The Cambridge Dictionary of Philosophy* (3rd edition). Cambridge: Cambridge University Press. doi: 10.1017/CBO9781139057509.

Aviezer, H., Trope, Y., & Todorov, A. (2012). Body cues, not facial expressions, discriminate between intense positive and negative emotions. *Science*, 338(6111): 1225–9.

Axline, V. M., & Rogers, C. R. (1945). A teacher-therapist deals with a handicapped child. *The Journal of Abnormal and Social Psychology*, 40(2).

BACP (2018). *The BACP Ethical Framework for the Counselling Professions*. Lutterworth: British Association for Counselling and Psychotherapy.

BACP (2020). *A Guide to the BACP Counselling Skills Competence Framework: The Competences Required to use Counselling Skills in a Range of Different Roles and Settings*. Lutterworth: British Association for Counselling and Psychotherapy. Available at: www.bacp.co.uk/media/8889/bacp-counselling-skills-framework-user-guide-may20.pdf (accessed 6 April 2021).

Bandura, A. (1986). *Social Foundations of Thought and Action: A Social Cognitive Theory*. Englewood Cliffs, NJ: Prentice-Hall.

Batchelor, S. (2010). *Confession of a Buddhist Atheist*. New York: Random House, p. 165.

Beck, A. T. (1967). *The Diagnosis and Management of Depression*. Philadelphia, PA: University of Pennsylvania Press.

Bion, W. R. (1990). *Bion's Brazilian Lectures*. London: Karnac Books.

Bordin, E. S. (1979). The generalizability of the psychoanalytic concept of the working alliance. *Psychotherapy: Theory, Research & Practice*, 16(3): 252–60.

Branch, W. T., & Malik, T. K. (1993). Using 'windows of opportunities' in brief interviews to understand patients' concerns. *The Journal of the American Medical Association*, 269: 1667–8.

Brown, B. (2012). *Daring Greatly: How the Courage to Be Vulnerable Transforms the Way We Live, Love, Parent, and Lead*. Harmondsworth: Penguin, p. 68.

Brown, S. D., & Lent, R. W. (2009). *Handbook of Counselling Psychology* (4th edition). New York: Wiley.

Calaprice, A. (2005). *The New Quotable Einstein*. Princeton, NJ.: Princeton University Press.

Cardwell, M. (1996). *Dictionary of Psychology*. Chicago, IL: Fitzroy Dearborn.

Carkhuff, R. R. (1969). *Helping and Human Relations: A Primer for Lay and Professional Helpers: Volume I. Selection and Training*. New York: Holt, Rinehart & Winston.

Carnegie, Dale (1998). *How to Win Friends and Influence People*. New York: Gallery, p. 220.

Covey, S. R. (2004). *The 7 Habits of Highly Effective People: Powerful Lessons in Personal Change*. New York: Simon & Schuster, p. 253.

Darwin, C. (1872). *The Expression of Emotion in Man and Animals*. Oxford: Oxford University Press.

Duval, S., & Wicklund, R. A. (1972). *A Theory of Objective Self-awareness*. New York: Academic Press.

Eagleman, D. (2009). *Sum: Forty Tales from the Afterlives*. New York: Knopf Doubleday, p. 78.

Ebert, R. (2010). *Roger Ebert's Movie Yearbook 2011*. Kansas City, MO: Andrews McMeel Publishing, p. 1500.

Egan, G. (1998). *The Skilled Helper: A Problem Management Approach to Helping* (6th edition). Pacific Grove, CA: Brooks Cole.

Einstein, A. (2010). *The Ultimate Quotable Einstein*. Princeton, NJ: Princeton University Press, p. 252.

Ekman, P., Friesen, W. V., & Ellsworth, P. (1972). *Emotion in the Human Face: Guidelines for Research and an Integration of Findings*. New York: Pergamon Press.

Ellerman, D. (2001). *Helping People Help Themselves: Towards a Theory of Autonomy-Compatible Help*. World Bank, Policy Research Working Paper 2693. New York: World Bank.

Emerson, Ralph Waldo (n.d.). *BrainyQuote.com*. Retrieved from: www.brainyquote.com/quotes/ralph_waldo_emerson_103408 (accessed 14 November 2020).

Erakat, S. (2006). *The Upper Hand: Winning Strategies from World-class Negotiators*. Holbrook, MA: Adams Media, p. 225.

Erksine, R. G. (1998). Attunement and involvement: Therapeutic responses to relational needs. *International Journal of Psychotherapy*, 3(3).

Ferrett, S. (2008). *Peak Performance: Success in College and Beyond* (annotated instructor's edition). New York: McGraw-Hill.

Galaxy, J. (2012). *Cat Daddy: What the World's Most Incorrigible Cat Taught Me about Life, Love, and Coming Clean*. Harmondsworth: Penguin, p. 104.

Gandhi, M. (n.d.). *Quotes by Mahatma Gandhi*. Retrieved from: www.goodreads.com/author/show/5810891.Mahatma_Gandhi (accessed May 2016).

George, R. and Cristiani, T. (1995). *Counseling: Theory and Practice*. Boston, MA: Allyn and Bacon.

Gu, J., Cavanagh, K., Baer, R., & Strauss, C. (2017). An empirical examination of the factor structure of compassion. *PLoS One*, 12(2): e0172471. Published 17 February. doi:10.1371/journal.pone.0172471.

Hill, C. E. (2009). *Helping Skills: Facilitating, Exploration, Insight, and Action* (3rd edition). Washington, DC: American Psychological Association.

Hill, C. E., & Lent, R. W. (1996). A narrative and meta-analytic review of helping skills training: Time to revive a dormant area of inquiry. *Psychology: Theory Research, Practice, Training*, 43(2): 154–72.

Høigaard, R., & Mathisen, P. (2008). Informal situated counselling in a school context. *Counselling Psychology Quarterly*, 21: 293–9.

Homer (2008). *The Odyssey* (Easyread Large Edition). ReadHowYouWant.com, p. 146.

Jackson, S. W. (1999). *Care of the Psyche: A History of Psychosocial Healing*. New Haven, CT: Yale University Press.

Jamison, L. (2014). Contemplating other people's pain. *The New York Times*, March 2014.

Jansen, J., van Weert, J. C. M., de Groot, J., van Dulmen, S., Heeren, T. J., & Bensing, J. M. (2010). Emotional and informational patient cues: The impact of nurses' responses on recall. *Patient Education and Counselling*, 79: 218–24.

Kohut, H. (2009). *How Does Analysis Cure?* Chicago, IL: University of Chicago Press, p. 93.

Kohut, H. (2012). *The Restoration of the Self*. Chicago, IL: University of Chicago Press, p. 144.

Kreider, T. (2013). *We Learn Nothing: Essays*. New York: Simon & Schuster, p. 59.

Laing, R. D. (1960). *The Divided Self: An Existential Study in Sanity and Madness*. Harmondsworth: Penguin.

Luft, J., & Ingham, H. (1955). *The Johari Window: A Graphic Model of Interpersonal Awareness*. Proceedings of the Western Training Laboratory in Group Development. Los Angeles, CA: University of California, Los Angeles.

Martel, Y. (2003). *Life of Pi*. Boston, MA: Houghton Mifflin Harcourt, p. 132.

Martin, K. L., & Hodgson, D. (2006). The role of counselling and communication skills: How can they enhance a patient's 'first day' experience? *Journal of Radiotherapy in Practice*, 5(3): 157–64. doi: 10.1017/S1460396906000215.

Maslow, A. H. (1943). A theory of human motivation. *Psychological Review*, 50(4).

McLeod, J., & McLeod, J. (2011). *Counselling Skills: A Practical Guide for Counsellors and Helping Professionals* (2nd edition). Maidenhead: Open University Press.

McLeod, S. A. (2008). Prejudice and discrimination. *Simply Psychology*. Available at: www.simplypsychology.org/prejudice.html.

Miller, A. (2002). *For Your Own Good: Hidden Cruelty in Child-Rearing and the Roots of Violence*. London: Macmillan, p. 101.

Miller, W. R., & Rollnick, S. (1991). *Motivational Interviewing: Preparing People to Change Addictive Behavior*. New York: Guilford Press.

Newman, C. (2007). Boundary issues in the professional/client relationship. *Journal of Community Corrections*, 17(1): 9–11.

Nin, A. (1970). *The Diary of Anaïs Nin, Volume Two (1934–1939)*. Orlando, FL: Harcourt.

Paul, R., & Elder, L. (2006). *The Miniature Guide to Understanding the Foundations of Ethical Reasoning*. Tomales, CA: Foundation for Critical Thinking Free Press.

Paulmann, S., & Uskul, A. K. (2014). Cross-cultural emotional prosody recognition: Evidence from Chinese and British listeners. *Cognition and Emotion*, 28(2): 230–44.

Perlman, H. H. (1979). *Relationship: The Heart of Helping People*. Chicago, IL: University of Chicago Press.

Peterson, M. R. (1992). *At Personal Risk: Boundary Violations in Professional–Client Relationships*. New York: W.W. Norton.

Piercy, M. (2016). *Gone to Soldiers: A Novel*. New York: Open Road Media, p. 685.

Prochaska, J. O., & DiClemente, C. C. (1983). Stages and processes of self-change of smoking: Toward an integrative model of change. *Journal of Consulting and Clinical Psychology*, 51(3): 390–5. https://doi.org/10.1037/0022-006X.51.3.390

Prochaska, J. O., DiClemente, C. C., & Norcross, J. C. (1992). In search of how people change: Applications to the addictive behaviors. *American Psychologist*, 47: 1102–14. PMID: 1329589.

Riess, H. (2017). The Science of Empathy. *Journal of Patient Experience*, 9 May: 74–7. doi: 10.1177/2374373517699267.

Rochat, P. (2003). Five levels of self-awareness as they unfold early in life. *Consciousness and Cognition*, 12(4): 717–31. doi: 10.1016/s1053-8100(03)00081-3. PMID 14656513.

Rogers, C. R. (1957). The necessary and sufficient conditions of therapeutic personality change. *Journal of Consulting Psychology*, 21(2): 95–103.

Rogers, C. R. (1961). *On Becoming a Person*. Boston, MA: Houghton Mifflin.

Rogers, C. R. (1980). *A Way of Being*. Boston, MA: Houghton Mifflin Harcourt, p. 134.

Rosenberg, M. B. (2005). *Speak Peace in a World of Conflict: What You Say Next Will Change Your World*. Encinitas, CA: Puddle Dancer Press, p. 129.

Roth, A. D., & Pilling, S. (2008). Using an evidence-based methodology to identify the competences required to deliver effective cognitive and behavioural therapy for depression and anxiety disorders. *Behavioural and Cognitive Psychotherapy*, 36(2): 129–47. https://doi.org/10.1017/S1352465808004141

Roy, A. (2004). *The Ordinary Person's Guide to Empire*. London: Flamingo.

Schweitzer, A. (1958). *A Selection of Writings of and about Albert Schweitzer*. Boston, MA: H. N. Sawyer.

Shakespeare, W. (2005). *Hamlet* (Arden Shakespeare edition). Edited by H. Jenkins. London: The Arden Shakespeare, Thomson Learning, p. 277.

Smith, H., & Smith, M. K. (2008). *The Art of Helping Others: Being Around, Being There, Being Wise*. London: Jessica Kingsley.

Sobell, L. C., & Sobell, M. B. (2008). *Motivational Interviewing Strategies and Techniques: Rationales and Examples*. Retrieved from: www.nova.edu/gsc/forms/ mi_rationale_techniques.pdf

Steinbeck, J. (2002). *East of Eden*. Harmondsworth: Penguin, p. 391.

Tomkins, S. S. (1962). *Affect, Imagery, and Consciousness. Volume 1: The Positive Affects*. New York: Springer.

Tomkins, S. S. (1963). *Affect, Imagery, and Consciousness. Volume 2: The Negative Affects*. New York: Springer.

UKEssays (2018). *Professionalism and Ethics in Counselling*. [online]. Available from: www.ukessays.com/essays/social-work/defining-and-understanding-ethical-mindfulness-social-work-essay.php?vref=1 (accessed 1 November 2020).

Vinge, V. (2010). *A Fire upon the Deep*. Basingstoke: Macmillan, p. 454.

Young, M. E. (2005). *Learning the Art of Helping: Building Blocks and Techniques*. Hoboken, NJ: Pearson/Merrill Prentice-Hall.

Zur, O. (2011). *Self-Disclosure & Transparency in Psychotherapy and Counselling: To Disclose or Not to Disclose, This is the Question*. Retrieved from: www.zurinstitute.com/selfdisclosure1.html (accessed 23 May 2013).

Index

solicitation, 73
space, 21–22, 33, 112–113
stereotyping, 78–80
summarising, 37–39, 125–126, 128–129
supervision, 248–250
support dyad. *See* helping relationship (working alliance)
support sessions. *See* helping sessions

talking sticks, 12
teams, 248
therapeutic relationship. *See* helping relationship (working alliance)
therapeutically-informed services, use of term, 231
therapist's conditions. *See* core conditions
thoughts, 6–7
time, 101
timing, 126
Tomkins, S. S., 31
touch, 32–33, 36, 113

training, 250–252
transtheoretical model (cycle of change), 132–135, *133*
trustworthiness, 106, 235

UK Essays, 114
unconditional positive regard (UPR), 72, 119–120, 121, **122–123**, 125–126
unknown self, 172, *172*

values, 169–170, 234
vicarious trauma, 183–184
virtues, 236
voice, 33–34

warm attention, 125–126
why questions, 44
wisdom, 107–108, 237
working alliance (helping relationship), 3, 91–100, **98**, 185–186, 192–193, 214–215. *See also* helping sessions
working with colleagues, 248

Zur, O., 46–47

www.ingramcontent.com/pod-product-compliance
Lightning Source LLC
Chambersburg PA
CBHW080556030426
42336CB00019B/3209